SUCCESSFUL
BUSINESS PLANNING
in
30 DAYS

A STEP-BY-STEP GUIDE FOR WRITING A BUSINESS PLAN
AND STARTING YOUR OWN BUSINESS

Peter J. Patsula

Successful Business Planning in 30 Days

A Step-by-Step Guide for Writing a Business Plan and Starting Your Own Business

Printed in the United States of America.

First published in 2000
Reprinted in 2002

Publisher's – Cataloging In Publication

Patsula, Peter Joseph, 1962–
    Successful business planning in 30 days : a step-by-step guide for writing a business plan and starting your own business / Peter J. Patsula ; edited by William Nowik
    p. cm.
    Includes index.
    LCCN: 00-190077
    ISBN: 0-9678402-0-1 (paperback)
    1. Business planning–Handbooks, manuals, etc. 2. Business–Handbooks, manuals, etc. 3. New business enterprises–Planning. I. Title.
HD30.28.P38   658.4'012   2000

Ordering Information:

                To order online visit:
                www.businessplan30days.com

Printed and bound by:

                BookMasters Inc.
                2541 Ashland Rd., P.O. Box 2139, Mansfield, OH 44905

Published by:

                Patsula Media
                Email: books@patsula.com
                URL: www.patsulamedia.com

Notice

The author and publisher shall have neither liability nor responsibility to any person or entity with respect to any loss or damage caused, or alleged to be caused, directly or indirectly by any information contained in this book. Although this publication is designed to provide accurate and timely information concerning the subject matter covered, it is sold with the understanding that the author and publisher are not engaged in rendering legal, accounting, or other professional services. You are urged to read as much as possible on the subject of planning and starting a small business and tailor your research to your individual needs. If legal advice or other expert assistance is required, the services of a competent professional should be consulted.

Contents

Action Plan

Preface

Author's Note

WHAT you are about to read and explore is the end product of eight years of intensive labor. It is difficult for me to fathom that the original conception of this guide was a considerably humbler version. But, after exhaustive research, and many revisions, the original conception grew and blossomed into **91** online guidebooks from *The Entrepreneur's Guidebook Series* (available at www.businessplanguides.com) and what you have now!

It's impossible to thank all the authors, professionals, businesswomen, and businessmen who inspired the various sections of this guide. Suffice to say that I am indebted to hundreds, if not thousands of mentors, unsung oarsmen who kept propelling me on to create something bigger and better than my original conception.

Use this guide to plan your business. Use *The Entrepreneur's Guidebook Series* if you need more helpful tips and information (see page xi for a detailed listing of our guidebooks). And visit our www.smallbusinesstown.com website for access to hundreds of helpful business resources and free software links.

With that said, I wish you the best in your entrepreneurial journey, and sincerely hope that *Successful Business Planning in 30 Days* takes you where you want to go.

–Peter J. Patsula

Peter J. Patsula has been a successful educator for over 12 years in Asia, Africa, and North America. Creator and author of "The Entrepreneur's Guidebook Series," he is currently residing in Seoul, Korea.

Editor's Note

Here is a book that can change your life. Study it, follow its directions, implement the business plan outline, add to it some sweat and inspiration, and you just might gain financial independence.

Successful Business Planning in 30 Days is written in a very straightforward manner, using clear language and step-by-step instructions. When you get into the nitty-gritty of planning your business, you will discover that Peter J. Patsula has left nothing to the imagination. Everything you need to know about starting and operating a successful business is here.

This is simply the best book of its kind.

–William Nowik

William Nowik has authored numerous books and creative media productions. His skill and craft has been greatly appreciated in the editing of this text.

Introduction

STARTING and running a successful business in today's rapidly changing world is a considerable challenge. If adequate planning and control measures are not established early, any venture can soon find itself raging out of control. To prevent this, it is necessary to put together a well thought-out, well-researched business plan – your blueprint for survival.

Writing a business plan is THE fundamental starting point for ALL entrepreneurial efforts. Time and time again, it has proven itself to be one of the single most controllable factors relevant to the success of any business.

What is a Business Plan?

A *Business Plan* is primarily an organizing tool used to simplify and clarify business goals and strategies, which might otherwise appear complex and intimidating. A business plan is also a sales tool. If it cannot convince at least one other person of the value of your business idea, then either your idea is not worth pursing, or your plan needs major rewriting. In addition to being simple and clear, a business plan is persuasive.

A business plan is factual, concise, well written, and arranged in a logical sequence. It contains all the pertinent information regarding your business and uses simple straightforward language that will not tax your readers. It does not contain unsupported statements, nor information that is ambiguous or poorly explained.

The mood of your business plan is calm and clear, with just the right dab of excitement! It is inspirational and positive, and is not full of empty promises.

Why Write a Business Plan?

A business plan is needed to consolidate your research, serve as a guide during the lifetime of your business, and make sure you take an objective and unemotional look at your entire business. It also provides potential investors and lenders with detailed information about your company's past, current and future operations.

A good business plan:

- Gives you a list of goals and steps to follow.

- Helps uncover obstacles you might have otherwise overlooked.

- Improves your management capabilities by giving you practice in anticipating situations both good and bad for your business.

- Trains you to analyze, organize and make better business decisions.

- Transforms you into a respected professional.

> *A good business plan transforms you into a respected professional.*

You can also use your plan to communicate more effectively with suppliers, advertisers, lawyers, accountants, auditors, business consultants and other interested parties who need to clearly understand the exact nature of your business.

> *To START a small business, you need an idea! To STAY in business, you need a PLAN!*

Essential Elements of a Business Plan

THERE are five essential elements every business plan should have:

I. Business Plan Overview (Introductory Section)

II. Company Plan

III. Marketing Plan

IV. Financial Plan

V. Supporting Documents

> *The content and organization of a business plan depends on its purpose.*

These five essential elements are guided by one omnipresent rule:

WHAT you put in your business plan and HOW you organize it, depends on WHY you need it and WHO it is for.

This guide is based on the business plan format suggested by the U.S. Small Business Administration (SBA). This format has been further refined and improved upon by researching the works of dozens of experts and adding their insights and recommendations. It is simple in structure, yet comprehensive in detail. It is packed full of information and strategies to help you make better decisions once your business is under way. It is inspired under the belief that potential entrepreneurs must first **saturate** their brain with business facts and concepts before taking the entrepreneurial plunge. Its goal is to immerse you in the language of business and train you to think and act as an entrepreneur.

Writing a Business Plan in 30 Days

Each planning day in this guide covers one or more "Key Areas" of a business plan. Although some days are more demanding than others, if you work full-time every day on your plan, you should be able to complete it in about a month. Nevertheless, if you find the workload too much, slow down, and take two or three months. It is also a good idea, before starting, to set aside some time to reflect upon your personal strengths and weaknesses, as well as conduct some preliminary research, by surveying market needs and assessing possible product and service solutions.

List, in point form, your research goals for the next four weeks:

Week 1	Week 2	Week 3	Week 4
Read through guide.			
Highlight "Key Areas"			

After completing your plan, use the information and data collected to prepare a formal business plan. Use the checklist on the back cover to review your research. Determine whether your answers are clear and complete. Evaluate the information from the standpoint of a prospective investor or lending agency and ask yourself how satisfactory your responses are. Find an expert or colleague to review your plan who is willing to offer constructive criticism. Your business plan is not finished until at least one other knowledgeable person carefully examines it.

Business Planning in 16 Weeks - The outline below has been provided as an alternative approach to planning your business. There is no reason not to follow our 30-day step-by-step approach, but it is worth keeping in mind that business planning, like entrepreneurship, is flexible, and can be adapted to suit your needs if ever so required.

> *Our goal is to immerse you in the language of business and train you to think like an entrepreneur.*

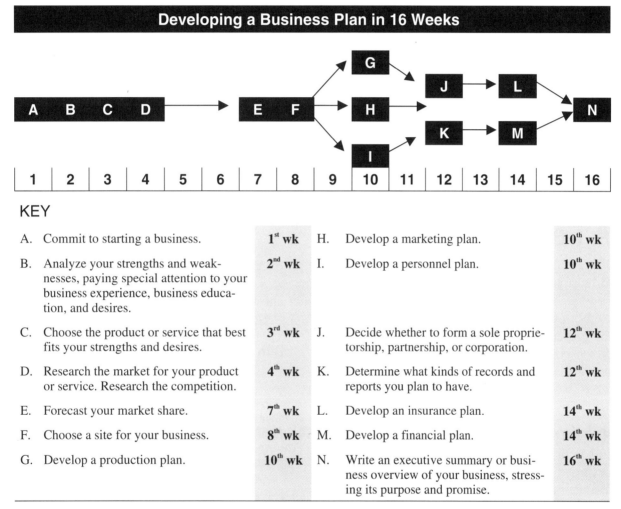

KEY

A.	Commit to starting a business.	**1st wk**	H.	Develop a marketing plan.	**10th wk**
B.	Analyze your strengths and weaknesses, paying special attention to your business experience, business education, and desires.	**2nd wk**	I.	Develop a personnel plan.	**10th wk**
C.	Choose the product or service that best fits your strengths and desires.	**3rd wk**	J.	Decide whether to form a sole proprietorship, partnership, or corporation.	**12th wk**
D.	Research the market for your product or service. Research the competition.	**4th wk**	K.	Determine what kinds of records and reports you plan to have.	**12th wk**
E.	Forecast your market share.	**7th wk**	L.	Develop an insurance plan.	**14th wk**
F.	Choose a site for your business.	**8th wk**	M.	Develop a financial plan.	**14th wk**
G.	Develop a production plan.	**10th wk**	N.	Write an executive summary or business overview of your business, stressing its purpose and promise.	**16th wk**

The above outline is based on an approach suggested by Nicholas, C. Siropolis in his text, *Small Business Management: A Guide to Entrepreneurship*, 2nd ed. (Boston: Houghton Mifflin Co., 1982, pp. 138-141).

How to Use this Guide

Successful Business Planning in 30 Days provides a comprehensive outline of section titles and headings that can be used to write a business plan. It examines all the "Key Areas" bankers and investors are most interested in, as well as other areas that are important to proper planning. This outline is also flexible. Change it, expand it, or rearrange it as you see fit, as long as your new outline is logical and better meets your needs and goals. Keep in mind that you do not have to research and explain every item outlined in this guide. Use common sense. This five-section comprehensive business plan guide is meant to help you, not frustrate you.

Start by reading this guide cover to cover. Use a marker to highlight "Key Areas" applicable to your business and those that require more detailed research. Underline key ideas. To save time, circle information and descriptive statements to be added to your final typewritten business plan (don't waste time writing down what has already been written for you). Next, study trends. Scout locations. Visit your library for reference material and review some of our online guides available at:

www.businessplanguides.com

After closely reading this guide, spend at least four weeks reflecting on your business goals, obstacles you might encounter, and the nature of your potential customers – their needs and wants. As soon as you have a fair idea of the type of business you want to start and where you want to go, jump into **DAY 1**: *Name your company. Design a logo.* Next, take your guide with you wherever you go. Don't leave home without it! Commit to completing your plan on schedule.

NOTE The forms and worksheets provided in this guide are intended for use as rough drafts only. Once completed, you will use your collected data and responses to prepare a formal, *typewritten* business plan (see page 205 for more "Business Plan Writing Strategies").

A Few Planning Tools

The *Daily Planner* found at the end of this guide on page 209 can be used to help your plan your business and organize your ideas. Print and photocopy as many copies as you need. The *Idea Sheet* shown below and on page xii can be used to supplement entries into this guide. You might also consider making a dozen copies or so of this sheet to fold up and put in your purse or wallet, so you can jot down ideas whenever inspiration or insight strikes you.

NOTE Don't be afraid to adapt this guide to suit your needs. Although this guide has been designed to be self-contained, you may wish to use a notebook to supplement entries, or perhaps incorporate additional planning forms from other sources. Make OUR *Business Planning Guide*, YOUR *Business Planning Guide*.

> *A lost "idea" is a lost "treasure."*

> *A "good business plan" is "good business."*

> *Spend at least four weeks reflecting on your business goals, obstacles you might encounter, and the nature of your potential customers – their needs and wants.*

Write heading title here.

IDEA SHEET

Page Reference #: [   ]   Heading Title: [   ]

Write guide page referred to.

Add content here.

Chart Title:

Graph/Sketch Title:

Use grids to sketch floor-plans, logos, designs, breakeven charts, graphs, etc.

Use chart to list ideas, products, companies, names, etc.

PERSONAL PLAN

1) Discovering if *YOU* Have Entrepreneurial Talent
2) Developing *MOTIVATIONAL* Skills
3) Developing *TIME MANAGEMENT* Skills
4) *STUDYING* the Lives of Successful People
5) Fine-tuning Leadership & *MANAGERIAL* Skills
6) Sharpening *SELLING* & Negotiating Skills
7) Creating a *RESOURCE* Reading Library
8) Designing a Customized Business *PLANNER*
9) Supercharging Promising Projects with a Plan of *ACTION*
10) Setting-up a Home *OFFICE*
11) Writing a *BUSINESS* Plan

COMPANY PLAN

12) Learning Why Companies *SUCCEED* and Why They Fail
13) Exploring *TOP* Businesses of the Future
14) Selecting *PROFITABLE* Small Business Products & Services
15) Researching *HOT NEW IDEAS* for Products & Services
16) *EVALUATING* Business Opportunities
17) Finding the Best Business *LOCATION*
18) Choosing the Right *LEGAL FORMATION*
19) *NAMING* Your Company & Products
20) Designing *LOGOS*, Business Cards & Business Stationary
21) Writing a Company *SLOGAN* & *MISSION* Statement
22) Opening *COMMUNICATION* Channels
23) Selecting Computer *SOFTWARE*
24) Buying Computer *HARDWARE*
25) Getting *CONNECTED*
26) Getting *PRINTED*
27) Avoiding the *COMPUTER BLUES*
28) Adopting an Easy-to-Use *ACCOUNTING* System
29) Managing *INVENTORY*
30) Setting-up an Efficient *ORDER ENTRY* System
31) Getting *INSURANCE*
32) Protecting Your Intellectual Property with *COPYRIGHTS, PATENTS & TRADEMARKS*
33) Understanding Business *LAWS*, Regulations & Ethical Codes
34) *LICENSING* Your Operations
35) Opening a Business Bank *ACCOUNT*
36) Finding and Hiring Qualified *PERSONNEL*
37) Using *TEMP* Services & Contract Labor
38) Weighing the Pros & Cons of *EXPANSION*
39) Establishing a Long-term *STRATEGIC* Plan
40) Starting & Operating a *MANUFACTURING* Business
41) Starting & Operating a *WHOLESALE* Business
42) Starting & Operating a *RETAIL* Business
43) Starting & Operating a *SERVICE* Business
44) Starting & Operating a *MAIL ORDER* Business
45) Starting & Operating an *IMPORT/EXPORT* Business

MARKETING PLAN

46) Understanding *WHY* People Buy
47) Spying on the *COMPETITION*
48) Pinpointing Target *MARKETS* with Unmet Needs
49) Uncovering New Consumer *TRENDS* & Demands
50) Building a *LIST* of Potential Customers
51) Developing a Customer *SERVICE* Plan
52) Establishing a *PRICING* Policy
53) Establishing a *CREDIT* Policy
54) Creating a Winning *PROMOTIONAL* Plan
55) Choosing an Advertising Design *THEME*
56) Selecting Advertising *MEDIA*
57) *WRITING* & Editing Like a Pro
58) Creating "Eye Catching" *GRAPHICS*
59) Using *WORDS* That Sell
60) Mastering *AD DESIGN* & Layout Techniques
61) *COLLECTING* Product Info to Help Write & Design Ads
62) Using *ODAC* - The "Advertiser's Soul-mate"
63) Creating *CLASSIFIED* Ads, Space Ads, Brochures & Catalogs
64) Creating *NEWSLETTER* & Direct Mail Promotions
65) Creating Award-Winning *RADIO & TV* Ads
66) Getting Free *PUBLICITY*
67) Designing *PACKAGING*
68) Preparing Advertising *RECORDS*
69) *TESTING* Promotions and Analyzing Results
70) Conducting *SURVEYS* to Improve Your Marketing Efforts
71) Opening *DISTRIBUTION* Channels
72) Fostering *REPEAT* Business
73) Creating *NEW MARKET OPPORTUNITIES*
74) *INNOVATING* Your Promotional Plan
75) *LICENSING* Successful Products & Services
76) *FRANCHISING* Your Operations
77) *NETWORKING* Your Markets

FINANCIAL PLAN

78) Estimating *START-UP COSTS*
79) Evaluating Renting, *LEASING*, Buying & Financing Options
80) Preparing a Breakeven Analysis, *CASH FLOW* Statement and Income Projection
81) *CAPITALIZING* Your Operations
82) *REDUCING* Business and Living Operating Expenses
83) Starting a *RETIREMENT* Plan
84) Building an *INVESTMENT* Portfolio
85) Investing in *REAL ESTATE*
86) Reducing Your *TAXES*
87) *SELLING* Your Company

SUPPORT PLAN

88) Getting *HELP* from the Government and Other Entrepreneurial Organizations
89) Finding a Good *ACCOUNTANT*, Banker, Insurance Agent & Lawyer
90) *ARMING* yourself with "Kamikaze Survival Techniques"
91) Consolidating Your Future with Thirty *GOLDEN* Rules

Online Guidebooks Available at:
Businessplanguides.com

IDEA SHEET

Page Reference #: [ ]   Heading Title: [ ]

Chart Title:

Graph/Sketch Title:

DAY 1
BUSINESS PLAN OVERVIEW

- Cover Sheet (see page 11)
- Table of Contents
- Executive Summary
- Fact Sheet

THE *Introductory Section* of a well-organized business plan, tells people:

☑ *who you are*   ☑ *what you are*   ☑ *what you want*

A business plan forces you to think through every aspect of your business and helps you recognize opportunities for growth and profit.

Use this section to grab attention, impress upon others that you have what it takes to be successful, and skillfully cater to the whims of potential investors by implying or stating what's in it for them if they read your plan.

NOTE A business plan is often used as a sales tool. However, be careful not to sound too much like a salesperson. Don't use fancy words to sell your business, let your ideas, research and facts do the persuading. Make your reader see the value of your plan without hitting them over the head with it or trying to pull the wool over their eyes.

Cover Sheet

Your *cover sheet* should be simple – kept to a single page – and most importantly, informative at a glance. Content can be placed anywhere on the page as long as it looks professional. Your cover sheet should also encourage readership and attract the attention of the target reader (see worksheet on page 11).

Harry's Pet Supplies
11604 - 102 Street
Edmonton, AB T5K 0R8
(403) 555-2345
(FAX) 555-1HPS

BUSINESS PLAN
for
**HARRY'S
PET SUPPLIES**

Harry Tegus, *President*
Sally Tegus, *Vice President*
#206 12210 - 103 Ave.
Edmonton, AB TS6 0W1
(403) 555-2225

Plan prepared October 1998
by Harry and Sally Tegus ©

Company Name

On your *cover sheet*, state the name of your company and have the words "Business Plan" written on it. Include your company's address, telephone number and Fax number (with area codes), E-mail address, URL address and the names, addresses and numbers of the people who can be contacted if further questions need to be answered.

Naming Your Company

Find a pen, a blank sheet of paper, and a quiet place to reflect. Jot down as many names as your can (the more the better), and from those select ten or so for closer analysis and criticism from third parties. Try to author a name that is exclusive yet inclusive, compact yet complete, and simple yet informative.

To help generate ideas, use the following strategies:

- **Associate your company with . . .**

  A favorite street, town, city, state, country or other geographical reference. E.g., *Bourbon Street* Bakery, *Canadian* Custom Engravers, *Paris* Furs.

  Animals. E.g., *Raven* Truck Box Liners & Woodcrafts, *Lion* Business Machines, *Shepherd* Security Systems, *Cardinal* Building Maintenance.

  Established Companies. E.g., *Xerox* Service Centre, *Ford* Auto Repair. Use the reputation of a larger company to add credibility to yours (get permission first).

  Mythical Figures. E.g., *Unicorn* Driving School, *Atlas* Muffler & Brake, *Midas* Mufflers, *Libra* Connection, *Odyssey* Outerwear.

  Quality and high standards of production. E.g., Muffler *Pro, Award* Building Maintenance, *Professional* Carpet Cleaning, Golf *Plus, Quality* Brake.

  Royalty, upper class social structures. E.g., *Lady* Ming, *Crown*tek, *King's* Crane Service, *Royal* Bank of Canada, *Master*clean.

  Well known historical figures, precious metals, gems, natural phenomena or famous objects. E.g., *Lincoln* Insurance, *Golden* Flooring Accessories.

- **Combine everyday words related to your business into one.** E.g., *Fabriozone* Cleaning Systems, *Weldangrind* Construction, *Heatilator* Fireplaces, *Safeway, U-Pak* Shipping & Moving, *Execucare* Services.

- **Combine the letters of owners.** E.g., *Alco* Roofing, owner's Allan & Collin; *Backice* Balloon Express, owner's Bob, Jack & Alice.

- **Create a fictional person.** E.g., *Ducky's* Office Supplies, *Jack the Stripper* Restoration Services, *Mr. Sweep* Chimney Cleaning.

- **Create a fictional place.** E.g., Tuxedo Junction, Sherwood Forest, Elephant's Castle.

- **Imply or state a major benefit of your product or service.** E.g., *Sunshade* Aluminum Products, Balloon *Express, Fresh* Food Experience, Club *Fit, Breath Easy* Furnace Cleaning, *Vision* Window Cleaning.

- **Inspire confidence and trust.** E.g., *Honest Abe's* Shoe Store.

- **Keep your name short.** Short names are easier to remember than long names. They also lend themselves better to logo design.

- **Look through directories, magazines, and the Yellow Pages.** Locate listings of the types of businesses you are interested in. Write down which names inspire you. Ask yourself why they stand out and then use their format as a guide to develop your own names.

- **Make your name sound bigger than you really are.** No one needs to know you're working in a kitchen, garage, or basement. E.g., Century *Towers.*

- **Make your name easy to remember.** E.g., *Builders First, Wired* for *Sound.* A company name is easy to remember if it is easy to pronounce, relate to, and spell, and has a nice ring to it, rolls easily off the tongue and is short.

- **Personalize your name then describe it.** E.g., *Salmon Arms* Fish & Tackle

House, *Picasso* Graphics Inc., *Beaver* Lumber, *Newman* Plumbing.

- **Qualify the type of business you are in with a descriptive noun.** E.g., Jim Burge & *Associates*, The Wig *Boutique*, Home Building *Centre*, Billingsgate Fish *Company*, Alps *Construction*, Cost-View *Consulting*.

- **Target your name to the people you want to sell to.** E.g., Weightwatchers, Bow Wow Dog Grooming, Lo-cost Furniture Warehouse.

- **Tell customers your business location.** E.g., *Campus* Eye Center, *River Valley* Equipment Sales, *Boyle Street* Clinic.

- **Use alliteration.** E.g., **D**rayden **D**evelopments, **I**carus **I**ndustries, **H**amilton **H**ouse or **S**un**s**hine **S**ecretary **S**ervices.

- **Use attractive letters.** A well-chosen company name represents itself well graphically. It is also easy to reproduce on signs and letterhead as a logo.

- **Use made-up words.** Add original words to your company name. E.g., *Atco* Red-Hat Valves, *Nutron* Manufacturing LTD.

- **Use your own name.** Avoid costly and time-consuming trademark searches. E.g., *Al Bundy's* Shoes, *Gundy* Inc., *Angela's* Hairstyling.

- **Write a name with catchy initials.** Three initials works best. E.g., *IBM*, Integrated Business Machines; *WEC*, Whitemud Equine Centre.

> *Many states prohibit using the words Corporation, Incorporated, Inc., Company or Co. unless your business is indeed such an entity.*

List key factors, important considerations and strategic objectives in naming your company:

List 10 possible company names for further consideration. Choose one:

My Company Name

Company Logo

Every company needs a logo! Place your logo on your cover page in a suitable eye-catching spot. However, be conservative about it by limiting its size. Also, resist the urge to get too colorful. Exhibitionism has no place in a business plan.

Why Every Company Needs a Logo?

Five reasons why every company needs a logo:

- **A logo gives your promotions continuity.** Using a logo exclusive to your firm consistently on all printed material unifies your marketing efforts and gives the impression that you know exactly who you are, and perhaps are a little bigger and better than you really are.

- **A logo give yours company an identity.** Developing an easily recognized logo gives you an identification advantage over your competition.

- **A logo is a tangible asset with a cash value.** Consumer trust is a hard thing to come by. When gained, it is extremely valuable to a company. This trust is often attached to a company's logo (or trademark) because people like symbols: they wear rings on their fingers; they drive cars more expensive than they can afford.

- **A logo is visible evidence that you have made an investment in your organization.** A well designed logo shows that management has a strong self-image, a definite direction for the future, and a commitment to the highest standards of quality and professionalism. A carelessly designed logo or no logo at all is often associated with organizations that are under-capitalized, poorly organized, and of uncertain longevity.

- **A logo makes your ads, letterheads, and envelopes stand out from the crowd.** People DO judge books by their covers. The billions of dollars spent every year on advertising and packaging prove this. A well-conceived logo makes it more difficult for customers to forget you. In the long run, it will generate better returns for your advertising dollars.

Designing a Company Logo in "Eight Steps"

STEP 1 – Gather all kinds of information and materials that will help inspire your design. This includes: ◆ your company's mission statement, action plan, marketing plan and expansion plan ◆ company goals and philosophies ◆ a directory of trademarks and logos ◆ as many competitive company logos as you can get your hands on (these can usually found in the Yellow Pages or magazine related to your specialty) ◆ graphics, photos, and any kind of physical object you feel may symbolize your company name.

STEP 2 – Determine how your logo will be used. Logos are meant to be versatile. Their design should lend themselves to any use imaginable. Imagine your logo being used in each of the following media: ◆ magazine and newspaper advertising ◆ billboards ◆ discount coupons ◆ brochures ◆ letterhead ◆ badges or buttons ◆ ball-point pens or pencils ◆ greeting cards ◆ postcards ◆ TV spots ◆ calendars or date books ◆ contests and other specialized promotions ◆ patches or decals ◆ actual products themselves ◆ giant 3-D sculptures outside your building.

KEY
CHEMICALS

STEP 3 – Decide what purpose your logo will have. Ask yourself: ✦ What kind of image do you want to create? ✦ Do you want your logo to be formal or informal? ✦ Will it be targeted towards consumers or business people? ✦ Do you want it to symbolize a company that stands for one thing or many things? ✦ Do you want it to jump out at people or slowly slip into their subconscious?

STEP 4 – Write the name of your company in the center of a sheet of paper. Keep in mind that logo design is an attempt to complement your company name, not overpower it. Words and meaning always comes first, graphics second.

STEP 5 – Sketch ten unique logo designs around your name. If, after experimenting with the techniques listed below, you cannot come up with a unique design, copy the logo design of competitors and other companies substituting your company name for theirs. If you like the result, to avoid infringing upon copyright and trademark laws, make enough changes to your final design so your logo could not possibly be mistaken for the one you copied.

Experiment with:

❑ length of name	❑ intertwined images and figures	❑ irregular shapes	❑ 3d-effects
❑ abbreviations		❑ shaded areas	❑ heavy borders
❑ initials	❑ circular shapes	❑ different colored areas	❑ light borders
❑ size of letters	❑ square shapes	❑ upside down views	❑ good old fashioned doodles
❑ lettering style	❑ triangular shapes	❑ sideways views	

STEP 6 – Scrap or modify your sketched designs based on the following logo design strategies:

EQUAL HOUSING
OPPORTUNITY

- *Scrap or modify all logo designs that don't have presence.* Logos that have presence can be placed on letterhead or in ads in a variety of positions, e.g., top, bottom, left, or right margins, and still look great.

- *Scrap or modify all logo designs that are cluttered with detail.* It is essential that your logo be easy to reproduce. Details can easily be lost in reproduction processes. Too much detail can also detract from your logo's message.

- *Scrap or modify all logo designs that do not seem versatile.* An effective logo will easily adapt itself to different media, with the addition or subtraction of a few lines, shapes and even letters, without destroying its basic appeal.

- *Scrap or modify all logo designs that use letters that are difficult to work with.* B, d, f, h, k, l, t, have ascenders that look good on paper. Words that have descenders like g, j, p, q and y take up more space and can cause problems graphically.

- *Scrap or modify all logo designs that do not have unity between graphics and lettering.* When lettering and graphics are placed together there is considerably room for disharmonious interaction. For example, a highly stylized letter will almost always end up competing with the symbol instead of complementing it. Your design will then look distracting and disorganized, implying your business is the same.

GOLDCORE
INVESTMENTS

- *Scrap or modify all logo designs that cannot be easily rendered in three dimensions.* When embossed on letterhead, a logo should make people want to

touch it. If turned into a charm, it should make people want to play with it in their hands. If turned into a sculpture, it should make people want to hug it.

● *Scrap or modify all logo designs with lettering style that does not complement your desired image.* Typestyles, like people, have individual characters. Some styles appear feminine, others masculine.

● *Scrap or modify all logo designs that do not look good in black and white.* If your logo only looks good when reproduced in full-color and embossed in gold, then you have a serious design problem.

● *Scrap or modify all logo designs with lines, shapes, patterns and letters that do not significantly add to its meaning.* In logo design, LESS is MORE.

● *Scrap or modify all logo designs that do not run letters into each other.* Letters combined together, so they touch each other, legally become graphic symbols and can be granted better protection under trademark laws.

● *Scrap or modify all logo designs that are too complex.* Keep your logo simple! The best logos leave a strong visual impression after being seen ONCE.

STEP 7 – Select three promising logo designs and prepare finished copies using transfer letter sheets and graphic artist techniques or, better yet, a computer drawing program. *Transfer Letter Sheets* can be found at stores that handle artist's materials and at most office supply stores. They come in various typestyles and sizes. Using transfer sheets, your chosen letters or graphics are applied to a poster board (or piece of high quality paper). Other details can then be added in with special black graphic markers and pens. To get the best, cleanest reproduction of your logo, draw it much larger than it will eventually appear on your stationery or other printed matter. Minor imperfections will disappear once it is reduced in size. A photographic negative can then be made of the final product (or use a photocopy machine to shrink it, then cut and paste it to media of your choice).

STEP 8 – Get critical feedback before selecting your final logo. Don't leave the image of your company in the hands of a few. Survey reactions from as many people as possible, preferably potential customers. Find out if they respond in the way you intended. Do they find your logo appealing, informative, and memorable? If they don't know your business, can they guess it?

Sketch at least 6 possible logo designs. Select and draw your final choice in the grids on the next page:

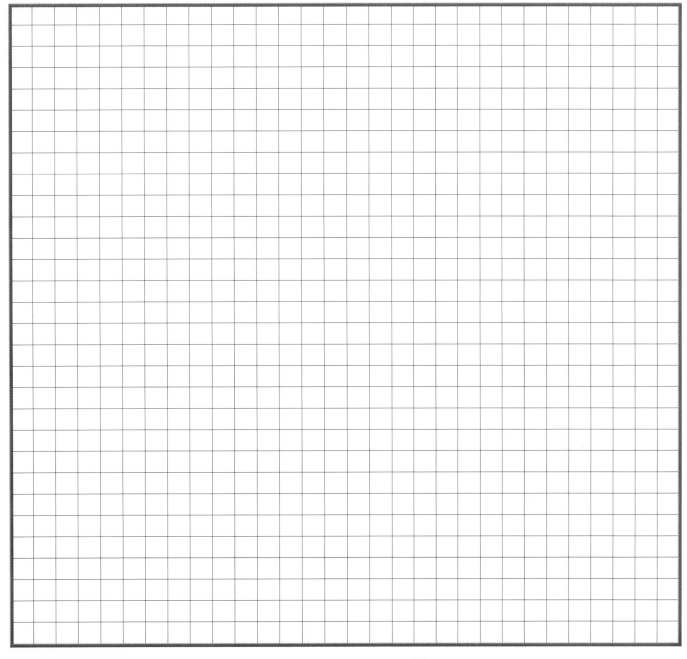

FINAL CHOICE

To Do List

**Business Plan
Overview**
Cover Sheet

✓ Company Mission
   Statement
✓ Copyright Notice
✓ Preparation Notice
✓ Principle Business
   Definition
✓ Summary of
   Business
   Proposition
✓ Targeted Reader
   Statement

*All truly great
successes have
had simple
strategies that
can be easily
communicated
to others.*

**TO WRITE A MISSION
STATEMENT STATE:**

WHO YOU ARE

Pure Passion
Pasta Shop

**MARKETS YOU
WILL SERVE**

individuals,
organizations
and restaurants
looking for fresh,
superior pasta
products

**PRODUCTS
YOU WILL SELL**

additive and
preservative free
pasta products

REASON WHY

to serve more
nutritious pasta

DAY 2

Company Mission Statement

A *Mission Statement* is an attempt to transform your goals and dreams into a single unified vision. It is aimed at getting all members of your organization pulling in the same direction and sharing the same view of your company goals, philosophy, and vision of the future. If given the consideration it deserves, it will reward you repeatedly by enhancing your identity and position in the marketplace. A mission statement is not a few loosely jotted down ideas, a long list of tasks to be completed, nor something that pops into your head while sipping a martini. It is a simple, clear, introspective yet practical statement of purpose that focuses your entire business and helps you recognize *exactly* what business you are in.

Every organization needs a mission statement and many require one for every business unit that is part of their organization. Some experts even go as far to say that all business decisions should be, in one manner or another, based on a mission statement. To more effectively position your company in the minds of your targeted readers, consider putting your mission statement on your cover page.

How Long Should Your Mission Statement Be?

While a plan of action or customer service policy may be many pages, a mission statement should be no more than 25 to 80 words and usually no more than one or two sentences. However, although short, keep in mind that a mission statement is a highly crafted work of ART that will demand a considerable amount of time and energy to refine and transform into the masterpiece it needs to be.

Writing a Mission Statement in "Four Steps"

To write a mission statement: state *who* you are, *where* you want to go, *how* you plan to get there, and *why* you need to do it. More specifically, state exactly what business you plan to go in, who you plan to sell to, and what it is you plan to sell. Summarize by linking these intentions to a compelling reason.

STEP 1 – State *who* you are (i.e., what business you plan to go in). State: ❏ your company name ❏ areas you will specialize in ❏ highlights of your customer service policy ❏ values that will guide your daily decisions.

STEP 2 – State *where* you want to go (i.e., who you plan to sell to). Clarify: ❏ markets you wish to target; your market niché ❏ clientele, individuals or businesses you hope to serve ❏ where your markets are located; their geography ❏ long-term goals; where you want your company to be in 5 or 10 years.

STEP 3 – State *how* you plan to get there (i.e., what you plan to sell). State: ❏ products & services you will offer ❏ customer needs you will meet ❏ key benefits of your products or services ❏ what skills and talents you have that make you superior to the competition ❏ how you plan to beat the competition.

STEP 4 – State *why* you need to do it (i.e., link your intentions to a compelling reason). There is an old saying: "If the *why* is important enough, no *how* is too difficult." Consider the following, few of us would parachute off the *Em-*

pire State Building for any sum of money. But if it meant saving our loved ones, somehow we would find the courage.

In other words, the key ingredient that turns a *mediocre* mission statement into one that makes you misty eyed whenever you think about it, is not a well thought-out list of company policies, targeted markets or amazing new products, but rather a *why* that makes it all worthwhile, a little piece of magic that comes to you in the middle of the night – a seed which allows motivation to blossom.

Sample Mission Statements

Example 1 – *A mission statement for a Pasta Shop*: (see chart on page 8) "We at Pure Passion Pasta will prepare and provide the finest quality all natural pasta products, made without additives or preservatives, to individuals, restaurants and organizations who choose to serve nutritious, delicious fresh pasta."

Example 2 – *Our mission statement:* "The Entrepreneur's Guidebook Series is dedicated to providing you with concise, easy-to-read information and ideas to help you understand the essentials of entrepreneurship."

Example 3 – *A mission statement for the original Star Trek series*: "These are the voyages of the Starship Enterprise. It's five-year mission, to seek out new worlds and new life. To boldly go where no one has gone before."

Example 4 – *A mission statement for Budget Travel*: "Budget Travel provides economical vacation travel and related services to customers in the greater Chicago area, who expect efficient, problem-free travel arrangements at a low cost."

Example 5 – *A mission statement for IBM*: "Our goal is simply stated. We want to be the best service organization in the world."

Example 6 – *A mission statement for Whitefield Markets*: "Whitefield Markets' goal is to be the lowest cost provider of quality foods and groceries in the West Orange area."

Write a draft copy of your mission statement:

FINAL VERSION: "Company Mission Statement"

In a business plan, salable and informative content is your primary concern. However, considering that venture companies receive several thousand business plans a year, an attention-grabbing cover sheet is worth developing.

Confidential Notice Statement

A confidential notice statement can be used to discourage unintended readers from reading your business plan. It is also a great way to generate curiosity.

Copyright Notice

A copyright notice © may be added to discourage people from copying your business plan and distributing it to others without your knowledge.

Preparation Notice

Your business plan should state the month and year it was prepared to give readers an idea of how current it is. It should also state who prepared the plan.

Principle Business Definition

A *Principle Business Definition* defines the nature of your business – what it *is* and what it *does*. It does not focus on your goals nor plans for the future. It focuses on facts. It can also be used to summarize company products or services, desired image, legal form, major business objectives, and/or targeted markets.

List important facts and key ideas of your Principle Business Definition:

Summary of Business Proposition

A *Summary of Business Proposition* unlike a *Mission Statement* or *Principal Business Definition* is aimed at zeroing in on the *needs* and interests of a targeted reader or prospect, as well as the *purpose* of your business plan.

Write a summary statement of your business proposition:

Targeted Reader Statement

In special circumstances, you may want to state the name of a banker, investor, or other specific person on the cover sheet of your business plan to attract their attention e.g., "for James T. Hill CEO of XYZ Inc."

List your targeted reader(s):

Use the following fill-in-the-blanks sheet to help design your cover page:

Company Name

Company LOGO

Company Name

Address

Phone/Fax

Email

URL

Business Plan

for

Company Name

❑ *Mission Statement* ❑ *Principle Business Definition*
❑ *Summary of Business Proposition* ❑ *Targeted Reader Statement*

Contact

Job Title

Address

Phone/Fax

Email

Name of Author   *Date*

Plan Prepared by

Copyright © 20____ by

Company Name or Author

DAY 3
Table of Contents

Your *Table of Contents* should be limited to one page. When designing your table of contents, keep in mind that many readers have "hot buttons." They like to read about cash flow, financial ratios, marketing strategies, or some other narrow interest. Make it easy for them to find the information they need.

Table of Contents – **Sample #1**

Table of Contents Based on SBA's Business Plan Guidelines – **Sample #2**

TABLE of CONTENTS

Use the following fill-in-the-blank sheet as a model to help you design your table of contents:

✓		Page #	✓		Page #
	BUSINESS PLAN OVERVIEW			**Competition Analysis**	
	Cover Sheet			❏ Competitor Descriptions	
	❏ Company Name			❏ Competitive Advantage	
	❏ Company Logo			❏ Competitive Position	
	❏ Company Mission Statement			**Selling Strategies**	
	❏ Confidential Notice Statement			❏ Business Cards	
	❏ Copyright Notice			❏ Company Slogans	
	❏ Preparation Notice			❏ Customer Service Plan	
	❏ Principle Business Definition			❏ Credit Extension Plan	
	❏ Summary of Business Proposition			❏ Distribution Plan	
	❏ Targeted Reader Statement			❏ Market Testing Plan	
	Table of Contents			❏ Pricing Policies	
	Executive Summary			❏ Promotion Plan	
	❏ Business Overview			❏ Publicity Plan	
	❏ Statement of Purpose			❏ Packaging Concept	
	❏ **Fact Sheet**			❏ Personal Selling Program	
	COMPANY PLAN			❏ Previous Marketing Methods	
	❏ **Company Description**			❏ Services & Products Mix	
	❏ Accomplishments			❏ Timing of Market Entry	
	❏ Buildings & Equipment Owned			❏ Warranty Policies	
	❏ Company Goals & Objectives			**Marketing Approach**	
	❏ Company History			**FINANCIAL PLAN**	
	❏ Company Philosophy			**Capitalization Plan**	
	❏ Contracts in Force			❏ Summary of Financial Needs	
	❏ Legal Structure			❏ Capital Required (Start-up Costs)	
	❏ Location			❏ Present Financial Structure (Capital Sources)	
	❏ Expansion Plan			❏ Loans Required	
	❏ Research & Development			**Uses of Funds Statement**	
	Merchandising Plan			**Pro Forma Financial Statements**	
	❏ Description of Principle Products & Services			❏ Twelve-month Income Projection	
	❏ Feasibility Study			❏ Three-year Income Projection	
	❏ Future Products & Services			❏ Cash Flow Statement	
	❏ Purchasing Plan			❏ Breakeven Analysis	
	❏ Proprietary & Exclusive Rights Obtained			❏ Pro Forma Balance Sheet	
	Operating Plan			**Current Financial Statements**	
	❏ Accounting System			❏ Current Income Statement	
	❏ Banking Plan			❏ Current Balance Sheet	
	❏ Buildings, Equipment & Other Purchases			❏ Current Asset Sheet	
	❏ Computerization Plan			❏ Other Financial Projection Statements	
	❏ Communications Set-up			**Business Financial History**	
	❏ Inventory Control			❏ Financial & Operating Ratios	
	❏ Order Entry Control			**Profit Planning**	
	❏ Operations Schedule			❏ Cost Reducing Measures	
	❏ Production/Manufacturing Plan			❏ Retirement Plan	
	❏ Quality Control			❏ Investment Plan	
	❏ Required Licenses & Legal Considerations			❏ Tax Plan	
	Organizational Plan			**Risk Assessment**	
	❏ Board of Directors			❏ Analysis of Competitor's Reactions	
	❏ Contract & Temporary Help			❏ Contingency Plans	
	❏ Management Team			❏ Insurance Plan	
	❏ Manpower Required			❏ Risk-Management Plan	
	❏ Organizational Chart			❏ Security Plan	
	❏ Ownership Structure			**Closing Statement**	
	❏ Professional Advisors			**SUPPORTING DOCUMENTS**	
	MARKETING PLAN			**Check Documents Required**	
	Market Description & Analysis			❏ Contracts & Lease Agreements	
	❏ Market & Industry Trends			❏ Credit Reports	
	❏ Needs Met			❏ Income Tax Returns	
	❏ Target Market Description			❏ Lease Agreements	
	❏ Target Market Analysis			❏ Letters of Reference	
	❏ Target Market Entry Strategy			❏ Personal Financial Statements	
	❏ Target Market Share			❏ Résumés of Management & Key Individuals	
	❏ Summary of Projected Sales			❏ Other Documents	

To Do List

**Business Plan
Overview**
*Executive
Summary*

✓ Executive Summary
✓ Business Overview
✓ Statement of
  Purpose
Fact Sheet
✓ Fact Sheet

DAY 4
Executive Summary

The purpose of an *Executive Summary* is to pique an investor's interest and to include the main highlights of your business plan. It is the heart of your business proposal and the first part that gets read. It is a mini-introduction to your company in which you try and capture the essence of your business in one or two pages (maximum three) using all the persuasion and excitement you can. If this part of your plan does not garner sufficient attention, chances are the rest won't either.

Suggested Executive Summary Topics

The following is a list of possible topics to cover in an *Executive Summary*:

Check topics you wish to cover:

- *Benefits of Your Product or Service* – Talk about the main need you want to meet and why you think that need exists.
- *Bottom Line Financial Figures* – Talk about sales, projected sales, earnings, and after tax profits.
- *Calculated Risks Involved* – Discuss the major risks that threaten the success of your business and how you plan to beat those threats.
- *Company Goals & Philosophies* – Elaborate upon your mission statement.
- *Competitive Pressures* – Talk about your competition and how you plan to beat them; i.e., your competitive advantage.
- *Funds Required* – Talk about the security offered to investors, plan for repayment of a loan, and plan for the use the funds.
- *Highlights of Your Marketing Plan* – Talk about why you have chosen the market you have; what its trends and risks are; where you fit into your particular industry; what will ensure a viable future for your business; what your expected market share is or will be; and who your customer are or will be.

- *Historical Perspectives of Your Business* – Talk about how your business came to be or how long it has lasted and why.
- *Important Facts & Figures* – Talk about or list key facts that may be of interest to your readers.
- *Key Products or Services* – Summarize what you plan to sell.
- *Key Suppliers* – List who you plan to get your merchandise from and what, if any, arrangements you have made to secure their services e.g., contracts.
- *Location of Business* and *Zoning Laws*
- *Other Businesses Your Own* – Describe all your existing or proposed businesses including dates of formation and proposed future operations if any.
- *Significant Trends* – Talk about technology, industry changes and perceptions, as well as significant buying trends; make assumptions on where you fit in to some of these large-scale trends.
- *What's in it for them* – An investor's main concern is: *"What's in it for me?"* Tell them in your first paragraph why they should read your proposal.

Sample Paragraphs for an "Executive Summary"

Use your "Executive Summary" to guide your research efforts. Rewrite it after all needed financial and marketing data is available.
BUSINESS PLAN WRITING TIP

(Company Name) was formed as a (proprietorship, partnership, corporation) in (Month, Year) in (City, State), by (Owners) in response to the following market conditions:

- (Start-up, growth) opportunities exist in the (Product/Service) industry.
- According to (research source), due to (reasons), there has been an increase in (verifiable fact or demographical data that supports growth statement).
- (Names of customers/clients) are willing to place large (orders/contracts) within the next (time period).

If your "Executive Summary" is less than a page, call it a "Business Overview" or "Statement of Purpose."
BUSINESS PLAN WRITING TIP

- Several other prospective (customers/clients), including (names of customers or clients), have expressed serious interest in doing business with us within the next (time period).

(I/We) previously (owned a company, worked within a company) that was active in the (Product/Service) industry. Over the past (time period), (I/we) have spent considerable effort researching ways to improve overall performance and increase profits in the (Product/Service) industry. (I/We) have developed ways to:

- advertise more effectively
- beat the competition's pricing
- expand the market
- increase quality
- lower unit costs

Financial Goals

	Year 1	Year 2	Year 3
Sales (000's)	650.00	3,880	16,649
Net Income	99.03	1,120.83	16,649
EPS	$.25	$2.80	$9.58

A total of ($) has been raised to launch (Company Name). (I/We) need an additional (loan, investment from private individuals and/or companies) of ($), which will be used to finance (working capital, plant equipment, real estate), and (_____).

Business Overview

If your *Executive Summary* is less than a page, it might more effectively be titled a *Business Overview*. A *Business Overview* summarizes key issues in your business plan. It also states what you want to accomplish by having someone read your business plan. It is shorter and more concise that an *Executive Summary*.

Statement of Purpose

A *Statement of Purpose* is similar to a *Business Overview* except that it is usually used when the purpose of your business plan is more specific, e.g., you want your readers to invest in your company, buy shares, give you a loan, become a partner, or extend you an operating line of credit. Below are key areas you should address in a *Statement of Purpose*:

- Describe **WHO** you are and what you sell (also describe where your are located and when your company was established).

- Explain **WHAT** your main objectives are (also explain how you plan to meet those objectives).

- Explain how and **WHY** your business will be successful (what is unique about your business and what your market niche is).

- If you need a loan, explain how **MUCH** you need, why you need it, and what specifically you plan to do with it (explain how it will make you successful).

- Detail **HOW** you plan to repay your loan (principle and interest).

Sample "Statement of Purpose"

(Harry's Pet Supplies), established in (1996) as a (Sole-proprietorship), is a (pet food and supply company) that caters to (pet owners) in the (Northwest Edmon-

Just as one would not think of sending a man to the moon without a flight plan, one should not think of launching a new small business without a business plan.

ton) area. The company is seeking (growth) capital in the amount of ($25,000) for the purpose of (purchasing machinery, which will allow the company to begin manufacturing, packaging and distributing its own brand of puppy chow).

This new product has been tested by current customers of (Harry's Pet Supplies) and has received an exceedingly positive response. Funding is required by (March of 1998). Repayment of the loan and interest can begin within (30 days) of receipt. This loan can be secured by company assets valued at ($80,000).

Check the summary method you will use to highlight the main points of your business plan:

Executive Summary ☐   Business Overview ☐   Statement of Purpose ☐

Outline the main points you wish to discuss in your "Executive Summary," "Business Overview," or "Statement of Purpose":

Year 1	Year 2	Year 3

List your Financial Goals.	Year 1	Year 2	Year 3
Sales ($000's)			
Net Income			
Profit			

Fact Sheet

A *Fact Sheet* is added to a business plan to summarize the basic and most important information of your venture. It should appear as a separate page after your *Executive Summary*. Fill-in what you can now and the rest when your business plan is complete:

Company		Address	

Contact		Phone		Fax		Email	

Form of business organization (proprietorship, partnership, or corporation)   Type of business and industry   Length of time in business

Number and name of founder/partners/shareholders		

Principal product or service line (Principle products and services)

Current and/or projected revenues	$	Current and/or projected market share	%

Funds invested in the business to date and their source

$		$	
$		$	

Additional financing required	$	Proposed terms and payback period	
Total value or net worth of business	$		

Registered patents or trademarks held

Business Advisors	Name	Address	Phone
Legal Counsel			
Accountant			
Insurance Agent			
Banker			

DAY 5
COMPANY PLAN

- Company Description

- Merchandising Plan

- Operating Plan

- Organizational Plan

IN YOUR *Company Plan* describe and summarize all the details of your business. Address as many of the topics outlined below as they relate to your business in an order that seems logical to you. Be prepared to back up your statements and justify any projections made with data in your *Supporting Documents* section.

Company Description

When describing your company in a business plan, refrain from trying to make it sound better or bigger than it really is. A company description should be factual not inspirational. Don't use this section to try and generate good PR.

Sample Company Description Statements

Begin this section with a half or full page summary addressing the most important "key areas" of your company.

In (Month, Year), (Company Name) was formed to (manufacture, distribute, service, consult, etc.) innovative (Products/Services) to (Market). This company is located in (City, State). (I/We) formed this company as a (proprietorship, partnership, corporation). Others involved in this business include: (list names).

The main goal of this company is to . . . (explain).

Initial, financing was arranged through (home equity loans, savings, venture capital, friends and family, etc.) (explain terms, rates and ability to repay).

Our venture has been very successful in generating and increasing sales, as well as effective in achieving profitability. This is due to the following:

- (Reason 1)

- (Reason 2)

- (Reason 3)

Provide a background of your company and details of any other ventures in which individuals on your team or yourself have been involved in.

OR – (Company Name) was recently conceived and is still in the beginning stages. To this point the following has been accomplished:

- A team consisting of (list names and primary responsibility, i.e. Bill Smith - Production), has been formed.

- A prospective (customer/client) list has been drawn up.

- Strategic Planning meetings are being held every Tuesday evening.

- Market research has been conducted in the following areas: (list areas).

List 6 major points you wish to summarize in your company description:

Accomplishments

Outline what your business has accomplished. Be specific. Give your investors something tangible to think about.

Describe and list any success your business has achieved to date. Include successful projects, promotions or R&D:

	Estimated Total Annual Market (Year)	Company Sales (Year)	Market Share (%)
Product/service 1	$ units	$ units	
Product/service 2	$ units	$ units	

Buildings & Equipment Owned

List and describe building(s) owned by your company. Include descriptions, conditions, renovations & remodeling required, interior layouts, and interior designs. List and outline your current company assets as well as your inventory in terms of size, value, rate of turnover and marketability.

List and describe building(s) owned. Describe value, condition and key features. Explain lease agreement (if applicable):

Building	Value $	Condition/Features	Description

Describe your most important company assets. Describe value, condition, make, and lease agreement or financing arrangement (if applicable). Describe how this asset is beneficial to your business:

Asset	Value $	Condition/Features	Description

Company Goals & Objectives

Clearly state the long-term goals of your business by examining strengths, weaknesses, opportunities and threats. Break down each long-term goal into more definable short-term goals and objectives. Quantify your goals by stating time limits if applicable and specific growth projections. If necessary, provide proof how your goals can be reached.

Establishing Long-term Goals & Objectives

To establish long-term company goals (over a year), take a serious look at all the past, present, and future internal and external factors impacting your company. Conduct a SWOT Analysis by examining in detail the strengths, weaknesses, opportunities, and threats facing your business.

Identifying Strengths & Weaknesses

1) *Look at how your company will operate.* Consider factors like your location, equipment, order processing efficiency, storage facilities, and other functions that affect operations.

2) *Look at your financial position.* Consider factors like your bookkeeping method, cash flow, sales revenues and profits.

3) *Look at your staff.* Consider factors like staff turnover rate, sales performance records, and customer service. Determine where individuals are personally the most effective, whether in marketing, product development, sales and customer relations, or management.

Strengths & Weaknesses of Bonachelli's Bakery – The following example outlines the strengths and weakness of a firm that specializes in providing fresh, whole-wheat baked goods for local retail and wholesale clients.

Strengths – ◆ We have excellent quality control for everything we manufacture because of our personal standards and modern facilities and equipment. ◆ We have a well set-up bookkeeping information system that helps us keep track of our performance so we can make better decisions.

Weaknesses – ◆ Some members of our baking staff need more training. ◆ An-

> *The secret of business is to know something that nobody else knows.*
> **ARISTOTLE ONASSIS**

> *Whenever you start a new business venture or expand into new territory, ask yourself the following: (1)* **Who** *is my market? (2)* **What** *can I sell them? (3)* **How** *can I make them want to buy? (4)* **How** *can I start small but think big i.e., minimize my risk and maximize my profit potential?*
> **BUSINESS TIP**

other salesperson would help increase and improve business. ◆ Sometimes delivery is later than promised. ◆ The market does not always seem to know how much healthier our whole grain products are over enriched white flour products.

List strengths:	List weaknesses:

Identifying Opportunities & Threats

1) *Look at your competition.* Consider factors like their location, market share, facilities, equipment, services and products.

2) *Look at local and national economic conditions.* Consider factors like housing starts, retail auto sales, real disposable personal income, unemployment rates and any other factors than may signal a change in the future demand for your goods and services.

3) *Look at emerging trends.* Consider factors like new technology, new markets and changing spending habits of your customers.

Opportunities & Threats of Bonachelli's Bakery –

Opportunities – ◆ Jasper's Bakery down the street has just moved to a new location. We may be able to win over some of their old customers.

Threats – ◆ The opening of a new fast-food restaurant near our location may reduce the amount of doughnuts we sell. ◆ Bad wheat harvests in the last two years, and dangerously low wheat reserves, will likely send flour prices skyrocketing.

List opportunities:	List threats:

Defining Long-term Goals

> *We are not managing this company for the next quarter. We are building it for the next generation.*
> **SAMUEL JOHNSON**
> Chairman, S.C. Johnson and Sons

Now that you have a clearer idea of your company's strengths, weaknesses, opportunities and threats, you will be able to more effectively define precisely what your organization must achieve results in, to achieve the kind of growth desired. Your long-term goals should be realistic, challenging and attainable statements of where you want your company to be in 3 to 5 years following the direction outlined in your mission statement. Long-term goals function as starting and organizational points, to make it easier to process, prioritize, allocate resources, and coordinate related short-term goals and objectives.

Check goals that reflect your long-term plans:

❑ Achieve a 15% rate of return on investment.	❑ Improve distributor or supplier relationships.
❑ Achieve a business net worth of $1 million after 3 years.	❑ Improve financial position.
❑ Build new plants or warehouses.	❑ Improve internal communications.
❑ Capitalize on location, parking and other facilities.	❑ Improve labor relations and personnel training.
❑ Enhance insurance coverage.	❑ Improve the effectiveness of ads and promotions.
❑ Enhance the quality of products and services.	❑ Increase market share within area by 10% in 6 months.
❑ Establish a research & development budget.	❑ Increase revenues.
❑ Foster repeat business.	❑ Open new retail locations.

Quantifying Long-term Goals

After your long-term goals are agreed upon, the next phase of your session is to quantify those that are overly general and vague and make them more meaningful from a practical point of view. This means giving a general goal, a more specific results orientated description. Three examples are illustrated below:

> A committee is something that keeps minutes but wastes hours.
> **ANON**

Example 1 – The goal of "Foster Repeat Business" could be described more specifically as – "We will foster repeat business by becoming more customer-oriented, making it easier for customers to find what they want, offering more competitive prices, and by training staff to make sure customers leave with the feeling their needs have been satisfied and that they want to come back."

Example 2 – The goal of "Improve Financial Position" could be described more specifically as – "We will improve our company's financial position by finding ways to increase our liquidity, solvency and profitability to the following target values: By Dec. 31, 1998, we want to achieve a working capital position of $_____, a net worth of $_____, and a pre tax profit margin of $_____."

Example 3 – The goal of "Increase Revenues" could be described more specifically as – "We will increase revenues by generating new customers, expanding sales to existing customers, acquiring other related businesses, opening new branches, marketing new products & services, and investing income to achieve $_____ in Revenues by Dec. 31, 1996."

List 2 future long-term goals. Quantify these goals:

Establishing Short-term Goals & Objectives

After your long-term goals are prioritized and quantified, you are ready to establish short-term goals and objectives (under a year) to support them. Short-term goals and objectives are aimed at supporting your long-term goals or objectives by specifying how, when, and what you need to do to achieve those goals. They make your long-term goals more realistic by being more specific, measurable, consistent, and time limited (see page 73 "Operations Schedule"). If your long-term goal is to "Increase Sales by 10% in the next year," some short-terms goals you might implement to achieve this goal include:

❑ Change company logo (remove a legal threat) ❑ Develop and market a new service or product (take advantage of an opportunity) ❑ Emphasize the competitive advantage of products in all promotional materials (correct a weakness)	❑ Improve customer relations with major restaurant clients through increased personal contact (correct a weakness) ❑ Retrain sales staff or replace weak sales staff (correct a weakness) ❑ Revise traffic flow of store (correct a weakness)

Sample Goals & Objectives Statements

We at (Company Name) believe very strongly in *financial*, *marketing* and *operational* excellence. To reflect these beliefs we have set the following goals:

We want to be considered as the market leader. To this end we will seek:

☑ trade industry awards ☑ solid financial ratios ☑ a major market share

The present market for (Product/Service) is estimated at $(XXX). Our goal for market share is (XX)%.

In the short term, we have the following market share goals:

1st Year (XX)% 2nd Year (XX)% 3rd Year (XX)% 4th Year (XX)%

> *Microsoft's only factory asset is the human imagination.*
> **FRED MOODY**

> *A "Company History" section should be no longer than two pages.*

To further establish (Company Name) as a market leader, we also plan to: ❑ Aggressively recruit of the best technical staff in the industry. ❑ Budget for computer training for new applications. ❑ Budget for necessary seminars and continuing job-specific education. ❑ (Decrease, Maintain) costs through acquisition of new plant and equipment. ❑ Increase productivity by investing in employee training and education. ❑ Maintain a state-of-the-art accounting system. ❑ (Set up, Maintain) an employee benefit program for continuing college education. ❑ Support company involvement in various local and national charity events.

Company History

Provide a background of your company and a description of any other ventures in which individuals on your team or yourself have been involved in.

State date business was established:

List other key dates and other company background information:

List founders and other key individuals (add résumé's to Supplementary Documents). Describe other ventures you or they were involved in:

Company Philosophy

A "philosophy statement" elaborates on a company's "mission statement." Describe how you wish your company to be perceived. Describe its present image or desired image of the future. Try and capture the spirit of your company without sounding overly dramatic.

Elaborate in more detail 3 critical points expressed in your company's mission statement:

Contracts in Force

List contracts and agreements in force including management contracts, shareholder or partnership agreements, franchiser service agreements, and service contracts. Indicate which ones are included in your supporting documents section.

List and describe key contracts and agreements in force:

Legal Structure

Describe the legal structure of your company and reasons for choosing that structure. If a partnership, list the names and addresses of owners and what percentage of the business they own. If a corporation, give dates of commencement as well as state/province of incorporation. Also, list principal shareholders and share distribution. If you plan to change your legal structure in the future, explain reasons, when the change will take place, and how the change will benefit your company.

NOTE Depending on whether you are a proprietorship, partnership or corporation, include a copy of your business license, partnership agreement, or incorporation charter, articles and bylaws, in the supporting documents section.

Sole Proprietorships

A sole proprietorship is a form of business where one person assumes complete liability for all actions of the business. About seventy percent of the thirteen million businesses in the United States are in this category.

PROS – ❑ absolute control over decision making (no bosses to issue orders, supervise your coming and goings, challenge your decisions, or gawk over your shoulder) ❑ ease of formation ❑ easy to terminate ❑ flexibility of management ❑ low startup costs ❑ possible tax advantages ❑ relative freedom from government control ❑ sole ownership of profits (all profits go straight to you the owner, profits become your personal income and are taxed as such).

CONS – ❑ difficulty in obtaining long-term financing or start-up capital (banks consider you a higher risk than corporations or partnerships) ❑ highly subjective decision making (limited by your own skills, experience & management capabilities) ❑ less available capital ❑ limited business deductions ❑ personal affairs often get mixed up with businesses affairs ❑ unlimited liability (if your business fails your creditors can take away your home, automobile, bank accounts, and any other personal assets you hold until all the debts are fully satisfied) ❑ unstable business life (What happens if you become seriously ill for an extended period?).

General Partnerships

A general partnership is created when two or more individuals, other partnerships or corporations, decide to combine their financial and intellectual resources to create and run a new company. There is no limit to the type of partners or number of partners. The primary advantage of this business formation is the pooling of talent, experience and capital. However, dual and multiple ownership can lead to serious complications if the relationships between individuals break down. Quite often the *pool* becomes a *drain*.

PROS – ❑ avoids double taxation (unlike corporations, the profits from partnerships are not taxed twice) ❑ broader array of skills and talents ❑ direct ownership of profits ❑ easier to obtain investment capital (investors and formal venture capital organizations are more comfortable with teams, rather than individual en-

Comparison of Legal Entities	Difficulty & cost to form	Difficulty & cost to maintain	Risk of owner liability	Difficulty of tax preparation	Flexibility of ownership	Cost of terminating business
Sole Proprietorship	low	low	high	low	low	low
Partnership	low to moderate	low	high	moderate	moderate	high
Corporation	high	high	low	high	high	high
Subchapter S-Corporation	high	high	low	high	low	high

trepreneurs) ❑ emotional support flexibility (a partnership is more flexible than a corporation, but less flexible than a proprietorship).

CONS – ❑ complex partnership agreement required (a partnership agreement should specify: objectives of partnership, date of commencement, amount of investment contributed by each partner, how profits and losses will be shared, provisions in the event of death, duties and responsibilities of each partner, how decisions will be made, duration of agreement, transfer of ownership procedures, dissolution of partnership, and other special clauses) ❑ difficulty in finding a suitable partner ❑ difficulty in obtaining long-term financing (partnerships cannot obtain long-term or short-term financing as readily as a corporation) ❑ divided authority (there's nothing worse than three guys or gals driving the same car) ❑ general partnership interest can not be sold without consent of the other partners.

Corporations

A corporation – sometimes called a "C-Corporation," "Incorporated Company," or "Limited Company" – is a legal entity that is chartered by and subject to the laws of the state or province in which incorporated in and is separate and distinct from the person(s) who own(s) it. The owners of the corporation, known as its shareholder or stockholder, are not personally responsible for the losses of the business. A corporation may own property, borrow money, incur debts, enter into contracts, sue or be sued. Generally speaking, the higher the risk and liability, the more money involved, and the larger the scope of your business, the more you should consider the corporate structure.

PROS – ❑ delegated authority of management (a board of directors and officers gives structure to the decision-making process) ❑ ease of securing funds (corporations have a significantly easier time attracting investors or securing capital in large amounts and from many investors including banks and individuals) ❑ flexible staffing ❑ founders can semi-retire more easily ❑ larger management base ❑ limited liability (shareholders are generally protected from liability and can lose only the money they have invested in the corporation) ❑ ownership is readily transferable ❑ possible tax advantages ❑ stability (a corporation is distinct from the individuals who own it and has a continuous existence despite management or ownership changes, or even the death of key shareholders or founding members).

CONS – ❑ complex management structure required (need to elect a board of directors; write a charter, articles, and bylaws; hire officers of the corporation e.g., CEO, VP, financial officer, etc.) ❑ corporate activities limited by numerous laws ❑ costly to maintain ❑ more government reporting and bookkeeping.

Describe legal structure and reasons for choosing that structure:

Sole proprietorship ❑   Partnership ❑   Corporation ❑   Other ❑

To Do List

Company Plan
Company Description

✓ Location Analysis

A city is like a magnet – the bigger it is, the greater the drawing power.
S. TENENBAUM

DAY 6

Location

Finding the right location for your business is a challenging task. A business will often flounder or flourish simply because a bad or prime location is found. Be prepared, before making any long-term financial commitments, and before investing any amount of time and energy developing a site, to roll up your sleeves and conduct some serious research into all the factors that might affect the success of your decision. A little sweat now can prevent a big headache later on.

NOTE Include photos or drawings of the location and building in your supporting documents section.

Check important factors:

Choosing the AREA	Choosing the SITE
❑ *Accessibility to Customers* – Is it easy for your target market to drive, bus or walk to your site? If the site is in a remote location, will savings in rent offset the inconvenience?	❑ *Building Appearance* – Does the building have an attractive exterior, adequate storefront, highly visible display windows etc.? Are sidewalks in good repair?
❑ *Age, Family & Income Demographics* – Are the demographics of the community agreeable? Is the population growing? Is the area supported by a strong economic base?	❑ *Building Design and Layout* – Does the physical site, fencing, roadways, and the design and layout of the building suit your needs? Does it have special lighting, heating or ventilation features that you need?
❑ *Area Trends* – Is their good potential for economic growth? Is the area new and growing? Are new industries scheduled to open in the next several months?	❑ *Building Site Utilities and Communications Access & Conditions* – Are water, soil, sewer, power and other utility conditions are favorable? Is the street lighting good?
❑ *Availability of Employee Housing* – If you need to provide employees with housing, is it available at a reasonable price?	❑ *Competitor Saturation* – Are competition levels healthy and even beneficial? Will you have a competitive advantage?
❑ *Community Services* – Are there good schools, hospitals, and recreation facilities in the area?	❑ *Convenience to Related Businesses* – Are related businesses, which encourage customer traffic, close by?
❑ *Construction Costs* – If you have to build are construction and labor costs reasonable?	❑ *Customer's Perceptions* – Does the building and area fit in with the perceptions of your customers?
❑ *Distance to Suppliers* – Are you close to suppliers & raw materials?	❑ *Expansion Potential* – Is their expansion potential?
❑ *Environmental Restrictions* – Are there any special environment restrictions?	❑ *Future Land Value* – Will the land retain its value and appreciate over the years?
❑ *Friendliness of Business Climate* – Has the neighborhood or area supported other businesses like yours in the past?	❑ *Leasing Costs & Conditions* – Can the site be rented or leased? What are the costs and terms? Is the per sq. ft charge competitive? Does the landlord provide helpful services?
❑ *Insurance Costs* – Are insurance rates for the area reasonable?	❑ *Occupancy History* – Were previous businesses successful? Is there a low business failure rate on nearby sites?
❑ *Labor Pool & Market* – Is there a convenient source of labor from which to hire skilled and unskilled workers?	❑ *Parking* – Is their adequate parking convenient to your store?
❑ *Media Channels* – Are advertising & publicity opportunities cost effective? Are there any cooperative advertising programs?	❑ *Renovations Required* – Are minimal renovations required?
❑ *Mortgage Costs* – If you need to build or buy in the area, can you get good terms for a loan or mortgage?	❑ *Site Location* – Is the site on the sunny side of the street? Is the location close to a main artery? How close is the building to bus stops and other transportation?
❑ *Municipal Services* – Is there adequate water and sewer services? Is there adequate fire and police protection?	❑ *Storage Available* – Are there adequate on-premises facilities? If not, are affordable and available warehouse facilities nearby?
❑ *Quality of Residency* – Is their little air, noise and water pollution?	❑ *Success Potential* – Do nearby businesses look prosperous?
❑ *Support Systems* – Do you have easy access to banking, communication, professional, janitorial and other services?	❑ *Traffic Flow* – Is their enough pedestrians and/or automobiles passing? Does the location look conducive to drop-in customers? Do pedestrians look like prospective customers? Is street traffic fairly heavy all day?
❑ *Tax Advantages* –Are there any incentives for startups?	❑ *Zoning Regulations* – Is the site free from local ordinances or special zoning regulations that would restrict your business?
❑ *Trade Support* – Is there a local Chamber of Commerce, Merchants' Association or other pertinent trade group?	
❑ *Trading Area Size* – Is the "trading area" large enough?	
❑ *Transportation Routes* – Is their easy access to highways, buses, taxies, railways etc.? Are any super highways or throughways planned for the area?	

More advertising and promotion dollars will be needed to support a poor location.

Sample Location Description

(Company Name) will be operated at (Address). This location is desirable because: ❑ Traffic flow has been rated high. ❑ Rent is below market. ❑ Building has the necessary facilities to operate this business. ❑ Location is convenient for our customers. ❑ Location is convenient for our freight companies, suppliers, clients and employees. ❑ Possibility of expansion if needed in the future.

We are renting this building on a (XX) year lease. We will be renovating at a cost of $(X) based upon 3 estimates. The building is zoned (R-3, commercial use).

State address of location. Describe general location area and site features:

Describe unique site features:

Describe the main advantages of your location:

Describe the main disadvantages of your location:

Describe the neighborhood:

Describe the costs of the location and whether it is leased or owned:

Describe traffic flow patterns and location visibility:

Summarize the zoning situation, and list any relevant zoning restrictions:

Describe accessibility to customers (describe convenience of transportation facilities)

Describe accessibility to suppliers (of particular importance to manufacturing firms):

Describe availability of transport service (of particular importance to manufacturing firms):

Describe other businesses in the area:

Compare your location to your competitors. What is your competitive advantage?

Describe parking facilities. Draw a diagram if necessary:

Describe size and sales floor space:

Describe condition and renovations required:

Describe growth features:

```
[                                                              ]
[                                                              ]
```

Describe whether relocation will be necessary in the future (and if so, its effects on operating costs):

```
[                                                              ]
[                                                              ]
[                                                              ]
```

List any other outstanding reasons for choosing the location:

```
[                                                              ]
[                                                              ]
[                                                              ]
```

LOCATION ANALYSIS WORKSHEET

Address:		Name of Realtor/contact person:
Phone #:		Sq. footage/cost/month: $

History of location	
Location in relation to target market	
Location in comparison to your competition	
Traffic patterns for customers	
Traffic patterns for suppliers	
Availability of parking (draw diagram)	
Notes on walking tour of the area	
Neighboring shops & local business climate	
Availability of raw materials & supplies	
Availability of labor force	
Labor rate of pay for the area	
Housing availability for employees	
Crime rate for area	
Zoning regulations	
Quality of public services (e.g., police, fire)	
Adequacy of utilities (get info from company reps)	
Tax rates (state, county, payroll, special taxes)	

To Do List

Company Plan
Company Description

✓ Planned Expansion
✓ Research & Development

DAY 7

Expansion Plan

If you plan to expand your business at some point in the future, outline and support how you plan to do this. Keep in mind that market forces should ultimately determine the size of your company. When sales increase, allow your company to expand naturally, don't force it. Likewise when sales decrease, make sure your company can contract so fixed costs don't consume all your profits.

When Should You Actively Pursue Growth?

Before committing to expansion, determine whether you and your business are indeed ready to expand. Consider the following:

Expand only if your business is already profitable. Profitability is important to business growth because it makes it easier to obtain financing for expansion. However, this is the opposite of how accounting systems are normally operated for tax purposes. To reduce taxes, accountants and business owners often try to show a loss or as little profit as possible, which allows the business to retain more cash. From this standpoint, if you need financing, your business should be profitable for several years before initiating a growth phase.

Expand when you can project increased profits. To increase profits, you can increase the absolute $ amounts of sales or the profit as a % of sales. If these two can be achieved simultaneously, the resulting growth will be more rewarding.

Expand when you can spot *saturation* or *operational bottlenecks* in your present facility. Determine how many additional customers you could service by building up or out and compare the additional sales to the cost of construction and temporary inconvenience. For example, if you have noticed increasing numbers of abandoned carts in your grocery store, this could mean shoppers are leaving when they realize the checkout line is too long. To solve this problem, increase your number of checkouts.

Expand when you can spread existing fixed costs over a large sales volume. When expansion can result in spreading existing fixed costs over a large sales volume, the decision to increase size is justified. However, whenever you have to increase fixed costs to attain higher sales levels, carefully investigate the proportion of the increase before proceeding with growth plans.

> *Business is talking a pile of cash, doing something with it, and winding up with a bigger pile of cash.*
> **LEONARD SHAYKIN**
> Managing Partner

> *Many managers of unprofitable businesses believe to solve their problems they should grow to spread fixed costs over a larger number of units, thereby improving gross margin. This is mistake. Fix your problem first. Don't make the hole bigger.*

Write down 3 reasons why your company is ready to expand, supported by 3 conditions in the marketplace, which support your reasons:

Protecting Your Company from Explosive Growth

Controlled growth is growth that is cautious, carefully charted, and carried along through regular planning sessions, progress reviews, and program modifications. On the other hand, explosive growth is growth that embraces a substantial element of peril that may actually destroy the potential of a budding company. When not backed by sales, it scares most bankers and investors and can lead to serious complications. Symptoms of dangerous explosive growth include:

- ❏ excessive numbers of employees
- ❏ climbing employee turnover rates
- ❏ loss of marketing coordination and control
- ❏ confused lines of authority
- ❏ general dissatisfaction and even dissension among customers and employees
- ❏ improperly trained department heads and supervisors
- ❏ proliferation of departments
- ❏ increased overhead
- ❏ runaway advertising costs
- ❏ slipping profits despite increasing sales

Write down any problems you anticipate if your company grows and how you plan to solve these problems:

> *Excellent firms don't believe in excellence – only in constant improvement and constant change.*
> **TOM PETERS**

> *Cartels are like babies: we tend to be against them until we have one of our own.*
> **LORD MANCROFT**

Sample Growth Strategy Statements

After having successfully introduced (Product Name) into the (Canadian) market, we will continue to expand in the following two market areas:

(Market Area #1)	(Market Area #2)

To increase sales in the (Canadian) market we will increase national advertising and begin targeting smaller accounts and specialty outlets. We also intend to offer our sales reps the opportunity to sell our products exclusively by joining our company, when we reach our first year sales goals. Those who desire to remain independent will be replaced with our own sales staff.

OR

After having successfully completed our entry phase into the (Vancouver) market, we will expand by: (a) enlarging telemarketing pool from 8 to 15; (b) doubling number of direct sales reps; (c) and franchising into neighboring cities, including (Seattle, Victoria and Portland).

Sample Targeting New Market Statements

To foster continued growth, we will use the following methods to expand our market and increase sales revenues: ◆ Develop closer customer contact to find out needs. ◆ Set up a customer referral system. ◆ Add complementary (Product/Service)s. ◆ Exhibit at trade shows. ◆ Register with (Organization). ◆ Follow-up on Federal and State Government trade leads. ◆ Conduct regional market surveys. ◆ Invest $(XXX) in R&D.

> *To stay profitable during expansion, a balance should be maintained between operating items on your income statement, and asset & liability items on your balance sheet. E.g., if sales average $500,000 per year and A/Rs on your balance sheet average $50,000, a balance of 10% exists. If growth is obtained by offering easier credit terms, the balance could be altered if sales are $1,000,000 and A/Rs average $150,000 (15%).*
> **BUSINESS TIP**

List and describe how you plan to expand your business:

❑ **Relocation** – If it appears unlikely that you can draw more customers to your present location (at a reasonable cost), consider moving closer to your customers. A location on *Main Street*, in a shopping mall or an industrial park may cost you more in rent, but if you gain exposure to new customers it may be a sound investment.	❑ **Downward Vertical Diversification** – If your profits depend on costs for raw materials, a profitable growth strategy may be to buy a farm or mine to produce your own materials. This strategy also makes sense if product quality is based on a consistent supply of goods of an acceptable quality level.
❑ **Upward Vertical Diversification** – Most manufacturing start-ups are forced to use existing marketing channels and sell through established manufacturer's reps, independent wholesales, etc. who have access to the market. However, as you grow, it makes sense to analyze your distribution system to see if you can improve your situation by hiring your own sales team, contracting distributors, buying a truck fleet, opening your own wholesale operation, or adding retail or factory outlet stores.	❑ **Horizontal Diversification** – Horizontal diversification involves adding other similar products or business lines. For example, a soft drink manufacturer sees a new market for bottled water. The bottled water is related to its current activity and uses some of the same equipment, thus reducing overhead costs.
	❑ **OTHERS** – Direct Marketing; Exporting; Joint Ventures; Network Marketing; Licensing; Franchising.

> *BIG is no good if your foundation is weak. A giant with skinny legs is an invitation to be tripped.*

> *During a growth phase, be prepared to experience increased personal commitment, increased pressure, and reductions in cash flow.*

Research & Development

Research and development is not only for high-tech startups and manufacturers. Service operations can also benefit from such efforts.

Sample Research & Development Statements

(I/We) have already spent a considerable amount of time researching and developing (my/our) (Product). So far (I/we) have been able to discover (Describe Discovery or Development), which has helped (Reduce Costs, Increase Sales). The largest achievement to date is the discovery of . . . (Describe Discovery). However, now that (my/our) research is becoming more experimental, (I/we) anticipate a considerable lag time before results can be realized. (I/We) have budgeted (X)% of revenues for the next four years for R&D.

(My/Our) next research project will center on . . . (Describe Next Project).

(My/Our) present joint research program with (Name of University or Institution) has proven very beneficial. (I/We) have also been investigating several government funding sources (Describe Programs).

Describe your research and development efforts:

To Do List
Company Plan
Merchandising Plan

✓ Description of
   Principle Products
   & Services

✓ Feasibility Study

✓ Future Products &
   Services

DAY 8
Merchandising Plan

A *Merchandising Plan*, also known as a *Sales Plan*, describes what products or services you will produce or provide. Merchandising plans also make projections based upon estimated sales to determine the amount of inventory needed. It also describes and compares the prices, quality and credit terms of potential suppliers.

Description of Principle Products & Services

Under this heading, provide a description of your products and services with an assessment of their strengths and weaknesses and marketability. If you have both a product and a service that work together to benefit your customers (such as a warranty service), make sure to mention this. Also, indicate the features and benefits that both you and the competition provide, those that some of the competition provide, and those that only you provide. Specific questions you may want to provide answers for in your product and service description include:

- What is special or unique about your product or service that separates it from the competition? Is it a specialty or uniqueness offered by none or few others?

- Will your prices be competitive in value? Will your product or service be competitive based on its quality, selection, price or location? Will your product or service lead to repeat business?

- What are the fixed costs associated with providing your product or service? What raw materials are used to make your product?

- What are the technologies used and technical advantages of your production techniques over your competitors?

- What special training or skill is necessary to provide the product or service? Do you have these skills?

Sample Product/Service Descriptions

(Company Name) intends to offer (Product/Service). This (Product/Service):

Product – ❏ offers the lowest price on the market ❏ is the most technically advanced ❏ offers more useful features than the competition ❏ saves customers time and money ❏ offers our users better value per dollar ❏ provides an alternative way to . . . (Describe Goal).

Service – ❏ provides a service which is not presently available in this area ❏ is strengthened by a team with combined experience of (XX) years.

We have a (Copyright, Trademark, Patent) and exclusive marketing rights for this (Product/Service) in the (Geographical Area). Our exclusive marketing rights will last until (XX) at which time they may be extended for (XX) years or terminated. Even though the technology used to create (Product) is new, we expect that others will be able to reproduce our results within (XX) years. To remain competitive, we will need to devote approximately (XX)% of revenues towards R&D.

The information compiled and organized in your merchandising plan makes great fodder for writing brochures and other promotional literature.

A man visiting a small boomtown called Cisco, Texas, noticed a lot of activity at the town's little hotel. Thinking that it was likely that ALL boomtown hotels did exceptionally well, he was immediately intrigued. This young man had always wanted to be a banker but put this idea on hold. His name: Conrad Hilton.
SUCCESS STORY

Describe your principle product and/or service:

Describe how your products complement your services and vice versa:

Provide details of other important products and services:

	Product/Service	Description	Unique Features	Stage of Development
1				
2				
3				

Describe patents or trademarks held or applied for:

Describe franchise or licensing agreements and regulatory, certification, or other requirements:

Discuss key success factors in your product(s) or service(s) and how you plan to exploit them:

Profitable Small Business Products & Services

The following two checklists describe factors and characteristics that help make a PRODUCT or SERVICE profitable:

Check the following factors and characteristics as they apply to your product:

❏ better than the competition ❏ comes complete with everything you need ❏ convenient to use ❏ costs three to four times less than its selling price ❏ does not demand more time than it is worth to develop or market ❏ durable, unbreakable ❏ easily understood through its advertising ❏ easy to mail and ship	❏ easy to maintain ❏ fully guaranteed ❏ hard to find in retail stores ❏ has a definite targetable market ❏ has no moving parts to break down (and if it does these moving parts are hermetically sealed against the probing fingers of three-year olds and other would-be adjusters of fine mechanisms) ❏ has sold well previously through mail order and retail	❏ has universal appeal ❏ made out of quality materials ❏ necessary to enjoy sports or other past-time activities ❏ novel and unusual ❏ recommended by experts or authorities ❏ safe to use ❏ satisfies a real customer need ❏ scientifically constructed ❏ will generate repeat orders

Check the following factors and characteristics as they apply to your service:

❏ has a definite targetable market ❏ has done well previously as a home or service business ❏ has general appeal	❏ has not saturated the market ❏ keeps customers coming back ❏ lends itself to the merchandising of related products	❏ produces long lasting results ❏ satisfies a real customer need ❏ does not demand more time than it is worth to develop or market

In 1942, Norman Edmund started his own scientific equipment business selling specialty lenses for $1 each through $9 classified ads. Now his company, Edmund Scientific produces more than $23 million in revenue per year and employs more than 160 people.
SUCCESS STORY

Researching Hot New Ideas for Products & Services

To hunt down new products & services, read consumer magazines, trade publications, and competitor's catalogs targeted towards consumers you wish to serve. Make it a habit of visiting libraries, government research centers, manufacturer's reps, trade fairs and anywhere particulars about people's buying habits and needs can be observed. Learn everything you can about your target market.

Realize that the key to knowing what can be sold tomorrow is understanding what is being sold today.

Get every easily available catalog or magazine targeted towards your chosen market. Interview friends, family and people on the streets who might be interested in the direction your business is taking. Ask them what products & services they want or need. Visit your local library and make a list of all their available resources and which of them are most useful to you. Find out if your library has a copy of: ❏ *Encyclopedia of Business Information* ❏ *Sources & Business Organizations, Agencies, and Publications Directory* ❏ *Small Business Sourcebook.*

List research sources for your products or services:

> *Criticism comes easier than craftsmanship.*
> **ZEUXIS**

Feasibility Study

Identify the product or service you plan to sell, and most importantly, what human need it satisfies. Describe whether this need is presently unfulfilled, whether demand can be easily influenced by advertising, and to what extent you will be entering a market where demand already exceeds supply. Use the following "80 Drill Questions" to help evaluate your ideas:

The following 80 questions are called "Drill Questions" because they should be answered quickly without second-guessing yourself. Eventually, you should become so familiar with them that they become second nature (i.e., drilled into you). Select those most applicable to your business:

| PROJECT IDEA | **80 Product & Service "Drill Questions"** |

MARKET DEMAND
❑ Does it have a definite targetable market?
❑ Is the target market responsive?
❑ Is the target market stable?
❑ Is the target market not yet saturated with competitive interests?
❑ Is the target market growing?
❑ Do you have enough experience and training to understand the needs of the target market?
❑ Are the strategies of other companies, who have already successfully catered to the target market, easy to duplicate?
❑ Can the target market be easily influenced by advertising?
❑ Is the target market more than large enough to make the project worthwhile?
❑ Are you genuinely interested in the typical customer representative of the target market?

PRODUCT/SERVICE VALUE
❑ Is it a quality product or service?
❑ Is it unique?
❑ Is it competitive?   ❑ Is it innovative?
❑ Does it offer real value to its customers?
❑ Will it be easy to sell?
❑ Does it have one easily desirable benefit of incredible value?
❑ Will you have no fear of financial loss if you give it an ironclad guarantee?
❑ Would you buy it yourself?
❑ Does it truly interest you?

COMPANY EASE OF FORMATION
❑ Is it compatible with your current mission statement and company philosophy?
❑ Does it easily lend itself to a catchy name?
❑ Does it easily lend itself to a catchy slogan?
❑ Can it be trademarked or branded?
❑ Will your logo look impressive attached to it?
❑ Is it photogenic?
❑ Can it be easily packaged?
❑ Is it not too revolutionary?
❑ Will it create customer apprehension?
❑ Does it fit in with your own personal image?

COMPANY SET-UP COSTS
❑ Can a company be set up to sell it with little capital investment?
❑ Will it generate a return on investment fast, so you won't suffer cash flow problems?
❑ Is there little red tape in selling it?
❑ Can the project be completed quickly?
❑ Will you be able to convince a bank to lend you money for it if you need it?
❑ Will you be able to convince friends, family, relatives and your spouse to support it?
❑ Can you accumulate resource material on it?
❑ Do you know people who would be willing to help you set-up a company to sell it?
❑ Does it allow you to take advantage of advanced technology?
❑ Can you run the business part-time so you don't have to quit your regular job?

ADVERTISING POTENTIAL
❑ Can you use cheap advertising to market it?
❑ Can you take advantage of as many forms of advertising as possible to market it?
❑ Can it be explained easily through words only?
❑ Will it live up to its advertising?
❑ Can it be explained easily through pictures in advertising?
❑ Will it give your customer, not just what they expected, but also something a little better?
❑ Can it be promoted well through direct marketing channels?
❑ Can it be made to appeal to a customer's basic instincts, desires and drives?
❑ Will it take little advertising before the consumer overcomes reservations about it?
❑ Will you be able to copy your competitor's advertising practices with little difficulty?

MARKET POTENTIAL
❑ Can it be tested without investing a large amount of capital?
❑ Does it lend itself to a variety of market testing strategies?
❑ Will the results of market testing be accurate?
❑ Can your friends or family test it for you and give you accurate feedback?
❑ Can recognized institutions test it for you and give you accurate feedback?
❑ Can you find a good mailing or customer list for it in which to test market response?
❑ Can you promote it at a trade show?
❑ Will you be able to test it within a short period of time?
❑ Is the market timing of it right?
❑ Can strangers test it for you and give you accurate feedback?

EXPANSION POTENTIAL
❑ Does it fit in with your long-range plans?
❑ If it takes off, do you have the resources to capitalize on it?
❑ Will it be easy to find the right kind of skilled labor if your company needs to hire?
❑ Can you easily train other to promote & sell it?
❑ Can it be sold through regular distribution channels?
❑ Would the government or large corporations be interested in it?
❑ Can you sell it internationally?
❑ Will it have a long sales life or is it just a fad?
❑ Can you improve upon it at a later date and offer a better version?
❑ Will you be able to sell the idea to other entrepreneur's?

PROFIT POTENTIAL
❑ Does it have a high mark up that people would be willing to pay for?
❑ Is it unlikely to be returned?
❑ Does it lend itself to repeat sales?
❑ Will company overhead be low?
❑ Will it be easy to transfer profits to other investments?
❑ If you tire of the business, will it be easy to sell?
❑ Are their tax advantages in selling it?
❑ Will you be able to build owner's equity by buying good quality commercial land?
❑ If sales start to lag, will you be able to cut you losses and start another project?
❑ Will it be easy to protect with patents, etc.?

*List factors that support **why** your business will be successful and **why** your proposition is feasible:*

Future Products and Services

The word "entrepreneur" means *to act*. Entrepreneurs thus *continuously search* for new areas of opportunity, envisioning what the future will be like, how it will change, and what needs may result. They learn how to search for unmet needs, exploit change, foster innovation, introduce new products, and enter new markets.

Creating New Market Opportunities

Search for the unmet need. Entrepreneurs are bloodhounds. But, instead of sniffing out lost children or escaped convicts, they learn how to sniff out the unmet needs of the people they wish to serve. To *win* new customers, ask yourself: "What's the unmet want and how can I meet this unmet want before someone else does?" To *keep them for life*, ask: "How can I anticipate their unmet wants before they even know they have them?" Below are 2 strategies for finding unmet needs and turning them into golden market opportunities.

- *Look for an existing network of distributors or dealers who do not have access to a product.* Sometimes, consumers can't get products because local distributors don't have them and can't get them due to circumstances out of their control e.g., a blizzard closes access to a city or town by road, hence essential items have to be flown in by air.

- *Look for the pain in people's lives and solve it.* Pain can be found by looking at routine activities and noticing their rhythms. Where does the rhythm fail, where does anxiety build? At that point, an opportunity waits.

Exploit change. There is no doubt that the entrepreneurs who prosper *tomorrow* are the ones who "adapt quickly to change" *today*. However, of more interest is the fact that the overwhelming majority of truly successful entrepreneurs are the ones who actually "seek & exploit change." Spotting change is a manner of having big ears and watchful eyes. It means jotting down notes everywhere you go hoping that one day they may add up to something no one else has yet recognized or taken advantage of. It means going to trade shows, business conferences and listening in office elevators. It means reading carefully the business pages of newspapers and watching for contracts received and personnel changes. It even means getting invited to your competitor's office parties by hook or by crook.

To exploit change and create new opportunities look for: ◆ an unexpected success or failure ◆ changes in perception ◆ changes inside or outside the structure of an industry ◆ changing values between suppliers and customers ◆ complacency ◆ converging technologies ◆ demographic changes ◆ intellectual arrogance ◆ industry regulation or deregulation ◆ lack of change ◆ rapid growth ◆ recession.

Foster innovation. Innovators are conservative in nature. They are not risk-focused; they are opportunity focused. Innovation is organized, systematic, and rational work that begins with the analysis of opportunities. These opportunities exist only in the marketplace. Profitable innovation is the result of an *effect* in the economy or society, a change in the *behavior* of customers, or a change in a *process*, i.e., how people work and produce something. Profitable innovation is always close to the market, focused on the market, and indeed inspired by the market. It begins by finding practical needs and then meeting those needs.

> *Business has only two basic functions – marketing and innovation.*
> **PETER DRUCKER**

> *Almost every advance in art, cooking, medicine, agriculture, engineering, and marketing, has occurred when someone challenged the rules and tried another approach.*

To foster innovation and create new market opportunities: ♦ allow your workers to develop ideas in small unified teams ♦ avoid tunnel vision ♦ be prepared to work hard ♦ carefully analyze all the necessary factors before you innovate ♦ develop a specialty skill ♦ don't be different for the sake of being different ♦ don't splinter your efforts ♦ don't try and innovate for the future – innovate for the present ♦ don't copy or steal – improve and emulate ♦ encourage free thought during meetings ♦ focus on actual progress, not on paperwork ♦ give a little to gain a lot ♦ keep funding low, deadline pressure high ♦ keep your innovations simple ♦ look, ask and listen ♦ nurture experimentation ♦ put together a "reverse engineering" team ♦ put yourself in the shoes of others to gain objectivity over your new innovation ♦ strive to be the market standard ♦ take advantage of someone else's innovation ♦ try not to be too clever ♦ urge your people to make at least ten mistakes a day ♦ when introducing an innovation, don't be tentative about it.

Enter a new market with an old product or introduce a new product to an old market. Entering a *new market* with a *new product* or *service* is very difficult for any business, especially for a new business. You can never be sure it will perform satisfactorily nor may you have the experience or market knowledge to be certain it will indeed meet the needs of your customers. Likely, you will end up with the impossible task of trying to sell something you have never sold before to people who have never bought anything from you. You may even lose old customers who are wondering where your loyalties went (see chart).

When entering a new market or introducing a new product, be cautious. When entering a *new market*, it is wiser (and more profitable) to sell *old products*. When introducing a *new product*, it is wiser to target an *old market*.

Entering New Markets

	Existing Product	Innovative Product	New Product
Existing Market	Women's Shampoo	*Alternative Greeting Cards*	Solid State Digital Camera
Identifiable Market (targetable)	Clothes for Professional Women	*Two Way Cable TV*	Specialty Sports Car
Unknown Market	Mobile Pet Grooming Service	*Personal Computers*	Video Disks

List 3 strategies you will use to find new products and services:

List and describe what kinds of future products and services you plan to provide:

To Do List

Company Plan
Merchandising Plan

✓ Purchasing Plan

✓ Proprietary & Exclusive Rights Obtained

DAY 9

Purchasing Plan

In this section of your business plan, explain when orders will be placed, when the first delivery will be received, when inventory will peak, when reorders will no longer be placed, and when key items will no longer be stocked. Also, describe where you get your inventory or raw materials from, buying terms, volume discount policies, and delivery policies. Discuss and list names and addresses of key suppliers. Describe where they are located, why you chose them, and other qualities unique to each supplier. Include cost breakdowns and rate sheets to back up your statements. Outline any plans or policies you have for dealing with suppliers.

Summarize key points in your purchasing plan:

Choosing Suppliers

Finding a good supplier is critical to your business survival and prosperity. However, don't make the mistake of relying on one supplier and one supplier only. Try and find at least two or three suppliers for each product you sell. Let them compete against each other for your business.

List and compare suppliers:

Comparing Suppliers	**Name of Item(s):**						
Name of Supplier	**Address of Supplier**	**Phone/Fax Number**	**Cost**	**Discounts Offered**	**Delivery Time**	**Shipping & Del. Costs**	**Reorder Policies**

Cost of Goods & Discounts – How competitive are the prices of the supplier? What quantity discounts are offered?	**Delivery Time** – How many days or weeks does it take the supplier to deliver the merchandise to your store? How long does it take to reorder?	**Shipping & Delivery Costs** – Who pays for freight, you or the supplier (these costs are a big expense item)? Where is the F.O.B. point?	**Reorder Policies** – What is the supplier's policy on reorders? Do you have to buy hundreds, a dozen or can you buy only two or three items?

> *When a man is trying to sell you something, don't imagine he is that polite all the time.*
> **EDGAR WATSON HOWE**

Getting the Most Out of Your Suppliers

To get the most out of your suppliers, use the following strategies: ◆ ask suppliers if they have a program to contribute to advertising costs ◆ buy from suppliers during their slow periods to get discounts or better terms ◆ buy in volume for discounts ◆ buy only the amount you expect to sell regardless of how favorable the price or credit terms ◆ establish your credit by paying on time ◆ offer partial and/or advance payment in return for discounts ◆ don't always pay what your suppliers ask – negotiate for the best price ◆ negotiate and sign a favorable supply contract ◆ prepare a written policy for dealing with suppliers ◆ maintain good business relations with all suppliers ◆ develop multiple supply sources and alternate sources of raw materials ◆ take advantage of discounts for early payment ◆ to keep your cash a bit longer, send your payment checks just before they are due.

*Where do you plan to buy your **floor stock** for resale (product/service firm)? Where do you plan to buy your raw materials and component parts (manufacturing firm)? List details of key inventory items, raw materials and parts you will order from your suppliers:*

Name of Item/ Raw Material/ Component	Name of Supplier	Price	Order Policy	Discounts Offered	Delivery Time	Freight Costs	Back Order Policy
		$				$	

*Where do you plan to buy your **operating supplies & materials** (product/service firm)? Where do you plan to buy your consumable tools and shop supplies (manufacturing firm)? List details of key operating supplies and materials you will order from your suppliers:*

Name of Item/ Tool or Supplies	Name of Supplier	Price	Order Policy	Discounts Offered	Delivery Time	Freight Costs	Back Order Policy
		$				$	

> Having too many suppliers can lead to wasted time with sales people, costly bookkeeping, dup-lication of lines, and mixed up inventory. If you have only one supplier, list alternate suppliers. Explain how you will handle loss of your supplier or a sudden increase in orders.

Developing a Purchasing Budget

In developing your purchasing budget, start by making sales projections as accurate as possible. Also, make sure to leave enough room to maneuver to take advantage of current deals or discounts by incorporating a *reserve fund* into your budget.

Planning Stock Purchases with Sales – A good purchasing plan maintains inventory levels that relate closely to monthly sales. In this way, you avoid over- or under-buying. Stock levels will not remain the same each month of the year. Sales records will show peaks and valleys, and purchases must be precisely timed to move with customer buying. Stock levels must peak just before major customer buying periods, and diminish as demand tapers off. Failure to peak or diminish stocks at the right time can seriously affect sales and profits.

Remaining "Open to Buy" – "Open to buy" is a condition whereby the merchant leaves a portion of the purchasing budget to buy additional items as the season progresses. It provides a built-in flexibility to take advantage of special deals.

Outline your purchasing budget based on sales projections. Detail any assumptions or special considerations. Will you have a reserve fund?

	Actual Sales Last Year			Planned Sales This Year				Actual Sales Last Year			Planned Sales This Year		
	SALES	COST	% of Total	SALES	COST	% of Total		SALES	COST	% of Total	SALES	COST	% of Total
Jan.							Jul.						
Feb.							Aug.						
Mar.							Sep.						
Apr.							Oct.						
May							Nov.						
Jun.							Dec.						
Purchasing Budget							Total			100			100

Calculating a Profitable Reorder Point

A good purchasing plan outlines the exact point stock should be reordered so you don't run out of stock (and lose sales) or carry too much (and increase carrying costs). To determine your *reorder point*, that is the minimum stock level at which additional quantities need to be ordered, calculate your *Economic Order Quantity*, (EOQ) and how many days it takes to receive a new order (refer to page 65).

> During the summer months, if sales levels drop considerably, you should lengthen your reorder point. During the winter months, if sales levels peak, you should shorten your reorder point.
> **INVENTORY TIP**

Reorder Point for a Shoe Wholesaler – Sue Smith owns XYZ Shoes Inc. and sells 10,000 pairs of slippers per year. She calculates her EOQ for these slippers to be 3,162 units per order (see page 66). According to her EOQ, her inventory of slippers should turnover an average of 3.162 times a year or every 115 days. Since it takes 14 days to receive an order, she needs to reorder 3,162 pairs of slippers 101 days after receiving her last order. To keep from being overstocked, she reorders when her inventory records show that she has 385 pairs of slippers left. She calculates this value by finding the percentage of stock needed to last until a new order is received (total $ value of stock can be used instead of # of units):

$$\boxed{\begin{array}{c}\text{Reorder}\\\text{Point}\end{array}} = \text{EOQ} \times [\frac{\text{\# of days to receive order}}{\text{inventory turnover days}}] = 3{,}162 \text{ units} \times (14/115) = \textbf{385 units}$$

Calculate reorder points for key inventory items.   *Describe any additional reorder policies:*

Item(s)	Total Sales Year	EOQ	Turnover Days	# of Days to Receive Order	Reorder Point	

Establishing an Order Inspection Policy

The criteria and procedures used to inspect incoming raw materials and inventory should be documented and well publicized to all parties involved. An order inspection policy should outline: ◆ *what to do at time of delivery* e.g., each carton is carefully examined for damage and all merchandise is counted ◆ *what to do when damage is discovered* e.g., damaged materials are held at the point they are received ◆*procedures for carrier inspection of damaged items* e.g., steps are taken to make sure all damaged items are not moved before they are inspected by the carrier ◆ *what to do after inspection* e.g., damaged materials are kept until written authorization from the shipper/supplier is received to return the damage items. To facilitate the above task, the use of a "Receiving Report" is common practice.

The longer merchandise stays on shelves, the more it will cost and the less it is worth.

Damaged materials should not be used or disposed of without permission from the carrier.

Receiving Report

Report #		Date		Our P.O. #:	

	Received From:			For:	
Name:			Name:		
Address			Address:		
Phone/Fax:			Department		

Shipped VIA	Express	Transport	Mail	Delivery Charges	Prepaid	Collect	C.O.D. Charges	Bill of Lading #	No. of Packages	Total Weight
					☐	☐				

Quantity	Item #	✓	Weight	Accepted	Rejected	Description

Received by	Inspected by	Complete	Partial	NOTES:

> *Entrepreneurs do one thing and they do it consistently – they add value to peoples' lives.*

Establishing an Inventory Discontinuation Policy

The last part of a purchasing plan involves establishing a set of guidelines to help determine when to discontinue stocking an item. These guidelines will likely be based on criteria such as the following: ✦ a newer model of the product has come out making the old one obsolete ✦ the product failed to meet a pre-calculated sales quota ✦ the product's turnover rate is well below your average turnover rate ✦ the product's profit margin has shrunk well below your average profit margin per inventory item due to reasons such as increased product costs, price wars, surpluses within the industry, or the need for drastic discounting due to what can only be described as lack of consumer interest ✦ the dust on the product's packaging is thick enough to write your name on it.

Highlight the main points of your order inspection and inventory discontinuation policy:

```
┌──────────────────────────────────────────────────────────────────────┐
│                                                                        │
│                                                                        │
│                                                                        │
│                                                                        │
└──────────────────────────────────────────────────────────────────────┘
```

Proprietary & Exclusive Rights Obtained

If you have a great idea with the potential for making a lot of money, you can bet once it becomes public, others will seriously consider ways they can take advantage of it or even steal it. After all, being innovative, the most important business skill anyone can have is based upon taking an existing idea and changing it slightly to benefit yourself and others. Protecting your idea is therefore almost as important as coming up with it. The three most important ways you can legally protect your ideas is through copyrights, trademarks and patents:

❑ **Copyright Protection** – Protects a work created by an author, artist or composer such as a novel, screenplay, computer program, painting, photograph, choreographic work, sculpture, musical composition, or song lyrics. However, copyright law states quite clearly that there is no copyright in facts or ideas, only in the form or expression of an idea. Average copyright protection is the life of the creator plus 50 years.

❑ **Trademark Protection** – Protects words, phrases, numbers, letters, pictures, designs or combinations such as logos and insignias, that distinguish or differentiate one manufacturer's products and services from another. A product cannot use a common generic term as a trademark. Average trademark protection is 15 to 20 years from date registered and is usually renewable.

❑ **Patent Protection** – Protects an idea, process, way of making things, or invention that is essentially better in some way than what was made or done before. A patent excludes others from making or selling your ideas, inventions, or products. Average patent protection is 17 years from date of issue and is non-renewable.

Discuss and list in detail any proprietary rights, such as patents, copyrights, trademarks and industrial designs your company owns. Also discuss and other exclusive rights obtained such as franchise territories or licenses:

```
┌──────────────────────────────────────────────────────────────────────┐
│                                                                        │
│                                                                        │
│                                                                        │
│                                                                        │
│                                                                        │
└──────────────────────────────────────────────────────────────────────┘
```

DAY 10
Operating Plan

Begin this section with a summary covering accounting procedures, legal considerations, inventory control, computer systems, and other areas important to the operation of your business. Summarize production and operating processes, but don't get too technical. List key dates of your *Operations Schedule* (see page 74).

Summarize key points of your operating plan. To what extent is the success of your business dependent upon you?

Accounting System

Accounting is essentially the "counting" and "keeping track of" money. It is important that banks and investors know you are capable of doing this properly, not only so you can pay your taxes, but also be in a better position to monitor you cash flow, estimate profits, and pay off loans.

What Makes a Good Accounting System?

A good accounting system is simple to use, easy to learn, accurate and flexible to change. It protects your business from fraud and error; takes into consideration the size, nature and extent of your business as well as your accounting abilities; provides accurate information for every business transaction in a manner that allows no needless overlapping or repetition of procedures; gives information on a timely basis; is within budget to implement and maintain: and most importantly, consumes as little time as possible. A good accounting system also recognizes the following two important needs:

1) **The needs of Management.** A good accounting system compiles and organizes information to help improve management's decision-making process.

2) **The needs of Government.** A good accounting system meets the minimum record keeping requirements of government income tax laws.

What Kinds of Accounting Records Should You Keep?

As a general rule, tax departments do not specify the exact type of records you should keep, other than that they be permanent, contain a systematic account of all income and expenses to determine taxes payable, and be supported by vouchers or other source documents. To meet these basic requirements, your accounting system should keep track of: ❏ A/Ps and A/Rs ❏ assets, equipment and inven-

> Nowadays, you hear a lot about fancy accounting methods, like LIFO and FIFO, but back then we were using the ESP method, which really sped things along when it came time to close books. It's a pretty basic method: if you can't make your books balance you take however much they're off by and enter it under the heading ESP, which stands for Error Some Place.
> **SAM WALTON**

tory ❏ business expenses ❏ capital gains and losses ❏ cash disbursements and cash receipts ❏ employment taxes including income tax withholdings, social security, Medicare, and federal unemployment taxes ❏ employee expenses ❏ medical and dental expenses ❏ gross sales (all sources of income you receive from your business) ❏ travel, transportation, entertainment, and gift expenses.

SUPPORT VOUCHERS – To prove business transactions and verify income and expenses, file away canceled checks, account statements,, cash register tapes, and all vouchers such as receipts, sales slips, deposit slips, paid bills, and invoices. A check register, or even a checkbook with enough space to clearly identify sources of disbursements, can be used as a basic record for deductible expenses:

To verify **gross sales** file: ◆ cash register tapes ◆ bank deposit slips ◆ receipt books ◆ invoices ◆ credit card charge slips.	To verify **purchases** file: ◆ canceled checks ◆ cash register tape receipts ◆ credit card sales slips ◆ invoices.	To verify **expenses** file: ◆ canceled checks ◆ cash register tapes ◆ account statements ◆ credit card sales slips ◆ invoices ◆ petty cash record system.

Setting-up an Accounting System

Canceled checks are the best source documents along with receipts and sales slips to prove a business expense deduction.
ACCOUNTING TIP

There is no single accounting method required of all taxpayers, other than you clearly show all income and expenses, maintain adequate records so you can file a correct return, support your entries with receipts, invoices, etc., and use the same method from year to year. Your accounting systems could range from a simple single-entry journal system to a sophisticated computerized system supplemented with monthly consulting services by a financial accountant.

In a traditional accounting system:

FIRST, enter all transactions as they occur into a *General Journal*. File away any related documents to prove these transactions. This *Journal* must be protected at all costs (whether it be a computer file or a book purchased at a stationary store). It is the soul of your accounting system. If disaster strikes and your accounting records and calculations are completely wiped out, as long as you've kept your journal in a safe place, you can always rebuild your system.

SECOND, post journal entries to an appropriate account in your *General Ledger*. A *Ledger* is usually a hard cover book in which each individual type or group of transactions are maintained separately on different pages. These groups of related transactions are called ledger accounts. The chief function of a ledger is to record and keep track of the balances of individual accounts. It will typically contain anywhere from a dozen or so, to hundreds of asset, liability, equity, revenue or expense accounts, depending upon the your management needs and the size of your business. To set up your ledger, assign each account: (1) an account title, (2) an account number, and (3) a ledger page or pages. Next, create an index. This index is a list of all account titles and numbers used in your accounting system. It is called a **Chart of Accounts**. A *Chart of Accounts* is like a table of contents at the beginning of a book (see page 48 for a list of possible small business accounts). Account numbers are usually between 10 and 59, 100 and 599, 1000 and 5999 and so on, as shown on page 48.

THIRD, sum up and analyze account balances periodically.

Accounting: A respectable, conscious or unconscious way of disclosing, hiding or misrepresenting financial information to give a skillfully adapted economic picture of a company or its components.
PAULSSON FRENCKNER

In more detail, this process, known as the ACCOUNTING CYCLE, can be broken down into eight areas:

A. Transaction Occurs	E. Trial Balance Adjustments Made
B. Transaction Entered in General Journal	F. Financial Statements Prepared
C. Journal Entry Posted to General Ledger	G. Financial Statements Posted to Ledger
D. Trial Balance Prepared	H. Books Closed & Prepared for Next Cycle

NOTE The classified section of your telephone directory can lead you to accounting services which can help you choose and set-up an accounting system for your business (also see our online Guidebook 📖 #28 for more info).

General Journal

	p.1		*Harry's Pet Supplies*		☞ DEBIT ACCOUNT							☞ CREDIT ACCOUNT							P✓	
	DATE		**DESCRIPTIONS**	**AC#**																	
1	Jan	12	Merchandise	130		1	2	0	0	0	00								1/12/95		1
2			Accounts Payable	210									1	2	0	0	0	00			2
3			*Purchase of Bulk*																		3
4			*Puppy Chow*																		4

General Ledger

			Account Name and No.			☞ DEBIT (IN)						☞ CREDIT (OUT)						BAL						
	DATE		Merchandise AC#130	**P/R**																					
			DESCRIPTIONS																						
1	Jan	12	Purchase of Merch. on account	p. 1		1	2	0	0	0	00								1	2	0	0	0	00	1
2	Feb	12	Purchase of Merch. on account.	p. 2		5	0	0	0	00										5	0	0	0	00	2
3	Feb	13	Return of Merch. on account	p. 2								1	0	0	0	00			1	6	0	0	0	00	3
4	Feb	26	Purchase of Merch. on account	p. 3		6	0	0	00										1	6	6	0	0	00	4

Making Journal Entries

All transactions are entered into the journal the order in which they occur. Each entry requires that you:

FIRST, date the entry on the left edge.

SECOND, write the debit account title(s) as far to the left as you can as well as its corresponding $ amount in the left-hand money column (to ease posting to the ledger, also write the corresponding account number).

THIRD, write the credit account title(s) – indented a half-inch or so – and its corresponding $ amount in the right-hand money column (a debit can be entered in red ink and a credit in blank ink – don't reverse).

FOURTH, write a brief note of explanation regarding the transaction (see example above).

NOTE All journal entries require at least 3 lines on a page: ♦ at least one line for a debit entry ♦ at least one line for a credit entry ♦ a line for an explanation (sometimes, a single transaction can impact more than 2 accounts and thus take up more than 3 lines).

Making Ledger Entries

When making a ledger entry:

FIRST, write down an explanation.

SECOND, list a posting reference (P/R), referring back to the original entry in your journal (usually listed as a page number).

THIRD, *debit* or *credit* the accounts in question. Posting a transaction to the ledger is never a one shot deal. Each transaction represents both at least one debit and credit account.

FOURTH, after the transaction has been fully posted to all its appropriate accounts, make a check mark beside the column total in the journal to show that it has been posted.

NOTES (a) All entries are in ink except for the balance column. The balance entry may be kept in pencil in case an error is made. (b) Each account appears on a separate page and is numbered in accordance with your *Chart of Accounts*. (c) If you are using a computer program, most programs automatically post the journal entry to the appropriate ledger account thus saving time. (d) Post journal entries at a minimum four times a year when you make your quarterly tax installments.

Single-entry Cash Based Systems

Basic knowledge of accounting is, not only essential to the productive management of your business, but also a prerequisite to assuring profitability.
ACCOUNTING TIP

For a small home, service or contracting business, which uses part-time help and has no inventory for sale, the single-entry *cash method* of accounting is a good choice. This system consists of little more than a carefully annotated checkbook in which all receipts and expenditures are recorded, supported by a few forms of original entry (invoices, receipts, cash tickets, etc.). Sales are recorded when cash is actually received and expenses are recorded when they are actually paid. A single-entry cash based accounting system as illustrated in IRS publication 583 "Starting a Business and Keeping Records," suggests using: ♦ Daily Summary of Cash Receipts ♦ Monthly Summary of Cash Receipts ♦ Check Disbursement Journal ♦ Employee Compensation Record ♦ Annual Summary ♦ Depreciation Worksheet ♦ Bank Reconciliation (see GB📖 #28 for a sample of this system).

Chart of Accounts

BALANCE SHEET ACCOUNTS

Asset Accounts
100-199

Company assets are anything of value including cash and tangible real goods that are owned by or owed to your company and contribute to the net worth of your business. In the case of real goods, the full value of the asset is listed regardless of whether it is fully paid for or not (all assets accounts are considered debit accounts unless otherwise noted).

NOTE *Soft assets* include such intangibles as good will, patents, formulas, and capitalized research and development (R & D). Soft assets are more difficult to keep track of and value. They should be approached with caution when incorporated into any accounting system.

Current Asset Accounts

Current asset accounts are accounts that can be easily turned into cash if necessary within one year. They are listed in order of their liquidity.

100 Cash on Hand (Cash)
105 Petty Cash
110 Cash in Bank
115 Short-term Investments
116 Long-term Investments
120 Accounts Receivable
121 Interest Accrued Receivable
125 Allowance for Bad Debts
130 Merchandise
131 Merchandise Discount
132 Merchandise Returns & Allowances
135 Raw Materials
136 Finished Goods
137 Work in Progress
140 Supplies
145 Prepaid Expenses
146 Prepaid Insurance
147 Prepaid Property Tax
148 Prepaid Rent
149 Prepaid Supplies

Fixed Asset Accounts

Fixed assets (also called real or tangible assets) are difficult to turn into cash. Fixed assets are of a long-term or permanent nature such as land, buildings, automobiles and equipment. They are not intended for resale.

150 Land
160 Buildings
165 Leasehold Improvements
170 Equipment
175 Furniture & Fixtures
180 Allowance for Depreciation
181 Allowance for Depreciation of Buildings
182 Allowance for Depreciation of Leasehold Improvements
183 Allowance for Depreciation of Tools & Equipment
184 Allowance for Depreciation of Furniture and Fixtures

Liability Accounts
200-299

Liabilities are legal claims against a business by persons or corporations other than the owners. These claims come before the rights of the owners. They consist of money owed to suppliers or vendors for inventory or supplies; money owed to banks or loan companies for buildings or equipment purchases; money owed for taxes; and anything else bought on credit. Liability accounts normally have credit balances.

Current Liability Accounts

Current liabilities are obligations or that must be paid within the year (or one operating cycle).

210 Accounts Payable
220 Salaries Payable
230 Tax Payable
231 Federal Income Tax Payable
232 State Income Tax Payable
233 Self-**Employment** Tax Payable
234 Sales Tax Payable
235 Property Tax Payable
236 Payroll Payable
237 Payroll Taxes Payable
240 Short Term Loans Payable
245 Interest Payable
246 Dividends Payable

Long Term Liability Accounts

Long-term liabilities are funds a company owes (outstanding balances less current portion due) spread out over a period longer than a year.

250 Long Term Loans Payable
260 Mortgages Payable
270 Bonds Payable

Owner's Equity Accounts
300-399

An *equity* is any debt a business owes, whether to outsiders or to its owners. *Owner's Equity* refers specifically to the owner's claim to the net assets of the company (assets minus liabilities). An *Owner's Equity* account is often referred to as a *Capital* account, *Net Worth* or simply an *Equity* account. *Owner's Equity* accounts normally have credit balances.

300 Capital Stock
310 John Doe, Capital
315 John Doe, Drawing
320 Retained Earnings
346 Dividends Paid

INCOME STATEMENT ACCOUNTS

Revenue Accounts
300-399

Revenues are the earnings, income, or cash inflow of your business. Revenues can come from the sale of products or the sale of services whether they are in the form of cash or A/Rs. Your income records should show date, amount, source, and whether you received as payment cash, property, or services.

410 Sales Revenue
414 Sales Tax Collected
415 Sales and Sales Tax Refunds
416 Sales Discount
420 Service Revenue
430 Other Income
440 Interest Revenue
450 Dividends Revenue
460 Royalties Revenue
465 Rental Income
470 Gain from Sale of Fixed Assets
475 Gain from Sale of Marketable Securities
480 Loss from Sale of Fixed Assets
485 Loss from Sale of Marketable Securities
490 Recaptured Allowance for Depreciation
495 Retirement Loss

Expense Accounts
300-399

Expenses are the day-to day expenditures arising out of current business activities. It represents an asset that you have for a very short time. Setting up a special expense account is easy. Just give it a title and a name.

510 Salaries Expense
512 Factory Labor Expense
520 Rent Expense
522 Mortgage Expense
525 Bad Debts Expense
530 Income Tax Expense
532 Property Tax Expense
535 Office Supplies Expense
540 Supplies Expense
550 Telephone
560 Utilities
565 Advertising
570 Insurance
575 Interest Expense
580 Depreciation Expense
585 Cost of Goods Sold
586 Factory Overhead
587 Selling Expenses
588 Administrative Expenses
590 Miscellaneous Expenses

Double-entry Accrual Based Systems

As your business grows, switch to the *accrual method*. Under this method, you record sales and expenses when they are incurred rather than when they are collected or paid. It is also recommended that you switch to a double-entry system. Using a double-entry system, ALL transactions are entered first in your *General Journal*, and next posted to at least two balancing *debit* and *credit* accounts in your *General Ledger*. A double-entry accrual based system should be used by a business that makes cash sales each day, has credit customers, holds inventory items, and hires employees. One such system, as illustrated in an Alberta government publication titled "Bookkeeping for a Small Business," suggests using: ◆ Daily Cash Sheet ◆ Synoptic Ledger ◆ Accounts Receivable Ledger ◆ Accounts Payable Ledger ◆ Weekly Summary Payroll ◆ Bank Reconciliation ◆ Asset Depreciation Records ◆ GST (Federal Tax) Records (see GB▦ #28).

Condensed Single-entry Accounting Systems

Special condensed single-entry journals, available at stationary stores for a variety of businesses, can be used to group common types of journal entries and simplify bookkeeping. These journals are single-purpose versions of the *General Journal* in which the explanation line is omitted and only one line is used to enter debit and credit accounts (see GB▦ #28 for a "Weekly Sales & Cash Report").

Envelope Journal Systems – If you own a small part-time business and have only a few transactions per day, week or month, consider photocopying and stapling on to a full size 9 by 12 envelope any single-entry journal page. Every time a transaction occurs put the receipt into the envelope, then make an entry on the journal page. When the page is full, or at the end of a specified period (a week or month), file the envelope and start a new one. Receipts from transactions can also be stored in a safe place, like a cash box, and then recorded and put inside the envelope when convenient. All expenses are paid by check. At the end of the year, total the envelope summaries and prepare financial summary statements.

NOTE Although condensed single-entry journals can reduce the chore of bookkeeping, they lack room to record vital pieces of information particular to individual transactions. This can become a serious problem if you need to track down a receipt to verify a record. To control this problem, file all checks, vouchers, and support documents according to dates. If you then need to verify an ad expense of $37.50 paid on Monday, April 12th, then all you should have to do is look in your file cabinet and pull out the file that contains all the receipts for April 12th.

Single-entry Income & Expense Journal Systems

Instead of using a *Daily Cash Sheet* and a *Synoptic Ledger*, record your income and expenses using an *Income Journal* (also called a *Sales* or *Cash Receipts Journal*) and an *Expense Journal* (also called a *Cash Payments* or *Disbursements Journal*). It is quite common for businesses to base their entire accounting system around these two journals. Both can be purchased at stationary stores.

Using an Income Journal
The *Income Journal* is used for recording all incoming revenue, whether cash or check. Entries for Harry's Pet Supplies are shown on the next page:

Not using checks makes it difficult to monitor expenses, increases the time spent on bookkeeping, increases the probability of double payments, and communicates to suppliers that your business is a marginal operation.
SBA

What advantages a merchant derives from double-entry bookkeeping! It is among the finest invention of the human mind; and every good householder should introduce it into his economy.
JOHANN WOLFGANG VON GOETHE

The accounting forms you use should allow easy routine processing. They should flow automatically to bookkeepers, computer staff, or other individuals who process them and enter them into your records, without increasing the likelihood of errors or misplacement.
ACCOUNTING TIP

Column 1-4 – On May 1, by examining the sales invoices and cash register tapes, Harry found he had cash sales of $430.00 and sales of $120.00 on account (these amounts include sales taxes collected). In his Income Journal, he recorded the *cash sales* in column 1 and the *credit sales* in column 2. In column 3, he shows $30 worth of returned merchandise. Column 4 then shows the total sales for the day, cash sales plus credit sales minus merchandise returned.

Column 5 – In column 5, Harry recorded cash received on previous credit sales. He did not include this amount in his daily sales figures, as he would have included it in the sales figure on the day the goods were actually sold on account.

Column 6 – In column 6, Harry recorded any cash or other income he received during the day. On May 1st, he received $10 in interest from an overdue A/R. On May 2nd, he received a deposit refund from a gas company that earlier had been recorded as a business expense. On May 3rd, he received $625 for selling his old company truck.

Column 7 – In column 7, Harry calculated how much he received during the day. As his daily sales figure may not necessarily be equal to the cash he received, this column ensures that he ends up with the correct amount of cash at the end of the day.

Column 8 – In column 8, Harry recorded his actual cash count.

Column 9 – In column 9, Harry recorded how much money he was short or over.

Column 10 – In column 10, Harry recorded how much he deposited into his bank account by subtracting from column 7 all his cash disbursements as noted in his Expense Journal (make a point of depositing the exact amount of cash received as noted in column 7, for then your Income Journal will provide an accurate record of the source of the funds you have deposited).

Other Procedures – Once Harry made the appropriate daily entries in his Income Journal:

a)   he added the sales on account (accounts receivables) for the day to the individual account cards of the people to whom he made the sales;

b)   he credited the cash received on account to the individual account cards of the people from whom he received it; and then

c)   he filed away cash register tapes, canceled checks, and copies of his sales invoices (and all other vouchers that document his sources of income e.g., bank statements and deposit slips), so that he could easily review them at a later date. At the end of each month, Harry then will total each column and then start a new sheet for the next month.

NOTE You can alter the format of your Income Journal to suit your business. If you operate a farm, for example, you may have twenty large sales in a year, instead of many small sales each day. In this case, you may wish to record your income as you make each sale, instead of recording daily totals.

Income Journal

Date	Particular	Cash Sales	Credit Sales	Merch. Returned	Total Sales (1 +2-3)	Cash Rec. on Credit Sales	Other Cash Received	Total Cash Received (1+5+6)	Actual Cash Count	Cash Short or Over	Bank Deposit (7-Exp.)
May 1	Daily Sales	430.00	120.00	30.00	520.00	240.00		650.00	648.00	(2.00)	505.00
May 2	A/R Interest						10.00				
May 2	Daily Sales	565.25	99.00		664.25	110.00		700.25	700.10	(.15)	700.25
May 2	Deposit Refund (Gas)						25.00				
May 3	Daily Sales	540.00			540.00	55.68		1,320.68	1,320.68		1,318.53
May 3	Auto Wreckers						625.00	625.00			

Using an Expense Journal

The *Expense Journal* is used for recording ALL business expenses. The simplest method of recording these expenses is a basic columnar sheet (see page 51).

NOTE As is true of reported income, business expenses must be substantiated with a sales invoice, an agreement of purchase, a receipt, or some other voucher.

Column 1 – In column 1, Harry recorded the number of the check used to pay for the expense as explained in the *Particulars* column. If cash was used, or if the purchase was on account, a note to this affect was also made. Afterwards, he took the bill he received and made a note on it that it was paid by check number 0407 on May 1. He then filed this bill away in an appropriately titled expense file. This file was a simple folder that would hold all his advertising bills for the year.

NOTE Retain your canceled checks once you receive them from the bank. This is part of your proof that the bill was paid or the asset purchased. As with the sale invoices and the bills, keep the canceled checks in an orderly manner so that anyone of them can be easily reviewed at a later date.

Column 2 – In column 2, Harry recorded his inventory or merchandise purchases. When he paid in credit he made sure he made a corresponding entry in his Accounts Payable record.

Column 3-8 – In columns 3 to 8, Harry recorded the amount of his expenses (you can modify these headings to suit the type of business you have).

Column 3-8 – In column 9, Harry recorded all his miscellaneous expenses. On May 3rd he put $2.15 back into his balance (change) fund to make up for money lost or stolen.

Column 10 – Harry recorded the amount paid for the large capital purchase of a used half-ton truck (at the end of each month, each column is totaled and a new sheet started for the next month).

Expense Journal

Date	Particular	Check Number	Inven. Purchases	Accoun. & Legal	Advert.	Insurance	Phone	Utilities	Salaries	Misc. Expenses	Capital Items
May 1	ABC radio	0407			300.00						
May 1	Salary for Sally	0408							565.00		
May 1	Window Decorations	(cash)								130.00	
May 1	Petty Cash Slips	(cash)								15.00	
May 2	Ottawa Insurance	0409				250.00					
May 3	Jim's Accounting	(credit)		240.00							
May 3	Wholesale Supply	0411	1729.14								
May 3	Ed's Used Cars	0412									1800.00
May 3	Bal. Fund Restored	(cash)								2.15	

Commercial Accounting Systems

Numerous commercial copyrighted accounting systems are available for small business owners to simplify bookkeeping. These systems are usually based on easy-to-use single-entry journals and come complete with instructions. You can examine many of them at office supply stores or send away for FREE catalogs. A list of companies which sell such systems include: ♦ Blackbourn's General Business Bookkeeping System ♦ Ideal Systems ♦ McBee Systems ♦ Safeguard Business Systems, Inc. ♦ The Johnson Systems (for a more extensive list, see SBA's *Recordkeeping in Small Business* Management Aid number FM 10 / 1.017 $2).

Computerized Accounting Systems

Accounting software and templates can be purchased in retail and mail order software houses, as well as, numerous book and stationary stores. Two of the most popular over the counter accounting packages for small businesses are *Quickbooks* and *M.Y.O.B.* Both packages are relatively easy to use and require very little knowledge of accounting terminology.

NOTE To keep federal tax authorities happy, at a minimum, your accounting system must produce legible records and provide the necessary information needed to determine your correct tax liability. You must also keep a complete description of the computerized portion of your accounting system. This description should outline applications being performed, procedures used in each application, controls used to ensure accurate and reliable processing, and controls used to prevent the unauthorized addition, alteration, or deletion of retained records.

Describe your accounting system or method of record keeping and explain why it was chosen. State who will handle daily bookkeeping. If you use an accountant, state their name, business name and address. Also, state who within your company is experienced at reading and analyzing financial statements and is thus able to implement changes to make your company more profitable after reviewing these statements.

Explain why you chose this system. Outline your time frame and schedule for the implementation of your accounting system:

<u>KEEPING RECORDS</u> – *Check the types of records you will keep and procedures you will implement:*

<u>ACCOUNTING TIPS</u> – *Check strategies and guidelines you will use to streamline your accounting and bookkeeping procedures:*

On a DAILY BASIS keep track of:

☐ *cash sales & receipts*
☐ *all funds disbursed* by cash or check
☐ *cash on hand & bank balance*
☐ *errors* – discovered in the recording of previous transactions
☐ *miscellaneous sources of income* – including income from professional fees, property, investments, capital gains, estates, trusts, employment, and pensions

On a WEEKLY BASIS keep track of:

☐ *accounts receivable* (A/Rs) – so you can take action on slow payers
☐ *accounts payable* (A/Ps) – so you can take advantage of discounts
☐ *amount of weekly payroll* – including name and address of employee, social security #, date ending the pay period, hours worked, rate of pay, total wages, total deductions, net pay & check #
☐ *all withholdings set aside for State and Federal Governments* – including sales tax, employee income tax withholdings, social security payments, pension plan payments, and unemployment insurance payments

On a MONTHLY BASIS keep track of:

☐ *amount of business done in cash and credit*

☐ *amount of business tied up in A/Rs*
☐ *amount of collections & losses from credit sales*
☐ *amount owed to creditors and suppliers*
☐ *total expenses*
☐ *gross profit*
☐ *net profit earned and taxes owed*
☐ *which products and services make a profit and which lose money*
☐ *amount of money invested in stock*

ALSO, at the END OF THE MONTH, make sure that:

☐ *all journal entries* are classified according to like elements and posted to the General Ledger
☐ a *Cash Flow Statement* is prepared
☐ an *Income Statement* and *Balance Sheet* for the month is available within a reasonable time, usually 10 to 15 days, following month's end – for small business semi-annual statements are sufficient
☐ *Petty Cash* account is in balance
☐ *The Bank Statement* is reconciled – the owner's books agree with the banks record of the cash balance
☐ all *Federal Tax Deposits*, Withheld Income and FICA Taxes (form 501) and State Taxes are made
☐ *A/Rs* are aged 30, 60, 90 days, or past due
☐ *Inventory* is inspected to determine which items need to be reordered and which need to be discounted due to slow turnover

❑ Always use pre-numbered checks instead of paying cash.

❑ Always use pre-numbered cash receipts or invoices.

❑ Always support accounting records with a paper trial (*paper* or *audit trails* consist of sales slips, invoices, receipts, canceled checks, or other pieces of paper that record business transactions; each transaction should contain the date of purchase, the name and address of the seller or supplier, the name and address of the purchaser, and a full description of the goods or services).

❑ Avoid setting up too many accounts in your "Chart of Accounts."

❑ Develop profit centers for different products or services.

❑ Don't encourage employee dishonesty with sloppy cash habits.

❑ Establish a filing system for all bills and sales invoices.

❑ Group entries of a similar nature (it is not necessary to enter each individual bills of sale from individual customers, who purchase items from your store).

❑ Keep business financial affairs separate from personal financial affairs.

❑ Keep records of assets bought and sold.

❑ Keep records for at least seven years after you have filed a tax return.

❑ Make detailed deposit slips and keep a copy.

❑ Never throw away canceled checks.

❑ Prepare a monthly bank reconciliation (it is highly recommended that you download GB📖 #28 for more detailed accounting information).

Banking Plan

One of the first things to do when you start a business is open a business checking account. Good business practice dictates that you keep your personal financial affairs separate from your business financial affairs. This section is particularly relevant if you are running a home-based business (you need to show that your personal and business financial affairs will indeed be separate).

Setting up a Business Checking Account

To open a business checking account you will need a copy of your business registration (DBA statement) to verify your business name, and you will need to find the *right* bank. To assist you in the latter task, consider the following guidelines:

STEP 1 – Avoid banks with unreasonable and expensive checking account policies. Good business practice dictates that every disbursement be made by pre-numbered checks. This will assure you of a formal record of all payments and expenses. Avoid banks that charge excessive checking fees. Try and stay away from commercial banks that are unwilling to offer interest on the balances in business and corporate accounts. Consider dealing instead with a trust company or Credit Union. These institutions are often willing to give you a daily-interest checking account with statement privileges. To attract depositors, they are also more likely to experiment with no-fee or low-fee accounts that further minimize extra charges.

STEP 2 – Choose a bank that offers *overdraft* protection. Considering the amount of checks you will write as a business owner, and the resulting wildly fluctuating balances, you will often inadvertently bounce checks. It is paramount that you protect yourself in such cases and avoid extra fees and the embarrassment to your suppliers and creditors. Talk to your bank or trust company branch manager in advance about overdraft protection and credit lines. Ask for an automatic overdraft protection of $1000 on your account, secured by your name only, that is without collateral. Most managers have the authority to do this, if you ask.

STEP 3 – Choose a bank that offers over the telephone services. Many banks now offer services that allow you to transfer money between accounts, make credit card inquiries, pay bills, and check account balances over the phone using a push button phone to enter account numbers and other pertinent information. These services can even be accessed via your cellular or car phone.

STEP 4 – Choose a bank that offers electronic banking services. The relatively new capacity of making financial transactions by computer over phone lines is destined to speed up cash flow more than any other current technology. Businesses are already using electronic order entry systems, which enable customers to reorder merchandise and check shipping dates directly. The next step will be the invoicing of customers via computer, and then receipt of payment electronically by wire transfer from the customer's bank to yours. To its advantage, electronic banking takes less paper and less transit time, reducing the work and cost of paper invoices, payroll, and bills and thus solving two of the biggest problems bothering commercial depositors. It also makes long-distance transactions as convenient as dealing with neighboring banks opening up the entire country to financial interfacing. Already, more and more banks are offering electronic bank-

ELEMENTS OF A POSITIVE CREDIT PROFILE
1. A positive up-to-date credit report
2. A home with a mortgage
3. An American Express card and/or Diner's Club card
4. A job you've held for a year or more
5. A current or paid-off bank loan
6. A Master Card or VISA
7. A department store credit card
8. A telephone in your name

ing privileges to small businesses, enabling them to have the convenience and cash management control enjoyed by larger corporations. Using these services, you can use your PC to check balances, transfer funds, consolidate cash between accounts, and pay bills. As encryption software improves, Internet Banking will also make further inroads into the banking industry and the way business is conducted. For entrepreneurs on the go, Internet Banking is a godsend.

STEP 5 – Also consider the following: ❑ *Banks' Riskiness* – Generally smaller banks in smaller communities tend to be more conservative in their lending practices and investment returns. ❑ *Availability of FDIC Deposit Insurance* – Covers up to $100,000 of a customer's account. ❑ *Maximum Loan Size* – Usually limited to 10% of the bank's capital account. ❑ *Interest Rate* – Review the interest rate paid on your deposits and rate charged on loans. ❑ *Minimum Balances*. Do you have to maintain a minimum amount of funds? ❑ *Specialization* – Larger banks can offer separate departments specializing in a variety of banking services. ❑ *Loyalty to Customer* – Will the bank pressure your business to liquidate a loan during an economic downturn? ❑ *Other Services* – Does the bank offer wire transfers, electronic banking, telephone banking, Internet banking, foreign currency deposit accounts, lockbox service etc.

Checking Account Strategies

To get the more out of your checking account, use the following **4** strategies: ❑ ALWAYS make payments by check to document business expenses. ❑ Use a checkbook that has enough room to write details of the check disbursement e.g., type of business expense. ❑ Write checks payable to yourself only when making withdrawals from your business for personal use. ❑ Avoid writing checks payable to cash. If you must write a check for cash to pay a business expense, include the receipt for the cash payment in your records. If you cannot get a receipt for cash payment, make an adequate explanation in your records.

Give the name and address of your bank. Describe any special services they offer that will help your business:

Eight Elements of a Positive Credit Profile

To improve your credit rating, consider the "8 Elements of a Positive Credit Profile" as shown above. These elements are listed from most important to least.

Outline your credit profile. Provide details that show you are a good credit risk:

To Do List

Company Plan
Operating Plan

✓ Buildings, Equip. &
  Other Purchases
  Required

✓ Computer Plan

✓ Communications

DAY 11

Buildings, Equipment & Other Purchases

To consider loan requests, banks want detailed information about all major purchases. List buildings, equipment, supplies, inventory, land, raw materials, vehicles and other purchases required. Give reasons why they are necessary and how they will improve your business. Include costs and whether you will buy or lease.

Buildings Required

List and describe any buildings that need to be purchased:

Describe physical needs, utility needs, floor and office space needs, and any renovations and leasehold improvements needed:

Indicate the space required or allocated to each of the following activities: (manufacturing firm):

Manufacturing Activity	Sq.ft	Other Activity	Sq.ft
Fabrication		Storage	
Machining		Shipping	
Assembly		Receiving	
Finishing		Office Areas	
Inspection		Restroom & Employee facilities	
		Total Space Required or Allocated (sq. ft.)	

Develop a scale drawing or floor plan of the physical layout of your store, warehouse, manufacturing plant, or facility:

What to Look for When Signing a Property Lease

Before signing a lease, be sure to check it thoroughly. Have an attorney or realtor familiar with lease agreements go over it. He or she might be helpful in tailoring a fair contract and in making useful suggestions on available options.

When signing a lease, go over and pay close attention to the following details (check important concerns):

❑ Are you able to keep your location if it proves successful?	❑ Who is responsible for insurance on the buildings and properties, including liability insurance?
❑ Are you free to move after a reasonable length of time if the location is not profitable (a short-term lease with an option to renew is desirable)? Can built-in equipment and fixtures be installed and removed?	❑ Who is responsible for payment of utilities?
	❑ What is the liability if you default on the lease?
	❑ What are the common charges?
❑ Who takes care of repairs such as plumbing, electrical or air conditioning?	❑ Are there any tenant association fees, promotion and/or mandatory advertising fees?
❑ Who is responsible for maintenance and supplies?	❑ Will you be able to expand if needed?
❑ Who is responsible for alterations?	❑ Can all 4or any of the property be sublet?

Describe the costs and terms of any leases signed:

Equipment & Supplies Required

Describe machinery required; fixtures; supplies required:

List fixtures & equipment required for a Product/Service firm; list machinery & equipment needed to perform manufacturing. Also indicate costs and installation charges. Indicate from who and where purchases are to be made:

Type of Fixture, Machinery, or Equipment	Buy or Lease From	Installation Charge	+ Number x Required	Unit Cost	= Total Cost
		$		$	$
		$		$	$
		$		$	$
		$		$	$
				Total Cost	$

Inventory & Raw Materials Required

Describe inventory required, amount, depth, quality level, and so forth. Also, list initial inventory and consumable supplies & tools:

Describe raw materials needed and whether they are readily available, their cost and quality:

Product Items, Raw Materials & Component Parts	Quantity	x Cost Per Unit =	Total Cost
		$	$

A) Total Cost $

Consumable Supplies & Tools	Quantity	x Cost Per Unit =	Total Cost
		$	$

B) Total Cost $

C) Total Opening Inventory Requirements (C = A + B) $

Land Required

Provide details of site plan, costs of land and buildings, including installation of services:

Vehicles Required

List the makes, models and costs of any cars or trucks you will need:

Other Purchases Required

Detail other important purchases. Describe these costs:

Computerization Plan

In this section, describe what kinds of computer software you will need and what kinds of computer equipment you need to run the software.

Selecting Computer Software

To create the perfect "computer solution," understand what it is you need to accomplish, and then match those needs with what the market has to offer. Computerizing your operations is usually a software problem first and a hardware problem second. Think of a computer without software, as a hammer without its head.

How can computerization help your business? Check factors that apply:

❑ analyzing market trends controlling inventory	❑ keeping transaction records for tax purposes	❑ organizing payroll
❑ designing & laying-out ads	❑ managing sales contacts	❑ placing & receiving orders from other businesses
❑ handling mass-correspondence	❑ managing client lists	❑ scheduling & tracking projects
❑ keeping track of product costs	❑ managing A/Rs and A/Ps	❑ storing & retrieving customer data

Indicate what kinds of computer software you need. Include cost and reasons for selecting software (see checklist on page 61):

System Requirements	#1	#2	#3	#4	#5
Hard Drive					
CPU					
RAM					
Other					
Cost	$	$	$	$	$

Selecting Computer Hardware

If your business is just getting under way, the purchase of a high-tech computer system can seriously tax your cash reserves. And perhaps worse, the time and energy required to learn how to use it could be better spent finding customers. However, properly incorporated into your everyday workflow, a computer can greatly improve the efficiency and effectiveness of your business. It is the *wheel* of the modern age. For most entrepreneurs, it is not a question of whether you should computerize, but when and how much should you spend – and then more specifically whether you should buy a brand name, a clone, or upgrade an old beast?

Outline your computer budget and main purchasing criteria. If you already have a computer system, describe your system:

<u>SYSTEM REQUIREMENTS</u> – *To help you make the right purchasing decision read through the following suggestions and component considerations for buying a computer (visit CNET's http://www.computers.com for the latest prices and specs):*

CPU (MHz)	RAM (MB)	Hard Disk Storage (GB)	Video Memory	Sound Card	CD-ROM, DVD-ROM	Monitor	Fax/Modem	Printer	Other Devices	Estimated Cost ($)

❑ *Computer Microprocessor* – For a solid middle-end system, don't buy anything less than an Intel Celeron 400 MHz, Intel Pentium II 350 MHz, AMD 400 MHz K6-III, or a Cyrix MII 366 MHz. The only used 486s worth considering, for low-end systems, are Intel's DX4/100 and AMD equivalents.

❑ *Motherboard* – PCI is the bus of choice. Insist on a motherboard with software upgradable flash BIOS.

❑ *RAM Memory* – Shoot for 64 MB of system memory, with 32 MB as a bare minimum.

❑ *Hard Drive* – Get at least a 4 GB EIDE (a.k.a. Fast ATA) hard drive. Choose the more expensive SCSI storage system if you need to use imaging peripherals such as scanners and handle large video and sound files.

❑ *Video Card* – To display true color (16.7 million colors) on a 15-inch or smaller display in 800 x 600 mode, your video card needs at least 2MB of video memory. On a larger screen monitor (17-inches and above), you need 4 MB of video memory. If you plan to use graphics intensive software, you need 8 MB or 16 MB of V-RAM.

❑ *Monitor* – Buy a 15-inch if you're content to work at 800 x 600 resolution. A 17-inch screen will give you more room to display multiple applications. Dot pitch should be 0.28 mm or less and support a non-interlaced refresh rate of 75Hz to 100 Hz (the higher the better; easier on the eyes).

❑ *CD-ROM, DVD-ROM* – A 20X or 32X CD-ROM is sufficient. Recordable CD-ROM drives are worth looking into if you need to archive large amounts of data. However, CD-ROM technology is on the downslide. DVD is the future. A 6X DVD-ROM is a better choice.

❑ *Sound Card* – Look for sound cards with 3D effects, wave-table synthesis, and full-duplex features. These cards produce real instrument sounds and can play and record simultaneously for real-time long-distance computer conferencing. Better games, better presentations.

❑ *Shielded Speakers* – To complete your multi-media system, you'll need powered, magnetically shielded speakers. Add a sub-woofer for deep bass sounds to make your presentations rumble. Your sound system is only as good as your speakers.

Rule-of-Thumb PC Configurations

USAGE	COST	CPU/RAM	Storage	Video/Display	Peripherals	Software
❑ *Home Business (economy)*	$750-$1,000	Celeron 466 MHz/64MB	8.4 GB	PCI 8MB 15" SVGA	6X DVD-ROM, Inkjet Printer, 56K fax/modem	MS Works, personal finance
❑ *Small Business (middle-end)*	$1,000-$1,500	Pent. III 600 MHz/ 128MB	13.5GB	PCI 16MB 17"	6X DVD-ROM, 600 DPI Laser, 56K fax/modem	MS Office 2000, Quicken
❑ *Power User (graphics)*	$1,500-$2,500	Anthalon 800 MHz /256MB	27GB	PCI 32MB 17"-21"	8X DVD-ROM, 600 DPI Laser, 56K fax/modem	Photoshop, CAD
❑ *LAN client/server*	$2,500+	2-Pent. III 600 MHz /256MB	2x9 GB SSCI	PCI 2MB 15"	40X CD-ROM, Network card, modem	LAN OS

Avoiding the Computer Blues

The fundamental rule for avoiding the computer blues is to "*plan* for the worst and *prevent* for the best." Avoiding the computer blues starts by selecting the right equipment and applications. It also involves training personnel, establishing security, maintaining equipment, and learning how to protect yourself from the multitude of computer gremlins out there just waiting for you to lower your guard.

CTS and low back pain now account for more lost days of work than any other single cause – almost 30 billion dollars a year in the U.S. alone.
COMPUTER MAGAZINE

Avoiding the *Hardware* Blues – Computer systems and associated equipment are extremely reliable. If they've been running for ten hours without mishap, they shouldn't need doctoring for a long time. Electronic components seem to either die almost immediately or last until external problems like heat, dust, moisture, power brown outs, and electrical disturbances do them in. To help avoid the *hardware blues*: ◆ break in your computer ◆ don't allow cables to form loops to induce electrical noise and current ◆ don't plug computer equipment into shared wall outlets to avoid nasty IC destroying power spikes from equipment containing motors ◆ keep your computer away from dust, cigarette smoke, airborne grease, liquids, food, and moisture ◆ keep your computer cool as excessive heat will kill electronic components faster than dirt and grease ◆ keep your computer safe from static electricity ◆ regularly vacuum, clean, and treat all computer electrical contact points ◆ turn your computer off during thunderstorms ◆ use proper electrical protection by purchasing an uninterruptible power supply (UPS.

Avoiding the *Software* Blues – Waiting for things to go wrong is the best way to give yourself a computer-induced ulcer. Avoiding the *software blues*, like avoiding the hardware blues, centers on careful planning and prevention strategies. You should also: ◆ back up regularly ◆ choose software carefully ◆ don't place floppies near strong magnetic fields ◆ protect from viruses.

Avoiding the *CTS & VDT* Blues – Study after study has been done in the last decade investigating the effect of long-term work with computers on our health. And what scientists have found is that like the problems associated with smoking, drinking and overeating, computer-related problems usually develop slowly over a long period of time, but when they arrive, they arrive with vengeance. Three of the most common problems are CTS (Carpal Tunnel Syndrome or wrist inflammation), VDT Syndrome (Video Display Terminal Syndrome e.g., eyestrain), and lower back pain. Out of the above three, CTS is the newest and most insidious. CTS is classified as a repetitive strain injury. It is derived from the repetition of nearly identical keystrokes at a high rate of speed, tens of thousand of times per day. Each keystroke causes the muscles to contract and the tendons to move; this in turn irritates the tendons as they slide over the bones in the back of the hand, eventually leading to pain and inflammation. Other physical problems linked to computer use include fatigue, shoulder and neck pain, nerve damage, angina or chest pain, blurred vision, chronic headaches, dizziness, facial rashes, irritability, nausea, shortened attention span, reduced productivity, sleep disturbances and sore toes (from having computer components accidentally dropped on to them). To help avoid the CTS and VDT blues: ◆ design an ergonomic workstation (*ergonomics* is the part of design that refers to the comfort and safety features of a product ◆ take planned breaks ◆ limit the time you spend in front of a computer ◆ quit when tired.

Avoiding the *Computer Crime* Blues – Computer crime can range from vandalism or burglary, to serious damage inflicted by disgruntled employees who use their access to divert money, goods, or destroy records – with surprisingly little chance of being caught. To protect yourself from computer crime: ◆ know the real costs of producing computer records and get coverage to compensate for those costs in case of tragedy ◆ assign security passwords to anyone who uses the computer to help prevent unauthorized users from stealing, modifying or destroying data ◆ change passwords frequently and on an irregular basis ◆ do not give too much control over company funds to any single employee without establishing checks and balances to monitor their work ◆ label all disks to identify contents ◆ keep a meticulous computer log and review it occasionally to make sure employees not authorized to work in certain areas do not overstep their bounds ◆ keep diskettes, removable hard drives and other vital data in a safe locked compartment

Make back-up copies of all vital material.	◆ make back-up copies of all vital material and store them in a fireproof, waterproof container, preferably off your business premises ◆ shred sensitive material from computer printouts ◆ spot-check usage of computers to reveal possible abuses of the system ◆ use file encryption software to scramble critical data so no one else can see it or use it unless they have the passwords to descramble it.

Indicate what steps you will take to protect your computer system and data:

Check applications you wish to purchase. Visit http://www.beyond.com for the latest prices and product information:

Buyer's Guide for Business Software

OPERATING SYSTEM SOFTWARE 🖫

❑ **Windows98** – *Launches* 36% faster than Win95. Allows you to store an average of 28% more on your hard drive. Requires at least a 486–66 MHz, 16 MB of RAM, preferably 32MB, and 150-200 MB on HD.

❑ **WindowsNT** – Although, WinNT is more expensive than Win98 and has fewer available applications, to its advantage it is more stable. It protects applications and the base operating system from crashes caused by other applications. This helps reduce data loss and lower software maintenance costs. WinNT is recommended for businesses both big and small. Requires at least a 486-66MHz, 32 MB of RAM, and 150-250 MB on HD.

❑ **LINUX** – LINUX is a free version of the UNIX operating system. CD-ROM starter kits, with manuals, are available for as little as $26.95. This is a serious operating system with a bright future. Microsoft considers LINUX a serious threat. Runs on a 386, 486 or Pentium. Requires 32 MB of RAM and over 300 MB on HD.

❑ **Mac OS 8.5** – Apple has a reputation for offering easy-to-use software. Mac OS 8.5 has more PowerPC-native code making the entire operating system faster. The disadvantage, compared to Win98, is less available software. However, the increasing popularity of the new iMac promises some hope in narrowing this gap. The Mac OS is still a popular choice for many DTP and graphic software users.

BASIC BUSINESS SOFTWARE 🖫

❑ **Database** – Leading Brands: *Access* by Microsoft, *Approach* by IBM, *FileMaker Pro* by Claris, *dBASE* by Borland, *Oracle*, *Paradox* by Corel, *SyBase*. *Oracle* is the world's largest database solutions provider. *FileMaker Pro* and *Access* are popular desktop solutions.

❑ **Spreadsheet** – Leading Brands: *Excel* by Microsoft. *Lotus 123* by IBM, *Quattro Pro* by Corel. *Excel* is the market standard. Offers the widest integration with other software.

❑ **Word Processor** – Market Leaders: *Word Perfect* by Corel, *Word Pro* by IBM/Lotus, *Word* by Microsoft. *Word* is the leading word processor. Highly recommended.

OTHER SOFTWARE WITH BUSINESS APPLICATIONS 🖫

❑ **Accounting Packages** – Leading Brands:

Personal Financing Packages
Quicken 4.0 .... $50
Money 99 Financial Suite $50

Entry Level Packages
DacEasy Accounting 9.0 for Win............. $165
Money Personal and Business 99............. $99
M.Y.O.B Accounting Plus 8.0 .... $161
Peachtree Accounting 7.0 for Windows... $124
QuickBooks Pro 99 .... $148

Mid-Range Packages
CYMA Small Business Edition................ $995
DacEasy Accounting V8.0 for Network... $373

High End Packages
AccPac/2000 .... $1,000+
Professional Accounting Series Plus ... $1,000+

QuickBooks Pro is a popular small business solution. M.Y.O.B. is another fine choice. Ask your accountant for their preference.

❑ **Contact Management** – Leading Brands: *ACT!* by Symantec, *Telemagic* by Sage U.S. Inc., *Maximizer* by Multiactive.

❑ **DTP** – Leading Brands: *Ventura* by Corel, *Microsoft Publisher* by Microsoft, *PageMaker* by Adobe, *QuarkXPress* by Quark. *QuarkXPress* is the #1 choice for printers & desktop publishers.

❑ **E-mail** – Leading Brands: Both Microsoft *Explorer* and Netscape *Communicator* include adequate email features in their Internet browsers. However, for serious email users, *Eudora PRO* is a better choice (available for less than $40). For network solutions, check out IBM's *Lotus cc:Mail* or Microsoft's *MS Mail*.

❑ **Graphics** – Leading Brands: *MacDraw*, Adobe *Illustrator*, *Canvas*, Aldus *FreeHand* (for Mac users); *Illustrator*, *Canvas*, *FreeHand*, *CorelDraw* (for PC users). *Illustrator* is the industry standard.

❑ **Integrated Packages** – Leading Brands: Microsoft *Works* and *Claris Works* for both Mac and PC users. These all-in-one packages include spreadsheet, database, and word processing; for users with straightforward needs.

❑ **Office Suites** – Leading Brands: *WordPerfect Office 2000* by Corel, *Smart Suite* by IBM/Lotus, *Office 2000* by Microsoft. *Office* has over 40 million end users. Keep your eyes open for discounted MS Office 97 and 98 CD-ROM clearances for under $100.

❑ **Photo** – Leading Brands: Adobe *Photoshop*, Adobe *ImageReady*, Microsoft *PhotoDraw2000*. For both Mac and PC users, *Photoshop* is the industry standard. *ImageReady* targets web page designers. Its most notable feature is the ability to optimize Jpegs and Gifs to speed up your site.

❑ **Presentation** – Leading Brands: *Freelance Graphics* by IBM/Lotus, *Corel Presentations* by Corel, *PowerPoint* by Microsoft.

❑ **Project Planner** – Leading Brands: *Project* by Microsoft. Helps plan and track projects more effectively. Useful in large organizations.

❑ **Virus Protection** – Leading Brands: *Norton AntiVirus* by Symantec and *VirusScan* by Mcafee. If you use the Internet, you must get virus protection; no if's, and's, or but's!

❑ **Web Browsers** – Leading Brands: *Netscape Communicator*, *Internet Explorer* by Microsoft. If you plan to have a homepage, you need to have both browsers on your computer to preview your site.

❑ **Web Page Design** – Leading Brands: *FrontPage* by Microsoft, *PageMill* by Adobe (for IBM and Mac), *Dreamweaver* by Macromedia, *HomeSite* by Allaire. Most website designers use *FrontPage*. *HomeSite* is increasing in popularity due to its simplicity and $99 list price.

Answering machines will never replace human beings. The fact is most people dislike leaving messages on machines especially if they have an urgent problem.
COMMUNICATIONS TIP

Communications Set-up

Perhaps a telephone, beeper, and answering machine are all you need to get a consulting business underway. But, considering that your first communication with a potential customer will likely be through the phone, fax or e-mail, and since first impressions create lasting impressions, make smart choices. Imagine what could happen to your professional image, if a client calls your home office and gets your four-year old son. *Good* communications is *good* business.

Answering Machines

One of the most useful functions of an answering machine it to provide clients with additional information about company hours, beeper numbers, fax numbers, or where key personnel can be reached during non-business hours. When recording your announcement, speak in a clear positive voice, giving the name of your company, and exactly what it is you want the potential customer or client to do. Customers like to know right away they have reached the right number and then specifically what is required of them.

An answering service or machine playing the old standard "You have Reached Jones & Associates. We're either with a client or on another call, so leave a message and we'll get back to you" is the oldest trick in the book and doesn't fool anyone.
COMMUNICATIONS TIP

Answering Services

Leaving a message with another human being especially during emergencies is far more reassuring to nervous clients than voice mail or answering machines. A professional answering service will answer your phone with the name of your company, followed by *Message Center*. Clients get the idea that there are 3 or 4 receptionists madly taking down messages, creating the impression that the business is larger than it really is. High-end outfits will also answer the phone exactly the way you ask them to, page you, or forward all your messages or only certain messages, or even hunt you down in an emergency. Before signing up with an answering service, talk to other entrepreneurs in your area who use the service. In many cases, you get what you pay for. Prices range from $40 to $100+ a month.

Cellular Phones

In the U.S. alone, there are over 55 million cellular phone users with figures growing at a rate of 30,000 new subscribers per day. Cellular phones are the ultimate communication tools of the 20th century. However, even though the cost of operation has been cut in half since 1990, they're still expensive (average cost per average user in 1997 was $42.78 per month). You also have to be careful of cellular phone crime. Clone phones that steal code numbers from telephone users, account for hundreds of millions of dollars a year in losses. Cellular phones are also addictive; too convenient. Airtime varies considerably from city to city with costs in the 40 to 80 cents per minute range, but you can reduce charges by shopping around for promotional, discounts, and packaged regional service plans, and using additional services such as call display, voice mail and call forwarding.

Fax machines are not high tech, but they are very user friendly when compared to other forms of high-tech communication. Everyone likes ripping the paper off a machine, even Grandpa.
COMMUNICATIONS TIP

Fax Machines

The fax revolution has virtually spelled the death of telex transmissions and has increased telephone revenue by about $2.5 billion a year. A fax machine can be used to send and take orders, ads, letters, news releases, instructions, or illustrated materials anywhere in the world, as long as recipients also have a fax machine.

Pagers

Before cellular phones came along, pagers were the fastest way to contact people on the go. Their use is still going strong for two reasons: they are smaller and much less expensive to operate, costing as little as $20 a month. Studies indicate that having a pager increases the probability of call completion to 90%. And some of today's pagers are so light and compact that you won't even know they're there – until you have to. The best-known pager service providers are AT&T, Skytel, AirTouch, PageMart, VoiceStream, GTE, MobileComm, and Sprint. Pagers can receive words, numbers, email, and a few of the latest ones even carry voice.

Telephone: Installing a Business Line

The telephone is often the first and only means of contact you will have with clients. Use it to make a favorable impression. If you work at home, install a separate business line. You can't afford to lose business when your phone is tied up with personal calls, but you will, if callers hear a busy signal every time you're on-line. The same is true if potential clients want to send a fax when you're not home but can only reach your answering machine. A business line also allows you to have a business listing in the Yellow Pages and, if you pay for it, a space ad.

Installation Procedures – Check whether your house or apartment is wired for an extra line by calling your phone company. If not, arrange for installation. Prices vary depending on where you live (starting at $68 in New York City, $37 in St. Louis). Basic phone service starts at $8 to $14 a month. The alternative to a residential line is a business line, which offers a free listing in the Yellow Pages. The downside is that you pay for every call you make (including local calls). Residential lines, on the other hand, offer plans with unlimited local calling for low flat rate. In California, setting up a business line will set you back $71 for installation, $85 if you need a wall jack, and $8 a month; local calls cost 6 cents for three minutes. In New York City, you'll pay for the installation of the line and then a deposit of $175 to $300 and $16 a month; a three-minute local call will cost you 8 cents. One way to save money is to install a business line for incoming calls and use your personal, residential line to make outgoing calls.

Describe how you will communicate with your customers, suppliers and business associates:

❑ Answering Machine   ❑ Answering Service   ❑ Cellular Phone   ❑ Fax Machines   ❑ Pager   ❑ Business Line

Indicate what kinds of equipment you will purchase to open communication channels. List monthly costs:

If you need Internet Access, describe monthly fees, per hour charges, web hosting charges, traffic charges, bandwidth and connection speed:

To Do List

Company Plan
Operating Plan

✓ Inventory Control
✓ Order Entry
  Control

DAY 12

Inventory Control

Consider your inventory carefully. Buying too little or too much, the wrong type or wrong size, can quickly lead to financial problems. It doesn't take long for excess inventory to become dated and hard to clear, nor does it take long for customers to become dissatisfied with your selection, or rather lack of selection, and take their business elsewhere. To help prevent these problems and maximize your profits, set up an inventory control and management system that outlines your ideal inventory level, establishes inventory purchasing policies, and informs you quickly what your inventory status is. To do this, follow these 4 steps:

STEP 1 – Determine your ideal inventory level. ❑ Find out average inventory turnover rate for industry (see trade journals). ❑ Determine ideal inventory level based on factors such as amount of capital available, consumer demand, historical sales patterns, quantity discounts, storage space, and supply levels. ❑ Calculate inventory carrying costs. ❑ Calculate EOQ & inventory turnover rate.

STEP 2 – Establish a purchasing plan. ❑ Establish guidelines for buying and selling inventory items. ❑ Find suppliers. ❑ Establish an incoming order inspection policy. ❑ Calculate reorder points for each item in your inventory. ❑ Establish a discontinuation policy (see page 44).

STEP 3 – Set-up an inventory record keeping system. ❑ Pick an inventory control system and record keeping method. ❑ Develop an "Inventory In-stock Record" & "Period Ending Inventory Record."

STEP 4 – Evaluate other concerns. ❑ Establish a markdown policy for products that don't move quickly enough at normal price levels. ❑ Establish a policy for valuating inventory to determine cost of goods sold.

Determining Your Ideal Inventory Level

Inventory must be maintained at a proper level and provided in a timely fashion, otherwise production efficiencies will erode, as in the case of a service or manufacturing business, or sales will plummet, as in the case of a wholesaling or retailing business. To find the right inventory level, an owner-manager must find a *balance* between: ◆ maintaining a wide assortment of stock **but** not spreading popular goods too thin ◆ increasing inventory turnover **but** not sacrificing service ◆ keeping stocks low **but** not sacrificing production efficiency ◆ making volume purchases to get lower prices **but** not ending up with slow-moving inventory ◆ having an adequate inventory on hand **but** not getting caught with obsolete items.

> *Large inventories consume cash, increase the investment in the business, and can bankrupt a business if not properly controlled. It is thus an important objective of every inventory control and management system to keep the financial investment in inventories just sufficient to supply the business – no more, no less.*
> **INVENTORY TIP**

Summarize your method of inventory management including expected rates of inventory turnover and seasonal fluctuations:

Outline your inventory control procedures. What is your mark down policy?

Describe which factors bear the most importance in determining your ideal inventory level:

❑ **Amount of Capital or Financing Available** – How much capital is available to purchase inventory? How will financing charges affect your cash flow? Do you have a special reserve fund to meet sudden high demand for a particular product?

❑ **Consumer Demand & Projected Sales** – How much and what kind of consumer demand exists in the marketplace and how will this effect sales projections? Keep in mind that holding inventory levels at less than what is needed to support sales will cost your firm business, while holding more inventory than present demand will generate excessive inventory holding costs.

❑ **Historical Sales Patterns** – How much inventory have you sold in the past? Which key items will you need to order more frequently and when will you need to stock up to meet seasonal demands?

❑ **Industry Averages** – What are the average inventory level and corresponding stock turnover rates for your industry? Consult trade journals.

❑ **Inventory Carrying Costs** – What and how much are your inventory carrying costs and how do they increase as your inventory levels increase? Consider theft, deterioration, physical damage, and obsolescence costs, as well as tax expenses and the costs of keeping stock control records, ordering stock, and tracking, shipping and receiving stock.

❑ **Quantity Discounts** – Can quantity discounts actually save you money in the long run? Will discounts received for making large single orders of goods or raw materials rather than numerous smaller ones, more than compensate you for the resulting increased carrying costs and increased probability of spoilage and damage?

❑ **Storage Space** – How much space do you have to store and display inventory?

❑ **Supply Levels** – How much inventory do your suppliers have available to sell to you? It is especially important when launching a large promotion to make sure your suppliers have enough merchandise to meet your needs.

Calculating a Profitable Inventory Turnover Rate

WHAT DOES INVENTORY MEAN? *The term "inventory" includes retail/wholesale merchandise or stock, raw materials, work in process, finished products, and supplies that physically become a part of the item intended for sale.*

Since the goal of inventory management is to provide a sufficient amount of inventory to meet sales demand and maximize profitability, you need to develop an effective method for determining: ♦ the minimum annual cost of ordering and stocking each item in your inventory ♦ the average minimum cost of ordering and stocking all the items in your inventory ♦ the average number of times your inventory is sold within a specific period of time (your inventory turnover rate) ♦ how much money should be invested in inventory at any one time.

Using the EOQ Formula – If you are in the business of buying and reselling goods, a handy tool to help reduce inventory costs is the "Economic Order Quantity" (EOQ) formula. This formula calculates the minimum annual cost for ordering and stocking an inventory item (or group of items) by considering the total units sold per year, the cost of placing and receiving orders, and all inventory carrying costs for each item. By knowing your optimal order size for ALL inventory items, you can average these to calculate your average turnover rate.

Calculating your EOQ – The EOQ model states that given certain reasonable assumptions, the order quantity that minimizes total inventory cost can be found using the following formula:

$$EOQ = \left(\frac{2 \times F \times S}{C \times P} \right)^{1/2}$$

F is the cost of placing and receiving an order

S is the annual sales in units (or sales in units for a specified period)

C is carrying costs expressed as a percentage of inventory value (usually this cost is the interest rate charged for any borrowed funds used to buy the inventory)

P is the purchase price the firm must pay per unit of inventory.

EXAMPLE If you own a shoe wholesaling company and sell 10,000 pairs of slippers per year, where your purchase cost is $5 per pair, your fixed cost per order is $500, and your carrying costs have been calculated to be 20% of the inventory value for that particular item, then according to the EOQ model, the quantity of slippers you should order each time is:

$$[(2 \times \$500 \times 10{,}000) / (20\% \times \$5)]^{1/2} = [(\$10{,}000{,}000)/ (\$1)]^{1/2} =$$
3,162 pairs

Using a variation of the inventory turnover ratio (where units are substituted for dollar value), this gives you an inventory turnover rate of:

10,000 units per year / 3,162 units =
3.162 times per year

With an average turnover rate of 3.162 times a year, you should reorder new stock every 115 days (365 days per year / 3.162).

Using the "Total Sales Divided by Six" Rule: For most businesses, total inventory should turnover at least six times per year. Using this rule of thumb, to figure out how much capital you should have invested in inventory at anyone time, divide your yearly cost of goods sold by six. For example, if you project annual sales to be $400,000 at a cost of $240,000, then you should carry on average $40,000 worth of inventory.

NOTE If your plan to retail high-ticket items (which tend to have a slower turnover), a more realistic rule would be *total sales divided by four* or *four and a half*.

Calculating a Profitable Turnover Rate for a Manufacturing Business – For a manufacturing business, rather than figuring the amount of inventory it should carry in *dollars*, it's easier to figure it in terms of *days of sales*. Consider the following example: a shoe manufacturer plans to stock a minimum inventory of sandals equivalent to 3 weeks (15 working days) of the projected sales rate to ensure having enough to satisfy demand (the maximum inventory might be 6 weeks of the projected sales rate to limit the investment in raw materials). If the sales rate of sandals were 150 pairs per day, then the inventory days for the minimum inventory planned would be 2,250 pairs of sandals. If the sandals cost $10 a pair to manufacture then the minimum inventory planned would be $22,500 (2,250 units x $10 per unit) and the daily cost would be $1,500/day.

Calculate your EOQ for key inventory items. Calculate an average for your entire inventory. Compare with standard industry turnover rates:

F = cost of placing and receiving an order

S = annual sales in units

C = carrying costs expressed as a % of inventory value

P = purchase price the firm must pay per unit of inventory

Item(s)	F ($)	S (# of units)	C (%)	P ($/unit)	EOQ (units)	Turnover Rate	Turnover Days	Industry Standard
Average Turnover Rates for Entire Inventory								

Detail inventory carrying costs and other EOQ considerations. Comment on any differences between your turnover rate and industry standards:

Developing an Inventory Records System

An *inventory record keeping system* is primarily used to determine your company's *cost of goods sold* as well and provide information for financial statements. It helps you provide better service to your customers by helping you dispose of unwanted items, keep "hot" items in stock, and see that parts and materials are not lost through theft, shrinkage, error or waste. To meet these objectives, your records system needs to tell you the following 3 things:

1) *Approximately or exactly how much of an item you have in stock at any particular moment in time.* You need to know this information so that you are able to reorder and maintain sufficient quantities in stock to meet customer demand.

2) *Exactly how much inventory you have in stock and have sold at the end of the month, quarter or year.* You need to keep track of this information for accounting and sales information purposes.

3) *How much stock is on order.* You need to keep track of this information so you don't accidentally order the same item twice.

> *Displaying older inventory prominently and monitoring its turnover daily, can help prevent loses due to obsolete inventory.*

To get these 3 essential pieces of information: ♦ pick an inventory control system ♦ pick an inventory record keeping method ♦ develop an "Period Ending Inventory Record" form ♦ develop a "Perpetual Inventory Record" also known as an "Inventory In-stock Record".

As your company develops and matures, you should also take steps to: ♦ integrate your inventory record keeping system with other systems within your company that track sales, production and purchasing activities ♦ regularly compare projections with actual results and analyze the differences ♦ develop procedures to correct problems once spotted and improve business performance.

Perpetual Inventory Method

Activity	Value in Units
Beginning inventory	100
Sales	(75)
Production (purchases)	95
Ending inventory (calculated)	**120**

Inventory "In-Stock" Record

INVENTORY CARD for					Harry's Pet Supplies	
Item: *Dog Collar*					Model: *deluxe leather*	
	Received		Withdrawn		Balance	
Date	#	$	#	$	#	$
12/31/95					*20*	*140.00*
1/1/96	*80*	*560.00*			*100*	*700.00*
1/1/96			*10*	*70.00*	*90*	*630.00*

Periodic Inventory Method

Activity	Value in Units
Beginning inventory	1,500
Sales	(800)
Production (calculated)	900
Ending inventory	**1,600**

Period Ending Inventory Record

Periodic Inventory Record for		DATE	
Harry's Pet Supplies		*1/1/96*	
Item	**Description**	**Quantity**	**Amount**
Stock #101	*Deluxe Leather Dog Collars*	*90*	*$630*
Serial # 871	*Enamel Bird Cage*	*1*	*1,000*
Stock #511	*HPS Brand Canned Dog Food*	*350*	*402.50*
	*Other **misc**. items*	*23*	*1,145*
	Total Physical Inventory	*464*	*3,177.50*

Summarize your inventory record keeping system. What kinds of forms will you use? Will you computerize your inventory records system?

Establishing an Inventory Valuation Policy

> *To prepare for potential sales increases, it may be prudent to hold some level of "safety stock." The amount of safety stock is determined by comparing the cost of maintaining this additional inventory against potential sales losses.*
> **BUSINESS TIP**

At the end of each fiscal year you must determine your yearly income to calculate taxes owed. An essential step in achieving this objective is to prepare an annual inventory to determine your costs of goods sold. An annual inventory is usually a list of goods held for sale including, in the case of a manufacturers, raw materials and work-in-progress on hand (see "Period Ending Inventory Record" above).

Problems You are Likely to Encounter When Valuing your Inventory – Although counting in-stock quantities is straightforward, difficulties can present themselves when determining its exact value. One problem you might face is the evaluation of work-in-progress. This is because you have substantial leeway in valuation, derived from the variety of choices available to you as to the manner in which how goods flow through your establishment. The best advice here is to come up with as simple a method as possible and stick to it. Another problem created is when you have similar items of different costs as a result of being purchased at different times of the year or from different suppliers. Both of these above difficulties are further aggravated, since the values at which your inventories of merchandise, materials, work in process, and finished goods are recorded, have a dual significance: *first*, the amount shown in your balance sheet as a current asset is likely to be a significant working-capital component – shareholders and investors like to see a company with lots of working-capital. And *second*, the accounting valuation which you place on your inventories directly affects your net income for the period and hence your taxes.

Two Most Common Methods of Inventory Valuation – For income tax purposes, two acceptable methods of valuing your inventory are:

- *Cost Method* – Using this method you determine the value of your entire inventory at its cost (this valuation method is also known as the "identified cost method" of inventory valuation). (a) For merchandise on hand at the beginning of the year, *cost* means the inventory price of the goods. (b) For merchandise purchased during the year, *cost* means the invoice price less appropriate discounts plus transportation or other charges you incur in acquiring the goods. (c) For merchandise produced during the year, *cost* means all direct and indirect costs (in the U.S. these costs must be capitalized under the uniform capitalization rules).

- *Lower of Cost or Market Method* – Using this method you compare the "market value" of each item on hand at the inventory date with its cost and use the lower value as its inventory value. Under ordinary circumstances and for normal goods, *market value* means the usual bid price at the date of your inventory. This price is based on the volume of merchandise you usually buy.

EXAMPLE If at the end of the year you have the following items on hand as shown in the chart on the right, using the "Lower of Cost Method," the value of your closing inventory would be $800. If you use this method you must value each item in the inventory. You may not value the entire inventory at cost ($1,200) and at market ($850) and then use the lower figure of ($850).

Items	Cost	Market	Whichever is Lower
A	$300	$350	$300
B	$400	$250	$250
C	$500	$250	$250
Totals	**$1,200**	**$850**	**$800**

State which method you plan to use to value your inventory. Explain your reasons for doing so:

❏ *Cost* Method ❏ Lower of Cost or *Market* Method

Order Entry Control

The purpose of setting-up an order entry system is to help you process and keep track of your customer orders. However, a good system must do more. A good system simplifies the buying process for your customers based on an analysis of their buying habits and practices as they deal with the idiosyncrasies of your business. More specifically, it must recognize areas in the ordering process that hinder buying decisions and then offer solutions to remove these obstacles permanently.

Choosing an Order Entry System

There are 5 basic types of order entry systems: sales receipt based systems, cash register based systems, coupon based systems, form based systems, and computer based systems. Each of these systems are described in more detail below:

Describe your order entry system:

❏ Sales Receipt Based Systems	❏ Cash Register Based Systems	❏ Coupon Based Systems	❏ Order Form Based Systems	❏ Computer Based Systems

Types of Order Entry Systems

❏ **Sales Receipt Based Systems** – A sales receipt based order entry system is usually seen in a very small service firm in which services rendered and occasional purchases are always written on a receipt. The receipt becomes the order entry form and the record for accounting and tax purposes. The receipts are usually stored in a cash box along with the change fund and sales revenues. This type of system is very cheap to set-up and simple to operate, but very limited as a management tool.

❏ **Cash Register Based Systems** – In this type of system, the cash register is the initial point of entry and is used to keep track of total sales, and within limits, individual items sold to aid in inventory control. However, this system, originating in the 19th century, is not much use to a large retail chain and should only be considered if you operate a small restaurant, corner grocery store or small independently run retail outlet. It offers little help in controlling a large inventory. To its advantage, it is relatively easy to set-up and operate.

❏ **Coupon Based Systems** – A coupon based order entry system is often used by mail order operations, where newspapers and magazines are the chief promotional media. A coupon-based system uses coupons that can be mailed in as the initial point of entry. The coupons function as simplified order forms.

❏ **Order Form Based Systems** – Before computers came along, businesses used invoices, sales orders, and purchase orders (many businesses still do) to organize their orders and purchases, and keep track of their inventory for management and accounting purposes. Of special interest to mail order operators is a "Daily Record of Responses" (a copy of this form can be printed from GB▢ #8, Form #30). This form allows you to keep track of individual orders or inquiries, how much cash is received, and which advertising pulled in that order. This form can be used as your initial order entry point.

❏ **Computer Based Systems** – Not too long ago, computers revolutionized the back end of how a business works in the accounting area with spreadsheet programs. But now, with falling prices in hard drives, faster processors and the growth of the Internet, computers are learning how to better handle information and super-large databases with ease, thus encroaching ever more and more into the order entry area. Soon they will completely revolutionize the front end of the business as well. Computer based systems can range from simple order and receipt entry systems to highly complex systems that keep track of inventory and other factors needed by management – all automatically. It is potentially one of the most complete order entry systems available to the business owner and the most efficient.

Improving Your Order Handling Efficiency

It is difficult for a small product or service business to compete with big firms on areas like assortment, price, and promotion. However, selling effort and service, is one place where the small product or service business can compete with larger competitors – and win. To improve order handling efficiency: ◆ design a great order entry form ◆ train sales staff to handle orders better ◆ remove ordering "bottlenecks" ◆ computerize your operations. The first 3 of these 4 strategies are discussed below and on the next page:

Designing a Great Order Entry Form – If you plan to use an order form in your order entry system, and most likely you will, whether this form is a piece of

Desire to have things done quickly prevents them from being done thoroughly.
CONFUCIUS

paper or a computer interface, heed the following advice: poorly designed forms cost time, money and customers. According to a report published by a business communication newsletter, more than 5 billion forms are thrown away each year. This happens when people try to fill out forms, make mistakes and have to start over again. Likewise, in a survey of 3,800 *Modern Maturity* readers, it was found that 58% of people who try to fill out forms give up after their first attempt. To design a great order entry form:

- *Simplify entry points for customer information.* Consider using narrative fill-in-the-blanks points of entry, especially when targeting kids, such as: My name is *Jack Benign*. I live in *New York*. My street address is . . . etc.

- *Use words readers will understand.* Avoid fuzzy phrases such as, "payment recovery is voided" when you mean, "you can't get your money back." Also cut as much jargon as possible. Don't say, "charge for excess drip" when you mean, "charge for extending wire more than 500 feet from the premises."

Training Sales Staff to Take and Handle Orders More Efficiently – There are 3 types of sales personnel who handle orders and who need to be trained properly to perform at peak efficiency. These personnel are the order handler, the order taker, and the order getter. The characteristics of each of these types of sales personnel are described below and on the next page, as well as strategies you can use to get them to operate smarter and better.

Removing Ordering "Bottlenecks" – The ordering process can be broken down into five distinct areas: order writing, forwarding orders, receiving orders, processing orders and filling orders. Each of these processes harbors potential "bottlenecks." Chart-C on page 72 outlines procedures and strategies for overcoming or preventing potential *bottlenecks*.

A. _Order Entry Forms_ – *Describe order entry equipment and forms you will use and how it will coordinate with inventory control:*

Types of Retail Sales Personnel	
(classified by level of creative effort)	
Routine Effort ▢▨▧▨ Creative Effort	
Order Handler Order Taker Order Getter	

B. _Handling Orders_ – *Describe how you will write orders, forward orders, receive order, process order, fill orders, and ship orders:*

Order Handlers – Order handlers are the members of your sales staff who perform such tasks as taking tickets at a concert or checking out food at a grocery store. Generally, they are the people who receive your customer's money and the last people to deal with your customer's. They work in a routine selling environment. Due to the nature of their jobs, they'll be asked numerous questions by customers, as well as, hear complaints about prices and services. It is thus important to encourage them to be pleasant at all times and help keep them abreast of important facts within their industry. It is also important to make it easy for them to communicate to you, so you can more quickly recognize problems and find solutions.

	Order Takers – Order takers are the members of your sales staff who in addition to taking, handling and filling orders can be trained in the art of "suggestion selling." Suggestion selling can result in many additional sales. For example, a counter attendant at a fast food restaurant, after taking a customer's order, may then ask the customer if he or she would be interested in a hot apple pie, a milk shake, or perhaps a larger order of fries.
	Order Getters – Order getters are the members of your sales staff who operate at their wits end. They handle transactions and take orders just like other staff members, but more importantly are expected to go out and get orders. For many clothing, furniture, jewelry and appliance stores, their success rests solely on the creative efforts of their order getters. However, to make these order getters truly effective is no simple task. Training order getters in regards to store policies and acceptable selling techniques in an attempt to standardize the quality of your service is mandatory, but more than that, order getters must be encouraged to become "super sales staff." This can only be accomplished by setting up structures within your organization that rewards creativity, courtesy and exceptional customer service with bonuses, promotions, extra training and peer recognition.

*C. **Ordering Bottlenecks** – Describe steps you will to take to remove ordering "bottlenecks":*

❑ **Order Writing** – All sales reps should be thoroughly trained to complete the order form properly. This applies not only to the field sales force but also to any inside salespeople. Terms, discounts, names and addresses, delivery information, and all special instructions must be written legibly. Poorly written-out order forms, or forms with mistakes should be acted on immediately (a lot of time can be saved and careless omission or errors avoided when the order form itself is carefully tailored to the needs of your organization).

❑ **Forwarding Orders** – It's essential that orders gathered by the field sales office be transmitted as quickly as possible to the home office. A delay of even a day or two can result in customer dissatisfaction. If the sales rep's territory is within an hour's drive of the office, a good procedure is to have the salesperson deliver the day's orders in person, either immediately after completing rounds, or early the next morning. Of course, if the sales force operates at substantial distances from the home office, orders may be emailed or faxed.

❑ **Receiving Orders** – Regardless of the method employed in getting the orders to the office (in-person, mail, or telephone) there should be a central clerk to receive all orders. It is this person's responsibility to check orders for accuracy, clarity, and conformance with company policy. Those that contain mistakes or omissions should be put aside for rechecking later. This clerk should be instructed to record every order on an order sheet (which can be printed). Each day's sheet should have columns for writing in the order number, the time received, the customer's name, and the salesperson signature or stamp.

Give prompt attention and quick dependable service to incoming orders. Ideally, every incoming order should be filled and the merchandise sent on its way within 48 hours. Strategies should also be in place, when orders come in heavy quantities (as happens before a holiday season or specific holidays), or when there isn't enough labor available to fill them, or when the transportation facilities are overburdened.

❑ **Processing Orders** – If additional copies of the order are needed avoid transcribing the information. Use an office copier. Send copies first to the internal sales department where prices are checked, then to the credit desk for an okay. After approval, they're sent on to the warehouse for filling.

❑ **Filling Orders** – On receiving the order, the warehouse supervisor should register it in logbook and check over its details. At this point, priorities and routing considerations are taken into account. With respect to routing, transportation runs to different areas are usually scheduled for different days of the week or month. Orders destined for those areas can accumulate in difference boxes or trays. Orders are distributed, as the order pickers become available. Various types of handling equipment – dollies carts of different kinds, conveyors, and even moving belts – can facilitate movement of the merchandise from the warehouse, to the loading area (good warehouse layout and proper utilization of space is important).

Establish a procedure for double-checking all outgoing orders. All outgoing orders should be carefully double-checked before loading to prevent wasted time and money handling returns or reshipping missed items.

To Do List

Company Plan
Operating Plan

✓ Operations
  Schedule
✓ Production Plan
✓ Quality Control
✓ Required Licenses
  & Legal
  Considerations

DAY 13

Operations Schedule

An *Operations Schedule*, also referred to as an *Implementation Schedule* or *Work Schedule*, outlines dates assigned and expected dates of completion for key activities, objectives and *decision points* (e.g. the completion of a budget). It also describes steps that will be taken to meet goals related to management, public relations policies, guarantees, and personal objectives. Month by month or quarterly flow charts can be used to outline specific actions to be taken and by whom.

NOTE A *decision point* is a checkpoint for measuring your results. Significant dates, sales levels, and production levels can be listed as decision points.

To be great is to be misunderstood.
EMERSON

Setting Tasks & Monitoring Progress

Once your have established short- and long-term goals as outlined in DAY 5, *Company Goals & Objectives* (see page 20), you will need to establish objectives for each of these goals. Next, you will need to prioritize these objectives, assign responsibilities and establish target dates. When doing so, consider the following: (**a**) how each objective will impact revenues and expenses, particularly your monthly cash flow and yearly budget; and (**b**) how long employees figure it will take to complete assigned objectives.

Management by objectives works if you know the objectives. Ninety percent of the time you don't.
PETER F. DRUCKER

An objective of great importance, but equally great cost, may have to be implemented gradually as your budget allows or perhaps put on hold indefinitely. Don't get overly ambitious at assigning target dates. Allow the recipient of the delegated responsibility to tell the group how long it will take, and then within reason, accept that as the target date. Remember, in most cases, your employees will already have a full day's schedule and little spare time. If they are not given sufficient time to achieve the objectives assigned to them, your plans may quickly be viewed as impossible to accomplish and will become next to useless.

Summarize your most important goal/objective in your "Operations Schedule" and why it is important. Who is responsible to complete this task?

Summarize key decision points. Give dates:

Key Goals & Objectives	Tasks Required to Accomplish	Who is Responsible	Scheduled Completion

Provide a detailed work schedule with objectives, starting dates and deadlines by week and month for your first year of operation. Use the "Current Status" box to indicate how near the task is to completion (25%, 50%, 75%) or whether it is already finished (100%):

OPERATIONS SCHEDULE					
Starting Date	Task to be Completed	Target Date	Task Assigned To	Current STATUS	Priority
Notes					
Notes					
Notes					
Notes					
Notes					
Notes					
Notes					
Notes					

Production/Manufacturing Plan

Comment on how you will produce your product. Include a brief description of your production or manufacturing process (but don't get too technical). If you offer a service, title this section *Service Plan* and comment on how you will deliver your service.

Sample Production Plan Description

We will be using a (Method of Assembly or Construction) for our (Product). Our main supplier of component parts will be (Name of Primary Supplier, City, State). In the event that they are not able to ship according to our specifications our secondary supplier will be (Name of Secondary Supplier, City, State). These parts will be shipped to us by (Method of Transport).

The actual machinery used in the production line will be manufactured by (Steel Box Machine Tools of San Diego, California, Texas). They also will be doing all scheduled maintenance under a service contract. This machine will allow us to . . . (Describe how the equipment will improve operational efficiency).

With (Equipment Name) our labor and production costs will be reduced by (XX)%. We anticipate the following outlay for this capital equipment:

A&M Machines $(XXX)	Service Contract $(XXX)

List the basic operations and procedures your manufacturing or service firm will have to perform to produce or deliver your product or service:

Quality Control

Assuring continued quality levels in your products and services is critical for repeat business and for general overall business success. Describe how you plan to assure and maintain quality in your operations.

Describe how you will maintain quality in the production of your products or delivery of your service:

Required Licenses & Legal Considerations

The laws and regulations pertaining to small businesses are quite extensive and have a major impact on how you conduct your business. Under this heading, discuss licenses and permits required, important legal considerations, and necessary inspections. As well, develop a *Business Code of Ethics* and consider any ramifications it might have on how you conduct your business.

Registering Your Business

To register your business, contact your local small business center or tax assessment office. Find these numbers in your phone book under city, state/province, and federal government listings (in the U.S., phone 1-800-U-ASK-SBA). Ask what city, county, state, and federal forms, licenses and permits are required (a *license* is a privilege granted by a legislative body at its discretion; a *permit* is a right that anyone can obtain if the requirements of the granting agency are met). Be specific about what kind of business you are starting. In addition, although you are not expected to be a lawyer, you need a basic knowledge of the laws and legal matters affecting your business. Are you aware of: ❑ Occupational Safety & Health (OSHA) requirements, ❑ regulations covering hazardous material ❑ local ordinances covering signs and snow removal ❑ federal small business tax code provisions ❑ federal regulations on withholding taxes and social security ❑ state workmen's compensation laws ❑ special laws affecting your industry.

Review charts on the next 2 pages. Check licenses and permits required. List other important legal and licensing considerations and obstacles:

Businesses Frequently Requiring a License or Permit

❑ Alcohol – sale & distribution	❑ Commercial trucking and bus operations	❑ Farm implement dealers	❑ Lodging – hotels, guesthouses, inns, motels, bed & breakfasts,
❑ Amusement park, carnival ride, music & dance bar operations	❑ Concrete technicians – testing labs	❑ Firearms seller	❑ Mines, oil and gas drilling operations
❑ Appliance testing labs	❑ Dairy plants, operators and distributors	❑ Fishing, hunting &trapping operations	❑ Nursing home operators
❑ Asbestos abatement	❑ Dancing schools	❑ Fishing vessel operations	❑ Outdoor advertisers
❑ Auto body repair	❑ Detective & security agencies	❑ Fish market & processing operations	❑ Pet shops, riding schools, cattle dealers, & stables
❑ Auto sales – new & used	❑ Drinking water supply facility operations	❑ Food or beverage seller or preparer	❑ Pipeline builders
❑ Broadcasting stations	❑ Elevators & operators, escalators	❑ Funeral homes	❑ Private school operators
❑ Cemetery operations	❑ Employment agencies	❑ Game or bird farm	❑ Restricted pesticide dealers and applicators
❑ Child day care centers	❑ Engine fuel & lubricants	❑ Hawkers & peddlers of crafts, flowers balloons & souvenirs	❑ Sanitarium operators
❑ Cigarettes – wholesale and retail	❑ Engineering and related fields	❑ Hazardous chemicals or flammable waste disposers	❑ Sawmills & timber cutting operators
❑ Collection agencies and finance companies		❑ Junk dealers	

Municipal, Rural, State/Provincial, Federal Licenses, Regulations & Requirements

Municipal Licenses, Regulations & Requirements – Local governments have the authority to issue their own business licenses within their jurisdiction. Since there is no uniformity throughout the state/province regarding municipal licenses for business, it would be wise to consult with the appropriate local officials to determine if your business is affected by local regulations, licenses or zoning requirements. City business licenses are generally required to control businesses which pose special problems to health, fire, safety, disturbance to the physical and social environment and so on. Research the following areas:

❑ Building Codes & Building Permits
❑ Home Owner's Regulations
❑ Local Ordinances
❑ Occupant Permit
❑ Zoning Bylaws

Rural Licenses, Regulations & Requirements – Outside of all cities and towns, business development must confirm with zoning requirements. These requirements are administered by the local county concerned, the municipal district, the regional planning commission, or the Provincial/State Planning Board. Approval from one of these bodies is necessary to construct a commercial building in a rural area.

State/Province Licenses, Regulations & Requirements – The State or Province in which you plan to operate may require you to obtain the following licenses and/or meet the following regulations:

❑ Agricultural Licenses
❑ Consumer Protection Bonds
❑ Environment Restrictions & Regulations
❑ Highway Development Permits
❑ Limited Partnership & Trusts
❑ Liquor License
❑ Registering for Sales Taxes
❑ Retail Licenses

❑ State Employers' Registration (U.S.)
❑ State Seller's Permit (U.S.)
❑ Strategic Materials & Equipment Permits
❑ Using a "Fictitious Name" (DBA Statement) (U.S.)
❑ Worker's Compensation

Federal Licenses, Regulations & Requirements – The federal government has wide licensing powers within the fields of agriculture, manufacturing, communication and interstate/provincial and international transportation. The following list contains some of the more pertinent licenses, permits, regulations and requirements of the Federal Government:

❑ Agricultural Permits
❑ Business Number (Canada) – The BN is a numbering system designed to replace the multiple numbers that businesses require to deal with the Canadian government. Each business is assigned a unique registration number that stays the same no matter how many or what types of accounts it has. The BN consolidates corporate income tax, import/export, GST, and payroll deductions. BN registration can be conducted online at www.rc.gc.ca
❑ Broadcasting Licenses
❑ Employee Forms – In the U.S., you will need to have new employees fill out Form I-9 and Form W-4. If your employees qualify for advance payment of the earned income credit, they must complete Form W-5. In Canada, your main responsibility involves filling out T4 slips at the end of the tax year for each employee.
❑ Employer Identification Number (EIN), (U.S.)
❑ Export/Import Permit
❑ Hazardous Materials Regulations
❑ Labor Union Regulations
❑ Occupational Safety & Health Requirements (OSHA)
❑ Patents, Trademarks, Copyright & Industrial Designs Registration
❑ Payroll Deductions (Form 941 U.S.)
❑ Social Insurance Number (Canada)
❑ Social Security Number (U.S.)

List which licenses have already been obtained and which ones are being processed:

Permit, License, or Necessary Inspection	Date Obtained or Completed

License or Permit Issuing Bodies	
Department	**Authority**
Building	Construction, renovations, zoning, signage
Health	Food handling, rest rooms, sewer connections, septic systems
Council	Licenses and permits
Town Clerk	Business certificates
Police	Alarm and business registrations
Fire	Safety inspections, alarm registrations
Weights and Measures	Weighing and measuring, packaging and labeling
Conservation Commission	Wetland alterations, building and activity near wetlands
Historic	Signs, building and home alterations, business activities

Developing a Business Code of Ethics

Beyond all the laws and regulations that govern the legal actions of businesses, a responsible company goes one step further. A *Business Code of Ethics* governs how a company will handle the "gray areas" of the law. It also attempts to establish as set of values and moral guidelines for company management and staff.

List any important issues your business code of ethics will address, beyond that which the government regulates:

❑ **Demonstrations** – Be truthful at all times when performing demonstrations. There is no point and trying to trick your customer. Short-term trickery will be outweighed by the long-term loss of trust.

❑ **Environmental Concerns** – As a small business owner you should consider the impact your business will have on your local environment beyond that which the government regulates. As it is, every year fields and groves are being sprayed with pesticides and dusted with chemicals while poultry, cattle and other livestock are being raised on chemical fatteners. Lakes, streams, and rivers are quickly being contaminated with industrial waste while at the same time the atmosphere is being polluted with harmful levels of sulfur and carbon compounds from factories and from the millions of vehicles. And if that isn't enough, peoples' ears are assaulted everyday by the din of city traffic, roaring machinery and thundering aircraft overhead. As a business owner, what are you going to do to address some of these problems?

❑ **Exploitation of Children** – Promotions directed towards children should not exploit their credulity, lack of experience, or sense of loyalty.

❑ **Extending Goodwill** – Inherent in the concept of a democratic society is the belief that those who are more affluent are responsible for the less able and less fortunate, hence, the social security system, programs for the hard-core unemployed, anti-discrimination laws, and the welfare system. A successful company is ethically responsible for giving something back to the community it has become rich off of.

❑ **Honesty** – A business that ends up serving a respectable function in a community is a business that functions at a high level of ethical behavior. The honest and fair entrepreneur is one who upholds higher and nobler objectives, rather than merely aiming at earning profits at any cost.

❑ **Indecent Material** – Do not promote or sell material that would cause widespread offense due to the derogatory, vulgar or indecent nature of the material.

❑ **Social Concerns** – Modern managers and business owners, should be aware of any social issues that might have negative or positive publicity affects on their operations.

If self-regulation worked, Moses would have come down from Mount Sinai with the ten guidelines.
ANON

*An **EIN** is issued by the IRS in the following format:*

00-0000000

*An **SSN** is issued by the U.S. Social Security Administration in the following format:*

000-00-000

*A **SIN** is issued in Canada by Social Security Services in the following format:*

000-000-000
FUNFACT

Basic Procedures for Registering & Licensing a Business in the U.S.

❏ Develop a detailed business plan to determine the feasibility of your venture.

❏ For individual counseling, contact your local SCORE office.

❏ Use your business plan to shop for equity capital, venture capital, or financing.

❏ Obtain financial commitments before incurring any start-up costs.

❏ Obtain the proper state and federal licenses. For most businesses, this would mean contacting the licensing section of your local government or the Office of the Secretary of State.

❏ If you intend to operate as a sole proprietor or partnership, file a "fictitious name" statement (DBA) with your county office. If you plan to incorporate your business, contact your State corporate registration center.

❏ Contact the local zoning or licensing authority in your city, town or municipality to obtain local operating restrictions.

❏ Contact the IRS and file for an employer identification number (EIN). To do this you will need to fill out an SS-4 form.

❏ If you plan to hire employees, register your company with the Workers' Compensation Board.

❏ Obtain any additional special licenses or permits that you may require.

Basic Procedures for Registering & Licensing a Business in Canada

❏ Develop a detailed business plan to determine the feasibility of your venture.

❏ For individual counseling, contact your local Economic Development & Trade office.

❏ Use your business plan to shop for equity capital, venture capital, or financing.

❏ Obtain financial commitments before incurring any start-up costs.

❏ Obtain the proper provincial and federal licenses. For most businesses, this would mean contacting the licensing section of the Consumer Relations Division, of Consumer and Corporate Affairs.

❏ If you intend to operate as a sole proprietor or partnership, register your business name with Central Registry, Department of the Attorney General. If you are going to incorporate your business, contact the Corporate Registry, Consumer and Corporate Affairs.

❏ Contact the local zoning or licensing authority in your city, town or municipality to obtain local operating restrictions.

❏ If you plan to hire employees, register your company with the Workers' Compensation Board.

❏ Contact Revenue Canada, Sources Deductions Section, to obtain an employer's account # (BN) for Unemployment Insurance and Canada Pension Plan Deductions.

❏ If you employ 5 or more people, register with the Health Care Insurance Commission.

❏ Contact your provincial Employment Standards Branch to ensure that you comply with the pertinent labor regulations.

❏ Obtain any additional special licenses or permits that you may require.

Summarize any registration procedures not yet completed. Explain any special licensing or registration concerns that may cause difficulties in starting your business:

To Do List

Company Plan
Organizational Plan

✓ Board of Directors
✓ Contract & Temporary Help
✓ Management Team
✓ Manpower Required
✓ Organizational Chart
✓ Ownership Structure
✓ Professional Advisors

DAY 14
Organizational Plan

An *organizational plan* helps you delegate work, responsibility and authority. It describes who runs your company, controls day-to-day operations, influences decisions, and more specifically, who does all the work (this section could also me titled "Organization & Management Plan").

Summarize the most important points of your organizational plan:

> *You're only as good as the people you hire.*
> **RAY KROC**

Board of Directors

If your business is incorporated, list the people you have or expect to have on your board of directors (include addresses and role in company). Tell when they meet and whether they have a financial interest in your company.

Outline the size and composition of your board of directors. Detail meeting schedule:

Present a brief résumé of three individuals on your board who are not part of your management team. Indicate compensation received:

Individual Position on Board	Salary Fees or Bonuses	TOTAL Compensation	Qualifications & Experience
	$	$	
	$		
	$	$	
	$		
	$	$	
	$		

Contract & Temporary Help

List contracted professionals and consultants who can provide assistance when needed in specialized or deficient areas such as marketing, sales, or production. Also, list temporary help resources available to meet fluctuating labor needs.

If you don't have a board of directors, get one. It looks good on your business plan and good on the résumés of your directors. Many people will be glad to oblige.

Using TEMP Services & Contract Labor

It is usually recommended for a new or growing business that needs help in the design, production, or distribution stages of a project, to initially stay away from hiring permanent staff. This not only protects you from the dangers of over staffing and runaway overhead, but also saves paperwork and extra responsibilities. Whenever your future staffing needs are uncertain, it is cheaper, less risky, and ultimately wiser to contract out labor through a temp agency, an employee leasing agency or a private sub-contractor, rather than hire.

Understanding the Hidden Costs of Hiring Employees – On the surface, it may appear that TEMP services cost more than hiring additional employees, but there are many costs usually overlooked. Mandatory costs such as social security, unemployment insurance, and workers compensation amount to over 11% of the basic salary. Payments for time not worked, including vacations, holidays, and sick days, amounts to almost 9%. Then there are company paid benefits such as health insurance, pension plans and discounts, and record keeping, payroll and other paperwork which amount to another 6-7%. Total hidden costs are in the neighborhood of 42%, meaning a basic $300 weekly salary actually costs your company $426 (and that doesn't include the costs of recruiting and training).

Describe any contract or temporary help that will be used. E.g., "The accountant will be available on a part-time, hourly basis, as needed. The initial agreement calls for services not to exceed _____ hours per month at _____ per hour":

| |
| |
| |
| |

Management Team

Whenever you see a new company doing its own payroll rather than using an outside payroll service, such as "Paychex," you can be pretty sure they are doing something wrong. As a start-up business owner, your time is better spent concentrating on your product and marketing – bringing "in" money – not giving "out" money.
BUSINESS TIP

Provide brief management biographies of key personnel and owners. Include their ages, educational background, business experience, abilities & related skills, other credentials, and an outline of their responsibilities. If relevant, put this information in *Supporting Documents* (résumés should be no longer than a page). As well, don't forget to include your own qualifications, and how you plan to get help in areas that your are deficient in. Will you take a course(s)?

NOTE If your business is incorporated, give detailed information on all corporate officers. Who are they? What are their skills? Why were they chosen? If your business is a partnership, explain why certain partners where chosen, what they add to the company and how their skills and experience are complementary.

Sample Management Team Descriptions/Biographies

President – (Name), Chief Executive Officer since (Date). Director and President since (Date). (Name) is the founder of (Company Name). (He/She) has had experience in the (Product/Service) field with (his/her) own firm, (Johnson Inc, of Calgary, Alberta, from 19(XX) to 19(XX). This firm was sold to (Company), in 19(XX). Since then (Name) has held a (Job Type) position with (ABC Inc.). (Name) graduated from the (University) in (Date) with a (business degree in economics). ◆ Responsible for entire operation. Oversees management and all other executives. Salary – $50,000.

> *Quality people make a quality company. Recruit the best and you will be the best.*

> *As a general view, remuneration by fixed salaries does not in any class of functionaries produce the maximum amount of zeal.*
> **JOHN STUART MILL**

Chief Financial Officer – (Name), CPA, Chief Financial Officer, Treasurer and Director. (Name) joined (Company Name), Inc. on (Date) as a financial consultant. (He/She) was named CFO on (Date). (Name) served as corporate controller of (XYZ Shoe Company) from 19(XX) to 19(XX). (Name) graduated from (Athabasca University in Edmonton, Alberta in 19(XX) with a (bachelor's degree in accounting). Since (Date), (he/she) has been licensed as a Certified Public Accountant in the (Province of Alberta) and is a member of (the Canadian Association of Certified Public Accountants). ◆ Responsible for financial operations, A/Ps, A/Rs, interaction with auditors and investor relations. Salary – $40,000.

Vice President – (Name), Secretary, Executive Vice President and Director. (Name) supervises company's sales to our largest corporate customers, including (list names of corporate contracts). (Name) has served as Secretary and a Director since (Date), has been (VP of Operations) from 19(XX) to 19(XX), and Executive VP since 19(XX). (Name) has been involved since (Date) with (Company Name). (His/Her) duties included (managing the sales department). From 19(XX) to 19(XX) (he/she) was a (sales rep for ABC Company, Banff, Alberta). (Name) attended (the University of Calgary) from 19(XX) to 19(XX) where (he/she) received an (engineering degree in fluid mechanics). ◆ Responsible primarily for sales and sales support. Salary – $35,000.

Vice President of Marketing – (Name) Vice President of Marketing. (Name) has been the Company's VP of Marketing since (Date). From 19(XX) to 19(XX), (he/she) was involved in (sales & marketing for Toys'R Us, New York). From 19(XX) to 19(XX), (he/she) was self-employed as an (independent sales rep). (Name) graduated from (Harvard) in 19(XX) with a B.A. in Philosophy. (He/She) is employed by the Company on a part-time basis. ◆ Responsible for marketing, human resources and training. Salary – $25,000.

Total Executive Compensation – $150,000.

Present a brief résumé of important management team members. State name, job title, work experience, education, responsibilities & salary:

Name		Job Title		Compensation	$
Experience					
Education					
Responsibilities					

Name		Job Title		Compensation	$
Experience					
Education					
Responsibilities					

Name		Job Title		Compensation	$
Experience					
Education					
Responsibilities					

Manpower Required

In this section of your business plan, describe all full-time and part-time personnel required. Describe the skills each need and whether they are readily available to work in your location area. Include job descriptions of duties and responsibilities of important personnel, along with salary and wage schedules and any training programs you will offer. Also, list details of employee compensation, including plans for employee training and fringe benefits. Furthermore, describe what openings are not yet filled, and if important, how these positions will be filled. End this section by describing how you expect your organization to develop over the next few years and what your future personnel requirements will be.

Describe your general full-time & part-time personnel required. Summarize details of any plans for employee training:

```
┌──────────────────────────────────────────────────────┐
│                                                      │
│                                                      │
│                                                      │
│                                                      │
│                                                      │
│                                                      │
│                                                      │
└──────────────────────────────────────────────────────┘
```

> *The worker should have enough income to provide for himself and his family sufficient to live a life in keeping with their Christian dignity.*
> **POPE LEO XIII**

Writing a Job Description

It is useful to write a job description for each employee. Not only does this help set the framework for your personnel policies and determine more precisely your needs when recruiting personnel, but it establishes a record of job responsibilities in case they come into question in the future. Furthermore, it simplifies the placement and training of employees and improves communication. In addition, all the information gathered can be used to create a newspaper or bulletin board ad when the position needs to be filled (see examples below).

XYZ Inc. – JOB DESCRIPTION

Job Title: Retail Salesperson

Duties: Greets and waits on customers; acquires and communicates product knowledge; records sales and provides accurate change; wraps for shipping and bags items; keeps shelves stocked and organized; directs deliveries; responsible for opening and closing store when manager is away.

Responsible to: Store manager

Requirements: Applicants must be bondable; have good mathematical skills; have previous sales experience; be available to work nights and weekends; be able to learn the use of cash register and other store procedures.

Personal: Must have an easy manner with people; dress and be groomed appropriately; be punctual and reliable; and be able to withstand long hours on the floor.

XYZ Inc. – JOB COMPETITION # C2341

Competition Deadline: 5/12/95

Company Name: Harry's Pet Supplies

Job Title: Assistant Manager

Job Summary: Manager in a Pet Supply Shop.

Primary Duties & Responsibilities: The Assistant Manager will be responsible for opening and closing the store on weekends and assisting in all aspects of running the store. Some cleaning up at the end of the day required.

Skills & Qualifications Required: High School Diploma and 3 years management experience; University graduate with a degree in business (preferably sales)

Terms of Employment: Base salary is $1,200 a month. Commissions will be based on 5% of sales.

Prepared by: Harry Tegus

Approved by: Sally Tegus

Date Posted: 5/12/95

Parts of a Job Description

A *Job Description* specifies job duties and responsibilities. It may also indicate specialized skills, education, and qualifications required. By laying out these criteria, as well as others outlined below, you give your prospective applicants ample material to help them decide whether they meet the requirements of your job, and your personnel department, the necessary information to screen applicants.

Check information below you will include in your job descriptions. Outline additional information.

Parts of a Job Description

❑ **Name of Company or Organization –** The top of your job description should have your company name or organization.

❑ **Competition Number & Deadline –** The competition deadline, along with the competition number is often located at the top of the job description. Often used by large organizations and governments with large staffing requirements.

❑ **Job Title –** Following your company name should be the title of the Job in question. This is what makes the job different from other jobs.

❑ **Organization Unit –** If your company is large you may need to indicate which division, department, location, or section of your company needs to fill the position (e.g. assistant copywriter, advertising dept.).

❑ **Accountability –** Title of person to which the job reports.

❑ **Supervisor –** Name of person to which the job reports.

❑ **Job Summary –** A job summary may be a short statement outlining the purpose or mission of the job in question, or it may be quite involved touching upon many aspects of the job ranging from its basic function and work to be performed, to its supervisory, technical or administrative scope.

❑ **Compensation & Job Benefits –** Describe how employees will be paid e.g., commissions, pay period, shift bonuses etc. Also describe company benefits such as: ◆ vacations & holidays◆ groups insurance ◆ hospitalization & surgical ◆ free parking ◆ training programs ◆ Christmas bonus ◆ savings plan ◆ profit sharing plan ◆ suggestion awards ◆ jury duty ◆ military leave ◆ old age benefits ◆ unemployment compensation ◆ equal employment opportunity.

List key positions requiring job descriptions.

Qualifications	
Duties	
Responsibilities	
Compensation	$ Benefits

Qualifications	
Duties	
Responsibilities	
Compensation	$ Benefits

Qualifications	
Duties	
Responsibilities	
Compensation	$ Benefits

Summarize other positions in your operation:

Job	Duties & Responsibilities	Qualifications Required	Full-or Part-time	Compensation	Benefits
				$	

Organizational Chart

An *Organizational Chart* shows at a glance who is responsible for the major activities of your business and who reports to whom. It also summarizes your management structure and helps identify your staffing needs.

NOTE Initially, your organization will be built around yourself acting as the owner manager, and perhaps a few other co-owners or employees, ideally, each with different backgrounds and aptitudes. Your name can occur more than once, in your organizational chart, as you will likely have many diverse responsibilities.

Develop an organization chart indicating who is responsible for each of the major areas of activity in your business; list each function and indicate the name of the individual who will perform that function and to whom he or she will be responsible:

Function	Performed By:	Responsible To:
Sales		
Marketing		
Operations Management		
Bookkeeping and Accounting		
Personnel Management		
Research & Development		

The following organizational chart is set-up for a small manufacturing firm with 50 to 100 employees. Modify and fill-in as required:

Organizational Chart

```
                          ┌─────────────────────┐
                          │                     │
                          ├─────────────────────┤
                          │     PRESIDENT       │
                          │  General Manager    │
                          └─────────────────────┘
              ┌────────────────────┼────────────────────┐
     ┌────────────────┐   ┌────────────────┐   ┌────────────────┐
     │                │   │                │   │                │
     ├────────────────┤   ├────────────────┤   ├────────────────┤
     │  Sales Manager │   │Production Mgr. │   │Financial Mgr.  │
     └────────────────┘   └────────────────┘   └────────────────┘
      ┌──────┴──────┐                          ┌──────┴──────┐
 ┌────────┐  ┌────────┐                   ┌────────┐  ┌────────┐
 │        │  │        │                   │        │  │        │
 │ Sales  │  │Advert. │                   │Bookkeep│  │Payroll │
 └────────┘  └────────┘                   └────────┘  └────────┘
```

| Sales | Advertising | | Bookkeeping | Payroll |

| Purchasing | Assembly | Quality Control | Repairs & Maint. |

Ownership Structure

Describe the ownership structure of your business if your company is a partnership or corporation. This is especially important if shares have been issued.

Summarize the ownership structure of your business. Detail any special conditions:

| |
| |
| |
| |
| |

Individual	Types of Shares Held	% of Total Issued	# of Shares Held	x	Price Paid Per Share	=	Total
				$		$	

Total Capitalization | $ |

Indicate any options to acquire additional stock that may be held or could be earned by your management team or others:

| |
| |
| |

> *Bear in mind that your day-to-day relationship with the firm you choose will for the most part, involve one person or a small group of individuals within the larger unit. You should feel comfortable with the people assigned to you.*
> **BUSINESS TIP**

Professional Advisors

As a small company, you can function quite well without the full-time services of an accountant, banker, lawyer or insurance agent. However, once you start to deal with large amounts of money or develop plans for serious expansion, it is wise and essential that you seek the guidance and experience of professionals.

Judging the Personality of a Professional Firm

Companies have personalities that are usually determined by upper management's style and values. Accounting firms, banks, insurance agencies and law firms also have personalities. Some are aggressive, others are conservative; some are cautious, others are risk-takers; some are people oriented, others are stuffy and formal; some are willing to work with small new companies, others will consider you a nuisance. To learn the personality of a firm you wish to work with, talk to their present and former clients. Be candid during screening sessions.

Provide complete information regarding your professional advisors:

Advisor	Name	Address	Telephone	Fees or Retainers Paid
Accountant				
Banker				
Insurance Agent				
Legal counsel				

10 LARGEST CPA FIRMS IN THE U.S. (1994 Sales in $ millions) ♦ Arthur Andersen & Co., SC (3,317) ♦ Ernst & Young (2,543) ♦ Deloitte & Touché (2,230) ♦ KPMG Peat Marwick (*2,100) ♦ Coopers & Lybrand (1,783) ♦ Price Waterhouse (1,570) ♦ McGladrey & Pullen (230) ♦ Grant Thornton (229) ♦ BDO Seidman (201) ♦ Crowe, Chizek (78) ♦ Source: *Public Accounting Report*; August 31, 1995 * Estimate

10 LARGEST LAW FIRMS IN THE U.S. (1994 Sales in $ millions) ♦ Skadden Arps, Slate, Meagher & Flom (582.0) ♦ Baker & McKenzie (546.0) ♦ Jones, Day, Reavis & Pogue (384.0) ♦ Weil, Gotshal & Manges (311.0) ♦ Sullivan & Cromwell (298.0) ♦ Gibson, Dunn & Crutcher (278.0) ♦ Shearman & Sterling (268.0) ♦ Clearly, Gottlieb, Steen & Hamilton (265.0) ♦ Latham & Watkins (263.0) ♦ Mayer, Brown & Platt (263.0) ♦ Source: *The American Lawyer*, July/August 1995

To Do List

Marketing Plan
*Market
Description &
Analysis*

✓ Market & industry
  Trends
✓ Needs We Will
  Meet

DAY 15
MARKETING PLAN

- Market Description & Analysis
- Competition Analysis
- Selling Strategies
- Marketing Approach

IN THIS section of your business plan, explain:

1. **WHO your target market is.** How you researched and determined this. What you determined their unmet needs to be (*market description*).

2. **WHO your competitors are.** How you rank amongst them (*competitive analysis*).

3. **WHAT steps you will take to open new markets.** How you will solidify your target market. Why your customers will ultimately choose your company over both direct and indirect competitors (*marketing* or *selling strategy*).

4. **HOW you plan to combine all the above activities** (*marketing approach*).

*Begin this
section with a
half or full-page
summary
addressing all
the key areas of
your marketing
plan.*

Summarize the key points of your marketing plan. What gives your company a competitive edge?

| |
| |
| |
| |

*Finding a need that
isn't being met
doesn't guarantee
success. This need
must be tied into a
group large enough
to generate a profit.
If you develop a
drug that prevents
cancer, then your
market would be
cancer patients
worldwide. How-
ever, if the drug is
very expensive to
manufacture, then
your market may
be millionaires
only.*
BUSINESS TIP

Market Description & Analysis

No business plan is complete without a detailed description of target markets followed by an analysis of the trends and conditions of the general marketplace, and how these trends and conditions will affect the outcome and profitability of your business. You don't have to be a trained statistician to analyze the marketplace, nor does your analysis have to be costly. Analyzing the market is simply gathering as many facts as you can about potential customers to determine the demand for your product or service. The more information you gather, the better your chances of meeting their needs and capturing a segment of the market.

Market & Industry Trends

Discuss industry outlooks and growth potential, as well as new products or technological developments and influences that will affect your market. State your sources of information and how you plan to keep up with new developments. Discuss population shifts, consumer trends, economic indicators, environmental considerations, business cycles, cultural and social changes, changing tastes in markets, and other relevant market demographics such as age and income trends.

List prospects for the industry by estimating Total Industry Sales ($):

	Product/Service	3 Years Ago	2 Years Ago	Last Year	This Year	Next Year	In 2 Years	In 3 Years
1		$	$	$	$	$	$	$
2								
3								

What has the sales trend been for your principal product or service over the last five years? What do you expect the sales trend to be for your product or service in five years? Describe how these sales trends will affect the performance of your business:

Industry Trends – *Describe key industry trends and factors likely to affect these trends. Support your statements with industry facts:*

Uncovering New Consumer Trends & Demands

> There's a tremendous difference between what the public wants and what the critics want.
> **ALLAN STILLMAN**
> New York City
> Restaurateur

Forecasting the future is not as difficult as a psychic or fortuneteller would have you believe. Market researchers regularly uncover trends by analyzing patterns in technological advancements and discoveries, market supply and demand fluctuations, government and corporate research policies, and the moods, needs and spending habits of consumers. These patterns can be uncovered by the analysis of data taken from polls, surveys, news clippings, or any media where information can be accumulated. From these patterns – as well as knowledge of past tendencies, historical cycles, an empirical understanding of human nature, and primitive gut reactions – researchers can derive astoundingly accurate predictions. You can benefit from their hard work by searching for your own patterns in their predictions. In the end, you may never quite piece together exactly what the future will be like, but you can make pretty good guesses.

Consumer Trends – *Outline 3 important trends that indicate growth potential in your market area. Indicate sources for this information:*

What are you really selling?		
NEEDS BEING MET	**POTENTIAL MARKETS**	**SELL THEM**
security	people with expensive homes	patrol services, alarms, dogs
stress relief	9-5 workers	weekend getaways
increased harvest efficiency	farmers	new improved combines
increased productivity	service industry workers	computers, faxes, info services
Write Down Here		
NEED YOU WILL MEET	**MARKET YOU WILL TARGET**	**PRODUCT YOU WILL SELL**

NOTE Don't sell *products*, sell *needs* being met. E.g., Don't sell alarms; sell security. Don't sell beer; sell sex, fun, and the good life.

Needs Met

Under this heading, point out a problem in the marketplace. Point out the need for a solution. Show that you have a bona fide solution and convince readers that you also have the credibility to make the solution work. Use the following two strategies:

STRATEGY 1: Find a need that presently isn't being met. Research the marketplace for a specific need that the competition has ignored, doesn't know about, or can't seem to meet, or hasn't bothered to meet. For example, if you find an area with a high crime rate, then it is reasonable to assume that its inhabitants are concerned with safety. The need you can meet is the need for security. Your target market would be people with expensive homes or businesses with large amounts of inventory. Your most likely products or services would be alarms, watchdogs, and/or security patrol services.

STRATEGY 2: Determine how many people have this need. Find out if the market is big enough to justify the cost of developing a new product or service.

NOTE Customers don't like buying *things* as much as they like buying what a product or service *stands for* or rather, what it *really means* to them. As an advertiser, this means that if you want people to buy your products and services, pay particular attention to the *real need* the product or service meets (see chart).

Describe a need that presently isn't being met and how many people have this need:

```



```

Explain what you are "really" selling based on your customers' perceptions. What is the "real" need being met?

```



```

Show "how" and "why" you can meet this need in terms of your resources and strengths. Show that you truly can solve the problem:

```



```

To Do List

Marketing Plan
*Market
Description &
Analysis*

✓ Target Market
  Description
✓ Target Market
  Analysis
✓ Target Market
  Entry Strategy
✓ Target Market
  Share
✓ Summary of
  Projected Sales

INDUSTRIAL MARKETS
⇩
Producers:
Raw Material Extractors
⇩
Manufacturers
(goods & services)
⇩
Resellers:
Wholesaler Distributors
⇩
Retailer Distributors
⇩
CONSUMER MARKETS

❑ adventure seekers
❑ Americans
❑ blue-collar workers
❑ Californians
❑ country music lovers
❑ drivers of luxury cars
❑ elderly persons
❑ fitness addicts
❑ government workers
❑ hikers
❑ homeowners
❑ housewives
❑ pet owners
❑ retired couples
❑ single white females
❑ teenagers
❑ white-collar workers
❑ yuppies
❑ *any group of people that
  have needs that are similar*

DAY 16

Target Market

As a marketer, you can market to the masses or market to a select group of individuals who have common identifiable needs and desires – a target market. *Mass marketing* is a little like firing a shotgun into a flock of geese and hoping to hit a few. Although having the potential to be extremely profitable, it's often ineffective in today's highly sophisticated and segmented markets, and what's even worse, can easily set you back a small fortune. Mass marketing is usually reserved for big businesses with large promotional budgets, huge marketing and distribution departments, and production capacity able to keep up with sudden demand. It is for people who want to sell engine oil, shampoo, deodorant, chocolate bars, chewing gum, soda pop, life insurance, and beer.

On the other hand, *Target marketing*, your second choice, and the only reasonable choice for the fledgling entrepreneur, is a marketing strategy comparable to using a high-powered rifle to crush the head of a pin. Most likely, you have limited resources to spend on marketing activities. Concentrating your efforts on one or a few key market segments is more likely to lead to success, allowing you to extract a much higher order rate per advertising dollar than the typical mass marketer. Target marketing means you know your customer like your best friend. Target marketers believe if you think small – and tailor your product offerings, prices, distribution, promotional efforts, sales presentations, and ad copy towards serving a specific group of customers – you can win big, and beat the big guys!

NOTE Going after a target market larger than you ability to meet its needs, will likely lead to bankruptcy not fortune – greed is no substitute for good planning. On the other hand, going after a target market that is too small to support your business is just plain silly. A target market must be big enough for profit, but small enough to serve.

Sample Target Market Descriptions

Product – The (Product) was introduced into the market in (Date). (Product)s remained much the same until (Date) when (New Technology) showed that there could be some enhancements made to the basic (Product). The market for (Product) has closely followed the typical population growth. At this time, there are approximately (XX) companies worldwide making (Product)s.

Service – (Service) companies have enjoyed a period of steady growth over the past (XX) years. This demand is due to many factors, not the least of which is . . . (Describe the most important factor). In our proposed marketing area, there are (XX) (Service) services.

Customer Profiles

EXAMPLE 1 At *Hot Air Adventure Tours*, our target customers will be consumers comfortable with long distance shopping, and recently retired executives interested in adventure, socializing, good health, and the magazines "Jet Set at 60" and "Hot Air Ballooning." Our target customers need to escape a boring retired life.

EXAMPLE 2 At *BJ's Pasta Supreme* we will target 24 to 40 year old health conscious males and females who are vegetarians and athletes. We will also target restaurants, daycare centers and other businesses that prefer to serve fresh natural pasta products without additives or preservatives.

Check questions you wish to answer in your target market description:

- ❏ Where do your customers live, work and shop? Will your business be conveniently located for the people you plan to serve?
- ❏ What are their needs and desires?
- ❏ What common characteristics do customers in your target market share?
- ❏ How will they learn about the product or service?
- ❏ What kind of advertising are they responsive too?
- ❏ What do existing customers like best about your company or product?

- ❏ Who else has a need for the product? Where are they?
- ❏ Will you be offering the kind of products or services that they will buy?
- ❏ Are your target markets consumers or businesses? If they are other businesses: What do they produce or sell? Who is the contact? How are they being serviced now? What is their history?
- ❏ If you are in the business of selling and repairing computers, how many computers are owned with a certain radius of your shop?

State potential users of your product or service and how these users will be located.

Write a customer profile. Identify customers by age, sex, income, lifestyles, buying and shopping patterns, average purchase in dollars, wants and needs, and any other characteristic or behavior judged relevant (use the "Customer Profile Checklist" provided on page 94):

Target Market Analysis

Write a detailed market analysis for your major product/service offered. If necessary, write a market analysis for EACH major product/service offered.

Briefly describe your target market and prospective customers in terms of geography and other demographic characteristics (see page 94):

Describe how your target market might be broken down into segments and outline how these segments have changed over time and how they might be expected to change in the future:

Describe the principal factors your potential customers consider when deciding on a purchase of a product or service like yours. Outline the principal benefit they will receive from patronizing your firm rather than one of your competitors:

Describe any weekly, monthly, seasonal, or other sales patterns:

Target Market Entry Strategy

In the section of your business plan, summarize how you plan to introduce your product or service to your target market.

Sample Target Market Entry Strategies

Some business owners may feel uncomfortable about the concept of targeting for fear of missing out on business they could have had if their marketing efforts had been more general. However, it has been consistently shown that for almost all businesses, sales and profits come from a relatively small number of customers.
FUNFACT

Product – Our (Product) has been designed by (Name of Design Team). We are able to manufacture our (Product) on (Method of Production) using the latest in (New Technology). This gives us a tremendous price advantage.

We intend to market our (Product) through all the normal distribution channels available to this (Product). These include retail, wholesale, and (Other Methods). To penetrate our target market efficiently and swiftly, we intend to initially use commission sales representatives strategically located throughout the (Geographic Area). We also will start a (Local, National) advertising campaign targeting end users in various (Local, National) publications.

Our sales representatives will be chosen based on their own experience in the marketplace. It is our intention to hire the best and the brightest among those currently available. A list of sales representatives all ready contacted is included in the *Supporting Documents* section at the end of this business plan.

Service – Over the past few years, we have noticed an increase in demand for (Service). Our computerized office allows us to track our clients' needs and schedule house calls on one hour's notice. We intend to attack this market very aggressively through the use of: ❑ door to door flyers ❑ advertisements in local magazines ❑ house-to-house visits to neighbors of present clients ❑ radio advertisements on weekends ❑ sales calls on real estate management companies.

Summarize your target market entry strategy:

CUSTOMER PROFILE Checklist

1. Type of *shopper*
- ☐ retail
- ☐ long-distance

2. Type of *market*
- ☐ industrial
- ☐ consumer

3. Size of *market*
- ☐ < $1 Million
- ☐ $10 Million +
- ☐ $1-10 Million
- ☐ _____

4. Rate of *growth*
- ☐ decreasing
- ☐ 10-15%
- ☐ steady
- ☐ 15-20%
- ☐ 0-5%
- ☐ 25% +
- ☐ 5-10%
- ☐ _____

5. Projected market *responsiveness*
- ☐ moderate demand
- ☐ high demand

6. Planned marketing *strategy*
- ☐ mass marketing
- ☐ target marketing

INDUSTRIAL SEGMENTATION
(for Industrial Markets Only)

7. Type of *industry*
- ☐ producer
- ☐ service supplier
- ☐ manufacturer
- ☐ retailer
- ☐ reseller
- ☐ government
- ☐ wholesaler
- ☐ raw materials
- ☐ distributor
- ☐ _____

8. Type of *business*
- ☐ proprietorship
- ☐ corporation
- ☐ partnership
- ☐ _____

9. Number of *employees*
- ☐ 1 - 5
- ☐ 20 - 100
- ☐ 6 - 19
- ☐ 251+

10. Annual *sales volumes*
- ☐ < $1 Million
- ☐ $10 Million +
- ☐ $1-10 Million
- ☐ _____

GEOGRAPHICAL SEGMENTATION

11. Market *climate*
- ☐ hot
- ☐ dry
- ☐ cold
- ☐ windy
- ☐ warm
- ☐ rainy
- ☐ cool
- ☐ snowy
- ☐ humid
- ☐ _____

12. Market *geographical terrain*
- ☐ desert
- ☐ farming land
- ☐ mountains
- ☐ ocean
- ☐ valley
- ☐ _____

13. Market *location*
- ☐ urban
- ☐ local
- ☐ rural
- ☐ county

- ☐ state
- ☐ global
- ☐ national
- ☐ _____

DEMOGRAPHICAL SEGMENTATION

14. Customer *age*
- ☐ child (0 - 12)
- ☐ middle (35 - 59)
- ☐ teen (13 - 19)
- ☐ mature (60+)
- ☐ young (20-35)
- ☐ _____

15. Customer *sex*
- ☐ male
- ☐ female

16. Customer *marital status*
- ☐ single
- ☐ divorced
- ☐ married
- ☐ _____

17. Customer *life cycle*
- ☐ newly married
- ☐ married 20 yrs.
- ☐ married 10 yrs.
- ☐ _____

18. Customer *number of children*
- ☐ one
- ☐ two
- ☐ three +
- ☐ _____

19. Customer *ethnic background*
- ☐ African American
- ☐ Native American
- ☐ Asian
- ☐ _____
- ☐ Caucasian
- ☐ _____

20. Customer *education level*
- ☐ high school
- ☐ university
- ☐ trade school
- ☐ _____

21. Customer *income*
- ☐ $15-$25,000
- ☐ $40,000 +
- ☐ $25-$40,000
- ☐ _____

22. Customer *location*
- ☐ in same building
- ☐ out of area
- ☐ walking distance
- ☐ out of town
- ☐ 5 minutes by car
- ☐ _____

23. Customer *occupation*
- ☐ white collar
- ☐ retired
- ☐ blue collar
- ☐ entrepreneurs
- ☐ professional
- ☐ _____

24. Customer preferred *payment* method
- ☐ cash
- ☐ purchase order
- ☐ check
- ☐ financing
- ☐ credit card
- ☐ _____

PSYHCOGRAPHICAL SEGMENTATION

25. Customer *life style*
- ☐ conservative
- ☐ trendy
- ☐ exciting
- ☐ thrifty
- ☐ family orientated
- ☐ _____

26. Customer *attitudes*
- ☐ environmentalists
- ☐ security conscious
- ☐ religious
- ☐ _____

27. Customer *interests & activities*
- ☐ sports
- ☐ physical fitness
- ☐ reading / books
- ☐ weekend athletes
- ☐ shopping
- ☐ vegetarians
- ☐ walkman users
- ☐ computer users
- ☐ movie goers
- ☐ _____

28. Customer *social class*
- ☐ lower
- ☐ middle
- ☐ upper
- ☐ _____

29. Customer *opinions*
- ☐ easily led
- ☐ opinionated

30. Customer *level of desire*
Do your target customers want your product or will they need a great deal of persuasion?
- ☐ high
- ☐ low
- ☐ medium
- ☐ _____

31. Customer *advertising responsiveness*
Are your target customers easily influenced by advertising or rebellious towards it?
- ☐ easily influenced
- ☐ neutral
- ☐ indifferent
- ☐ rebellious

32. Customer *needs*
Are the needs of your customers new needs created by change or old needs presently being neglected?
- ☐ new
- ☐ neglected

33. Customer *benefits*
- ☐ economy
- ☐ luxury
- ☐ convenience
- ☐ high quality
- ☐ reliability
- ☐ performance
- ☐ easy access
- ☐ fast delivery
- ☐ _____
- ☐ _____

34. Customer *buying preferences*
- ☐ single orders
- ☐ bulk orders
- ☐ several orders
- ☐ _____

35. Customer *seasonal buying patterns*
- ☐ spring
- ☐ winter
- ☐ summer
- ☐ Christmas
- ☐ fall
- ☐ _____

36. Customer *reasons to buy from you*
- ☐ you're the best
- ☐ good service
- ☐ you're the cheapest
- ☐ no competition
- ☐ you're the fastest
- ☐ _____

37. Customer *usage*
- ☐ light users
- ☐ repeat users
- ☐ medium users
- ☐ presently non-users
- ☐ heavy users
- ☐ _____

Target Market Share

When making market share projections, be reasonable, don't exaggerate. Backup your findings with research studies and projections by industry experts. Determine: ❑ What % of total sales in your market area do you expect to obtain after your facility is in full operation? ❑ What % of the total market share must be taken away from your competition in order to reach your projected market share? ❑ What sales volume do you expect to reach with your products or services in one year? Two years? Five years?

Sample Target Market Share Statements

The (Asian) market for (Product/Service) is estimated at $(XXX) annual sales based on data furnished by (Name of Data Source). We estimate that we can achieve (XX)% market share within (XX) years. Marketing data for other markets is in the process of collection (use this same format for additional markets).

Estimate the present or projected size of your target market in total units or dollars and your present or projected share. Forecast how you expect your market share will grow or change over the next few years:

Building a List of Potential Customers

To approach the problem of building a growing body of satisfied customers, start by compiling a list of your present customers and then augmenting this list with lists from outside sources. A *customer* or *house* list will allow you to carry out promotional activities with catalogs and DM, inform established clients with a company newsletter about new product innovations and trends, and perform surveys to learn how to serve your customers better. To build your customer list: ◆ add anybody who buys goods or services from you, makes an inquiry, visits your business and signs in, writes in to request a catalog, or visits your trade show exhibit and leaves a business card ◆ have a contest to collect names ◆ offer free products or promotional items at reduced prices to get names ◆ place inquiry ads in classified sections offering free info ◆ seek out referrals (ask customers for friends and colleagues who might be interested in your products or services).

Build Your House List Using Compiled Lists

Compiled lists can be bought, rented, and found for free. Names from compiled lists can be tested, and if responsive, added to your house list. Sources of compiled lists include: ◆ the Yellow Pages ◆ Direct Mail Lists, Rates and Data (a directory that lists companies that offer lists for rent) ◆ Dun & Bradstreet (if you want to find people with certain kinds of credit) ◆ the federal government (the Government Printing Office publishes a free list called *Directories and Lists of Persons and Organizations*) ◆ local governments (public tax records, birth registrations, marriage licenses, and building records can be used to create customer lists) ◆ magazines (almost every magazine is willing to rent you its list of subscribers) ◆ mailing list brokers (can rent to you almost any list imaginable).

Fostering Repeat Business

All customers are not created equal. In many cases, 80% of your business will come from 20% of your customers – this is called *the 80/20-rule* i.e., one repeat customer is worth four one-timers. It therefore makes sense to focus 4/5th of your time and effort getting to know and serving the 1/5th of your customers who keep coming back and who ultimately will give you most of your profits.

To help you build good relationships with your customers and keep them coming back, make it a habit of looking at your business from their point of view; find as many ways as possible to give them what they really want and need – which is good value, good service and good follow-up; and always be reliable, credible, attractive, responsive and empathic. It is also important to: ◆ always plan what you are going to sell to your customers next (never send a package to a customer without including an order form for reorders and sales literature on other products you think they might need) ◆ constantly rediscover who your customer is (never forget your customer and they won't forget you) ◆ develop a line of products to complement existing products ◆ give your best customers occasional discounts or freebies, and make sure they know they're getting special treatment ◆ sell consumables i.e., products that are used up and need to be regularly replaced ◆ take surveys of your customer interests ◆ treat the *second order* as gold.

Summary of Projected Sales

Summarize major market segments by Product/Service Line & Market Segment.

Market Segment 1– Describe any weekly, monthly, seasonal, or other sales patterns (estimate sales by month in $ or units):

Product/Service Line	1	2	3	4	5	6	7	8	9	10	11	12	TOTAL

TOTAL

Market Segment 2– Describe any weekly, monthly, seasonal, or other sales patterns:

Product/Service Line	1	2	3	4	5	6	7	8	9	10	11	12	TOTAL

TOTAL

To Do List

Marketing Plan
Competition Analysis

✓ Competitor Descriptions
✓ Competitive Advantage
✓ Competitive Position

Ability is the art of getting credit for all the homeruns someone else hits.
CASEY STENGEL
Baseball Manager

Don't forget to research "indirect" competition e.g., an arcade may find competition from a bowling alley or pool hall.
BUSINESS TIP

COMPETITOR ASSESSMENT

EXAMPLE

Betty's Bakery has both direct and indirect competitors for her Whole Wheat Bread Products

Direct Competitors

● Local fresh bread producers
● Brand name bread manufacturers

Indirect Direct Competitors

● Rice, potatoes, fries and pasta
● Vegetarian food producers

DAY 17
Competition Analysis

No marketing plan is complete with out a detailed description of your competition and how they will affect your overall marketing strategy. *First*, describe them. *Second*, show how you plan to beat them.

Competitor Descriptions

List who your major competition is (if there is any), including estimates of their market shares and profit levels if possible (report who is doing well and who isn't). Include descriptions of their location, product and services they offer, computerization and technology used, equipment assets, promotional methods, personnel, reputation and position in the minds of customers, and anything else that may give them a competitive advantage or disadvantage.

Sample Competitor Descriptions

(Competitor Name) located at (Address) is our main competitor. Its strengths include: ❑ *Effective Location* – located on a major artery; next door to supplier ❑ *Competitive Pricing* – known for aggressive pricing policy; low cost producer ❑ *Fast Delivery* – ships overnight to most major cities anywhere in the world ❑ *Respected Management* – everyone in upper management has an MBA.

To its disadvantage, (Competitor) has: ❑ *Poor Service* – takes more than 3 months to receive spare parts ❑ *Questionable Dedication* – If sunny, management is out playing golf or hitting the ski slopes ❑ *Obsolete Machinery* – Unless replaced within six months ❑ *High Overhead* – Spend lavishly on company cars.

Studying the Competition

Never underestimate the importance of studying the competition *before* and *after* becoming well established. Those who fail to do so risk losing their market share, in some cases overnight. To stay ahead of your competition: develop strategies enabling you to react quickly and effectively to whatever your competition tries next, keep track of their selling activities and movements in the marketplace so you are constantly aware of the threat they pose to your business, and stay teachable – read, observe and listen.

Start by recognizing *exactly* who your competition is, both directly and indirectly. Next, identify the most successful of them and learn as much as possible about why they are succeeding. To do this: ◆ check the Yellow Pages ◆ conduct an informational interview with their present and former clients ◆ conduct a survey of people on the street ◆ get a hold of their products (analyze, dissect, evaluate, find weak points and strong points) ◆ get a hold of their advertising and promotional material ◆ keep a file on each competitor containing their ads, articles, brochures, newsletters etc ◆ recruit a researcher/spy ◆ seek out help from people who are running the same kind of business as you outside your city (people in other regions will probably consider you a colleague rather than competitor).

Evaluating the Competition

Evaluating your competition is a process of comparing strengths and weakness. Take a good look at competitors who have become superior due to better quality, service, promotion, location, pricing strategies, displays, packaging, and market timing. Next, look at any additional benefits competitors offer compared to your offerings, and closely examine, the nebulous, sometimes indefinable ingredient called, image. In business what you don't know *can* hurt you. Any strategy that gives you insights into the competition and ultimately the spending habits of consumers is more valuable than gold (use the *Competitor Profile Worksheet* on page 99 to make more detailed notes about individual competitors).

List and describe who your major competition is:

Describe their product and service offerings compared to yours:

Describe their competitive advantage or disadvantage:

Briefly describe other major industry participants:

Name & Location of Competitor	Estimated Sales	Estimated Market Share (%)	Principal Strengths & Weaknesses
	$		
	$		
	$		
	$		

Competitor Profile Worksheet	
Name of COMPETITOR:	
Location:	
Phone:	
Owner:	
Item	**Comments**
PRODUCTS & SERVICES OFFERED	
Size, Weight	
Durability, Versatility, Ease of Use	
Uniqueness of, Perceived Value of	
Pricing Structure	
METHODS of DISTRIBUTION	
Wholesale, Retail, Reps	
Mail Order, Personal Selling	
MARKET SHARE	
Growing, Stable or Declining	
Number of Customers	
Estimated Sales	
% Share of Market	
Location of Customers	
COMPANY IMAGE	
Packaging	
Promotional Materials	
Methods of Advertising	
COMPANY PERFORMANCE	
Competitive Advantages	
Location Advantages	
Profitability	
Do they have a Market Niche?	
STRENGTHS	
WEAKNESSES	

Competitive Advantage

Indicate how you plan to beat the competition by making a comparison of strengths and weaknesses and how in the end, you come out on top. Show that you have conducted studies or surveys that support your conclusions – it is not good enough to say you have a competitive advantage; you must convince yourself and your readers of your superiority with proof. If you can't come out on top, which is likely the case, since your company is new and unproven, then at least make a fair assessment of where you rank amongst the competition. Describe your major opportunities for growth and major threats. Also, indicate any special market appeal to your products or services that may put you on top in the future.

Sample Competitive Advantage Descriptions

The competitive advantages which (Company Name) brings to this market are:

Check competitive advantage statements that apply to your company:

- ❑ A level of *Capitalization* that will allow (me/us) to fully address our target market with comprehensive marketing and customer service plans.
- ❑ A quarterly newsletter directed at both current customers and prospective new customers.
- ❑ A toll-free national 800 number which can be used for customer orders and inquiries.
- ❑ As a unique (Product/Service) company, we will be able to keep our margins high, allowing us to provide internal financing for expansion.
- ❑ At (Company Name) our pricing structure considers our costs and what the market will pay.
- ❑ By purchasing in large amounts, (my/our) per unit costs and shipping costs decrease. Through these economies of scale, we can offer lower prices.
- ❑ Companies with which (I/we) have established contracts with are known to be financially secure.
- ❑ Experience in this market. (I/We) have (XX) years of hands-on experience in this industry.
- ❑ (I/We) have secured a 5-year lease at below market rates.
- ❑ I/We have secured a prime location.

- ❑ (I/We) will print complete four-color catalogs on a yearly basis. Price lists will be updated as needed.
- ❑ (I/We) have a history of innovative ideas (list your most meaningful ideas and any future ideas).
- ❑ Lower overhead will allow (me/us) to funnel profits back into operations thus avoiding high debt ratios or lost sales opportunities.
- ❑ (Product/Service) pricing will include a range of quantity discounts as well as an early payment discounts.
- ❑ Rather than being strictly local, (I/we) will expand into the national market.
- ❑ Sophistication in management, finance and distribution allows (me/us) to run an efficient and lean structure, yet still provide quality service to our clients and customers. This also results in (me/us) being the low cost supplier in a price sensitive market.
- ❑ To control foreign exchange risks, (I/we) will monitor the markets and hedge accordingly. (I/We) will also use overseas bank accounts.
- ❑ With (my/our) level of capitalization, should an unexpected downturn occur, (I/we) will be able to continue operations on a positive scale.

(I/we) will be able to reduce overhead as a percentage of sales thereby increasing the amount of profit retained. With (my/our) aggressive pricing policy, more people will purchase our merchandise thus increasing the size of (my/our) market share. (I/We) at (Company Name) propose to use (my/our) good solid business sense, economies of scale, and efficient financial techniques. This will allow (me/us) the following options: ◆ increase advertising ◆ increase customer service ◆ increase profits ◆ increase selection offered ◆ reduce prices.

This plan will give us tremendous flexibility to use any of these options or a mix of them to effectively attack our target markets and meet our long-term goals. (My/Our) combination of experience, sophistication, capitalization and innovation will assist (me/us) as (I/we) strive to reach (my/our) sales and profit objectives.

Compare the advantages and disadvantages of your business with two other competitors:

Factor	Your Company	Competitor A	Competitor B
Price			
Convenience of Location			
Availability of Parking			
Image			
Breadth of product/service line			
Depth of product/service line			
Credit policy			
Display and fixtures			
Sales training & effectiveness			
Sales support			
Availability of delivery			
Breadth of product line			
Depth of product line			
Performance (for manufacturers):			
speed and accuracy			
durability			
versatility			
ease of operation or use			
ease of maintenance or repair			
ease or cost of installation			
size or weight			
design or appearance			

Indicate what, if anything, is unique about your product/service offering or firm situation:

Summarize the advantages of your operation compared with the competition. Show how you will beat the competition:

Competitive Position

If a prospective customer cannot tell the difference between your company's offerings and another, then you have a problem. Nothing is preventing them from seeing your promotion, loving it, and then going out and buying someone else's products or services. To overcome this problem, prove to them that your business, products or services are distinct from your competition's by finding and promoting something that gives you a competitive advantage or in the least makes you *appear* more competitive. Even when dealing in basic commodities like batteries or aspirin, marketing executives have gone to all sorts of extremes to create brand awareness and product differentiation e.g., the *Eveready Bunny*? "It keeps going and going . . ."

NOTE Market positioning theory can be summed up by answering the following three questions: (a) What's so special about your company? (b) How are you different from your competitors? (c) What is your uniqueness in the marketplace?

How Positioning Works in the Marketplace

Once customers have tried your products or services, they have a perception of your company in their minds. However, they will only become loyal customers once they fully believe that what you are selling is different and/or more beneficial than what your competitors are selling. Knowing this, the most successful businesses strive to determine exactly how their products and services are being perceived by their customers, and then take steps to position them more strongly in the marketplace, in comparison to competing products or services. They do this by specifically targeting their promotions to a key aspect of their product. For example, a bakery that offers fresh, better tasting, high quality whole wheat bread made without preservatives and additives will try to position itself in the marketplace as "a consistently good-tasting, healthy, whole wheat product."

NOTE If your product or service is properly positioned, prospective purchasers or users will more easily recognize its unique benefits and advantages and be better able to assess it in comparison to the offerings of your competition.

Ten Positioning Strategies

Listed in the chart on the next page are ten different approaches to positioning your company in the marketplace to gain a competitive advantage.

Summarize your competitive positioning strategy:

Describe how your positioning strategy will give you an edge in the marketplace:

```
┌─────────────────────────────────────────────────────────┐
│                                                         │
│                                                         │
│                                                         │
│                                                         │
│                                                         │
└─────────────────────────────────────────────────────────┘
```

Check which positioning strategies you will follow:

❏ **Compare your product or service favorably to a competitor's.** This type of positioning can involve implicit or explicit comparisons. Implicit comparisons never mention a competitor's name though the inference is obvious. Often the unmentioned competitor is made fun of or looked down upon. Explicit comparisons can make a comparison with a direct competitor (usually the market leader), with the goal of attracting their customers (e.g., the Pepsi Challenge); or it can use the compared product as a reference point with no attempt to attract the customers of the compared product e.g., the Volkswagen Dasher: "Picks up speed faster than a Mercedes and has a bigger trunk than a Rolls Royce."

❏ **Disassociate yourself completely from the product class.** This type of positioning is particularly effective when used to introduce new products amongst heavy competition. For example Intel with its recent Pentium Chip attempted to disassociate itself from its 8086, 286, 386, and 486 lineage in an effort to lessen the gains made by other chip manufacturers such as AMD and Cyrix. The name change also helped ward off the threat of the PowerPC chip being perceived as new 90's technology and Intel as old outdated 70's technology.

❏ **Offer a range of packages for the same product or service.** This type of positioning involves selling the same product in a range of packages of different sizes, design or even label as well as using different distribution channels to reach the various segments that each packaging variation targets. Beer, for example, can be sold in kegs, cases, twelve-packs six-packs, twelve-ounce cans and bottles, on tap, and by the pitcher. The beer in each container is exactly the same but appeals to separate market segments with different needs. Services can also package in a variety of ways e.g., skis can be rented in novice, intermediate or expert packages, and vacations can be sold in economy, family, honeymoon or deluxe packages.

❏ **Position against older products.** This type of positioning is particularly effective when used to introduce new products that differ from traditional products. Lead-free gasoline was at one time positioned against leaded gasoline as being cleaner burning and friendlier to the environment.

❏ **Promote a specific use for your product.** This type of positioning works best when you can easily teach your customers how to use your product via a promotional medium that allows a demonstration e.g., to promote egg consumption, using TV advertising, show how many ways to can cook an egg (scrambled, poached, boiled).

❏ **Promote a unique product or service benefit.** This type of positioning is generally more effective then positioning by features because it's easier to sell customers on what a product or service can do for them rather than explain how it does it.

❏ **Promote a unique product or service feature.** This type of positioning is very common whether you're selling services or manufactured goods, as long as your product or service has some unique features of real value to your customers. Even if your product or service does not have a unique feature, you may be able to gain an edge over your competitors, by studying and mapping the *perceptions* of consumers with regards to your products or services in relation to those of its major competitors. Any perceptions you discover to be in your favor should be exploited.

❏ **Satisfy a specific need.** This type of positioning is built around satisfying a special customer need in an innovative manner. Some experts say that this is the only reason for starting a business and about the only way to stay in business.

❏ **Target the user.** This type of positioning directs its efforts to using people in its advertising that the target customers can identify with. Models aren't necessarily gorgeous or handsome. They are more like everyday folk with everyday problems, and are always shown in a positive light after using a product or service.

❏ **Use a combination of strategies.** Incorporate elements from several of the above types of positioning. Most small business owners should use this approach especially if operating in a small trade area where there isn't a large enough customer base to justify the expense of separate marketing approaches.

To Do List

Marketing Plan
*Selling
Strategies*

✓ Business Cards
✓ Company Slogans

DAY 18
Selling Strategies

Lack of a selling or marketing strategy is a serious weakness in many plans. You must prove that you have given the marketing of your product or service a lot of thought by describing: ◆ how you expect to get customers to buy your product or service ◆ how you plan to gain a market share if the competition is tough ◆ what business are you *really* in (i.e., what will your customers really be buying) ◆ what do you do best (strengths) ◆ what do you need to work on (weaknesses).

Summarize the main points of your selling strategy:

Business Cards

A *Business Card* is important for every business. It sums up *who* you are and *how* you wish to be perceived. It is the first step in marketing your business.

5 Steps to Business Card Design

STEP 1 – Brainstorm for content. On a piece of paper, write down everything you might want on your business card.

STEP 2 – Separate optional and essential information. Now that everything is on paper, determine what's absolutely necessary and what's not.

STEP 3 – Experiment with design using essential information. Using only information that is absolutely essential, experiment with layout, logo and lettering size and create you basic business card design.

STEP 4 – Incorporate optional information into your basic design. Using your optional information, determine whether its incorporation into your basic business card design compliments it enough to warrant consideration.

Consider putting other info on your business card, not directly related to your business, like a calendar or a metric-imperial conversion chart. This way, your card has a better chance of becoming a permanent part of someone's wallet or purse.
BUSINESS TIP

Business Card Folding Designs

Horizontal	Vertical	Short Fold Horizontal	Short Fold Vertical	Tent Fold	Book Fold	Gate Fold	Z Fold

NOTE Make use of the back of your business card if you wish to summarize major services & product or give other detailed information. However, print only what is necessary and useful to your client or customer. Don't get carried away. If you need more space than the standard business card size permits, experiment with folding techniques (see examples on previous page). With proper design, you can turn an ordinary business card into a great mini-brochure.

STEP 5 – Produce final design. Printing shops can help you with your final design. Often you can simply browse through cards they have made for other clients, pick one you like, and have them substitute your information.

Describe how you want your business card to be perceived. Check information you want on your business card. List additional information:

| |
| |
| |

Essential Information	**Optional Information/Effects**
❑ YOUR NAME ❑ Title or position held ❑ Company name ❑ Phone number (personal and/or business) ❑ Toll free 800 number ❑ Fax number ❑ Pager number ❑ E-mail address ❑ Addresses (personal and/or business) ❑ URL address	❑ Company logo and company slogan ❑ Education and/or other qualifications ❑ Summary heading of products/services ❑ Detailed product and/or services information ❑ Special offers; discounts; promo material ❑ White space for handwritten product information ❑ Eye catching graphics ❑ Special effects like raised lettering or gold embossing

List additional information:

Sketch two possible designs for your business card (or front and back):

FINAL DESIGN

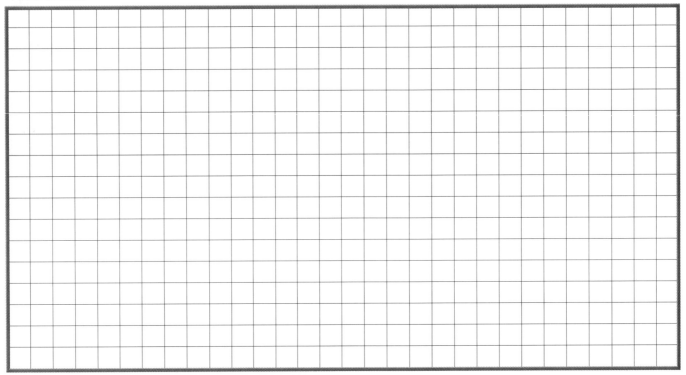

Company Slogans

One of the first steps in building a magnetic company identity is to come up with a company slogan. Slogans are words or phrases used to sum up and express the spirit or aim of your company, and unlike a company name, logo, or trademark, can easily be changed to reflect new marketing strategies. This is their greatest strength. More specifically, slogans can be used to: ◆ liven up letterhead ◆ add pizzazz to logos ◆ consolidate company philosophies ◆ supplement lack luster company names ◆ give details about what a company actually sells ◆ motivate customers to buy ◆ zero-in on target markets ◆ inspire entire promotions ◆ add punch to order forms ◆ single-handedly change the public's perception of a company from being "boring" and just like everybody else to that of being "cool" and finely tuned into their needs.

Every company should have a few slogans to help position their company in the minds of consumers.

Common Denominators of Great Slogans

Great Slogans are difficult to forget after being heard once. They are not forced, artificial or contrived, and are neither general enough that they don't mean anything nor specific enough that they pigeon hole your business. Furthermore, great slogans: ◆ beg to be chanted or sung ◆ create vivid pictures in their reader's mind ◆ get advertised free by word of mouth ◆ summarize completely your field yet also provide identity through uniqueness of ideas ◆ tend to reflect a company's mission statement ◆ tie in well with a companies name and logo ◆ use as few words as possible.

A proverb [slogan] is a short sentence based on long experience.
MIGUEL DE CERVANTES

FAMOUS SLOGANS

"Get a piece of the Rock."
Prudential

"Have you driven a Ford . . . lately?"
Ford Motor Co.

"The instrument of the immortals."
Steinway & Sons

Great Slogans ALSO . . . ❑ **Appeal to peoples' emotions or sense of pride in a positive manner.** "Known by the company it keeps." (Seagram's Canadian Vodka) *E. Seagram & Sons Inc. Liquors* ❑ **Direct people to act.** "Take a bite out of Crime." *Crime Prevention Coalition* ❑ **Feature great benefits.** "Mends everything but a broken heart." *Fix-All Liquid Cement Co.* ❑ **Invent new concepts.** "Welcome to Miller time." *Miller Brewing Co.* ❑ **Invent new words.** "Don't just fertilize . . . Spencerize." *Spencer Chemical Div., Gulf Oil Corp.* ❑ **Mention their company name.** "Everyone needs the Sun." *Sun Insurance Co.* ❑ **Mention their markets.** "America's best read weekly." *Liberty Magazine* ❑ **Mention their products.** "I saw the Haver Lite." (miniature flashlight) *Haverhills* ❑ **Mention their services.** "The greatest show on earth." *Barnum & Bailey Circus* ❑ **Use alliteration.** "Look to Lockheed for leadership." *Lockheed Corp.* ❑ **Use detail**. "99 44/100 % pure." *Ivory soap* ❑ **Use humor.** "Correct mistakes in any language." (erasers) *Eldon Roberts Rubber Co.* ◆ **Use movie titles.** "A diamond is forever." *DeBeers Consolidated Mines Ltd.* ❑ **Use rhymes.** "Takes a licking but keeps on ticking." *Timex Corp.* ❑ **Use the word people.** "The can opener people." *Dazey Products Co.* ❑ **Use the word you, yours, or yourself.** "Vote yourself a farm." *Abraham Lincoln (1860)* ❑ **Use puns cautiously.** "A pen is only as good as its point." *C. Howard Hunt Pen Co.*

Writing a Slogan for Your Company or Product

The following is a simplified format for writing a company or product slogan.

Company Name, followed by greatest benefit.

EX: "At ROBERTSON'S, our consultants save you money."

Write three slogans using the above format:

Write 7 more slogans using the above techniques. Check the three best. Test them on friends, family, relatives and customers:

MY COMPANY SLOGAN

Write your
FINAL CHOICE:

DAY 19
Customer Service Plan

Imagine you own a flower shop called *Flora's Boutique*. One day, your bell rings, and in walks a tall elegant woman in her mid-thirties. What do you suppose she is thinking and feeling when she first looks around, talks to one of your staff, buys an expensive crystal vase, and then on her way out trips over your welcome mat and smashes it into a thousand pieces? A *Customer Service Plan* attempts to provide answers or rather guidelines to these and other difficult questions. It attempts among other things to create a positive business environment, establish a company image, and build customer loyalty. Listed below are 4 guidelines:

Build customer loyalty. View your customer service plan as an opportunity to reward customer loyalty with unquestioning, all accepting, continuous positive reinforcement. Everyone likes to be treated special (see chart below).

Create a positive business environment. Making people feel good about themselves and your company makes it more conducive for them to spend their money. Offer free coffee, donuts, mints or suckers.

Establish a marketable company image. "Image is everything." At least that's what we have all grown to believe – largely influenced by companies with huge advertising budgets and little regard for truth. These companies feel that if you can't find a need, why not create it by manipulating our primeval urges. These companies believe that if you create the right image for yourself, you can pretty much sell anything at any price. And these companies are right! Cosmetic companies do it. Car companies do it. Beer and soft drink companies do it. So the question remaining is: If others can relax their moral standards in the pursuit of the almighty dollar, and have incredible success doing so, then why not you?

To create a professional image be reliable, courteous, and service orientated. Treat each customer with dignity and respect as if each was capable of giving you thousands of dollars in business, even if they only give you a few. This means treating a coal miner, who walks into your jewelry shop with dirt under his fingernails, like any other valued customer. Also, pay close attention to: ◆ appearance and attitude of staff ◆ displays ◆ entrance and parking ◆ location ◆ packaging ◆ prices ◆ publicity from news media ◆ quality of advertising and promotional programs ◆ quality of delivery and after sales service ◆ quality, appearance, and suitability of your stationery, invoices, envelopes, business cards and logos ◆ store layout and size ◆ tone of voice while on the phone (image is more important in a business of intangibles e.g., if you sell hair care services, your image is more important than if you sell TVs).

> *A positive image builds up gradually over many years. A negative one can hit fast and destroy your market position virtually overnight.*

> *At all times your image should be consistent with the needs and expectations of your target market.*

> *Always do what you say you are going to do. It is the glue and fiber that binds successful relationships.*
> **JEFFRY A. TIMMONS**

REWARDING CUSTOMERS
*The secret to winning and keeping customers for life is to "**reward**" them.*

When the Customer . . .	REWARD . . .
Appears, calls or inquires . . .	by being prompt and prepared
Is angry or defensive . . .	with kindness and empathy
Has special requests . . .	by customizing your service
Can't make up his mind . . .	with a specific recommendation
Raises objections to buying . . .	by agreeing, empathizing & showing value
Gives buying signals . . .	prompt response
Buys . . .	by delivering more than you promise
Refuses to buy . . .	with polite appreciation
Is going to be disappointed . . .	with positive perks
Complains . . .	with fast, positive action

> *In the United States, you say the customer is always right. In Japan, we say the customer is God. There is a big difference.*
> **JAPANESE BUSINESSMAN**

> *To eliminate the majority of hairs that stick to the average chicken wing, Fran Perdue, chairman of Perdue Farms, purchased a quarter-of-a million dollar jet engine to blow them off.*
> **FUNFACT**

Handle complaints right away. It's hard to remain calm when a hotheaded customer is yelling at you. But in any confrontational situation, let your customer blow off steam, and then calmly and coolly solve their problem. This, more than anything else is a sign of professionalism and management sensitivity. To handle complaints more effectively: ❑ Get people at the top actively involved in both listening to and resolving complaints. "Just a second let me talk to the manager." Is better than, "Sorry the manger won't be back until tomorrow." ❑ If you can't handle complaints right away, handle them within 24 hours. ❑ Make it easy to complain (a great way to get feedback). ❑ Set-up a suggestion box in private locations so people won't feel threatened to use it. ❑ Take every complaint seriously. ❑ Use the following technique (a) listen with understanding and sensitivity (b) paraphrase what the customer tells you so they know you are listening (c) find out what the customer wants (d) propose a solution – if the customer doesn't like your solution, ask what he or she would consider fair (e) make a follow-up call to insure satisfaction (f) whatever else you do, *never* let the customer lose face.

Provide extras that really impress people. Customizing your services or going beyond the call of duty shows people you really care, gives you and your team a source of pride and confidence, is great for generating repeat business, overcomes customer defensiveness, and virtually eliminates the competition by establishing you as best customer service provider in your field. Computerized print-outs, forms, and invoices, for example, can promote customer relations by making customers feel better informed. They don't have to decipher illegible handwriting.

Describe how you will provide quality service before purchases are made as well any special after-sale services:

Writing a Customer Service Maxim

Below is a list of customer service maxims or mini-philosophies you can use to help inspire your own customer service policy.

Check and write a customer maxim that seems to capture the essence of what you hope your company will become:

❑ **CUSTOMERS . . .** ARE human beings first, not business. They need to be treated like friends and guests.

❑ ARE the bosses, we are the employees.

❑ ARE to be treated like lifetime partners; as if we were going to see them every workday for the rest of our lives.

❑ ARE ultimately responsible for our business, our profits, and our success.

❑ BRING us their needs; it is our job to fulfill them to the best of our ability.

❑ DESERVE service with a smile.

❑ DESERVE the best value for their dollar.

❑ DESERVE what's best for them, even if it's not necessarily what's best for us.

❑ DO NOT interrupt our work; they are the reason for it.

❑ EXPECT us to make a positive and lasting impression by being committed, attentive to details, and by following up on whatever we promise.

❑ SHALL be rewarded for their loyalty.

❑ SHALL not be argued with, for nobody can ever win an argument with a customer.

Credit Extension Plan

Credit can be extended by your business to clients, companies, or large organization that usually do business with you on a regular basis, in the form of delayed payments, financing, or charge card services. These forms of credit can be defined respectively as: trade credit, financing, and charge card credit. In all cases, a business that offers these services is engaged in more than providing convenient payment options; the extension of credit and financing is a deliberate marketing strategy designed to stimulate business and give your company a competitive edge.

PROS & CONS of Extending Trade Credit

The advantage of extending trade credit is more customers and increased sales. In fact, most manufacturers and wholesalers find it imperative to offer credit terms to their customers, simply to survive. However, although selling on credit can boost sales, it can also increase direct and indirect costs, which must be weighed against potential benefits. By offering trade credit, you will require more extensive bookkeeping, invoicing, and collection procedures that often demand hiring additional staff just to manage the extra accounts. And what's worse, a definite percentage of the businesses you grant credit to, will not be able to pay.

Guidelines for Extending Credit

Before extending credit to any customer, develop a policy or criteria and procedures to weed out potential bad credit risks. Use the following 11 steps:

STEP 1 – Become a member of your local Credit Bureau. Credit Bureaus provide the resources to check out all applicants, and the latest up-to-date procedures and polices most companies are using.

STEP 2 – Set polices including standards for measuring each applicant. Not all customers should be allowed to apply for credit. Set a policy that allows you to make sure that credit is warranted before you grant it.

STEP 3 – Devise a credit application form. Before granting credit to a customer, have them fill out an application form. A lawyer can help you in preparing this form. A simple credit application form asks for the customer's name, address, telephone number, place of employment, and bank and credit references.

STEP 4 – Verify the data on the application form. The information provided in the application form should be checked carefully by mail or telephone, and/ or with a bank, credit bureau or mercantile agency, such as Dun & Bradstreet.

STEP 5 – Evaluate the application. A decision to extend credit to any specific client or company is generally based on what is called *The Five C's of Credit*:

Character – Are they willing to pay bills when due? (credit records must be studied to determine what kind of past behavior was evidenced by the applicant)

Capacity – Do they have the ability to pay debts? (if a company is suffering a serious cash flow problem, think twice about extending them credit)

Capital – What is the company's net worth? (a company with substantial assets, and a temporary cash flow problem, may not concern you that much)

Conditions – What are the current general economic conditions? Do they speak positively or negatively about granting credit to any customer?

Collateral – What collateral can they pledge to secure credit?

STEP 6 – Set a credit limit. If the application is approved set a credit limit for the customer (to control your losses in case the account goes delinquent). The limit you choose will depend upon your research and company policies.

STEP 7 – Establish terms of sale. When a firm offers trade credit, it usually offers a discount off the purchase price for early payment (to reduce its average collection period and improve cash flow), and states a limit as to how long the customer has until the bill must be paid. In the case of a wholesaler who ships goods to a retail firm, a typical "terms of sale" might be marked on the shipment's invoice 2/10, net 30. This means that the retailer is permitted thirty days of credit from the date of invoice. If the bill is paid promptly – within ten days have – the retailer is entitled to 2% off. Before you establish your terms of sale, check out what your competition is doing. In the least, offer similar terms.

STEP 8 – Set up an effective invoicing system. Invoices should be prepared and mailed promptly on a regular basis (monthly or bi-monthly) with all payment terms clearly stated. Set up an accurate, efficient and organized system for rendering these statements. Try and send an invoice with each shipment or invoice within two working days of filling the order.

STEP 9 – Monitor credit usage carefully. Monitoring your accounts receivable allows you to identify problems before they become serious credit risks. This is accomplished by setting up a system for aging all A/Rs. Pay particular attention to overdue accounts, not only to make sure that your customers have received their bills, but also to stop giving them credit in the future, or until their account has been brought up to date. When monitoring you A/Rs, make it a habit of comparing your average collection period (ACP) with industry averages, past experience, and changes to payment terms, as well as your monthly bad debt percentage.

- **A/R Dollar Value = average credit sales per day x average collection period** – If a business has credit sales of $500 per day and ACP of 20 days, it will have a total of: $500 x 20 days = $10,000 invested in receivables at any given time (if you are missing the values of certain variables you should be able to make reasonable projections using industry averages).

- **ACP = A/R Position/Daily Sales** – If a business has an A/R position of $2,000, (its customers owe $2,000 at that particular time) and annual credit sales of $40,000, its average collection period is ($2,000)/($40,000/365) or approximately 18 days.

STEP 10 – Establish a bad debts collection policy. Timely and effective debt collection is essential to generate positive cash flow and to increase profits by diminishing the need for short-term operating loans. All companies extending credit need to implement a systematic collection procedure to follow up on slow accounts. The purpose of this procedure is to help reduce "delinquency" without destroying the good will of good customers. You don't want to avoid losing potentially good customers by giving them a nasty or insensitive collections notice. A bad debts collection policy can be broken down into the following stages: (1) Fax a duplicate copy of the invoice. (2) Call the customer. (3) Send a form letter requesting payment. (4) Send a series of form letters requesting payment, each one becoming progressively stronger. (5) Hand the matter over to your attorney or collection agency.

Check polices established:

❏ **Monitor** A/R dollar amounts (A/R position) on an ongoing basis as well as calculate the percentage of total sales on credit.

❏ **Send** invoices immediately after the sale, rather than wait for the end of the month.

❏ **Offer** discounts for quick payments to improve our cash flow position.

❏ **Assess** a late payment fee from customers.

❏ **Age** A/Rs monthly.

❏ **Monitor** our average collection period & bad debts ratio.

❏ **Project**, monitor, and write off a percentage of bad debts.

❏ **Evaluate** the "Credit Worthiness" of customers using the 5 C's of credit.

❏ **Have** an effective collections policy.

❏ **Have** on file a series of increasingly pointed letters to collect from late or delinquent accounts.

❏ **Identify** prompt-paying customers and search for more like them.

❏ **Are** able to show that the costs of granting credit are offset by the benefits of higher sales.

There are three basic types of trade credit as listed below. Check type of trade credit you will extend to customers:

❏ **Open Credit** – Also referred to as open account, open book, or regular credit, this form extends short-term credit to customers without requiring any down payment and without adding either interest or carrying charges to the bill. It is usually extended for a thirty-day period.

❏ **Option-terms Credit** – This type of credit permits a customer to charge up to a limit and pay within thirty days of the billing date without penalty. A firm can assign a carrying charge for any amount not paid within that time period and release additional credit (up to the limit) as payments are made.

❏ **Revolving Charge Credit** – Revolving charge credit refers to the continuous releasing of credit to the credit ceiling as payments are made. This type of credit is the most common form of credit given to businesses.

Describe any additional credit extension polices. Also, discuss and special selling terms you will offer your customers:

Outline your credit collection procedure and collection procedures of overdue accounts:

DAY 20

Distribution Plan

Having access to good distribution is fundamental to good marketing. You need to be able to deliver your products and services to the right people, at the right time, in the right quantities, and at the lowest cost.

Choosing the Right Distributor

When deciding whether to use agents, wholesalers, brokers or retailers to distribute your products, consider the six factors as summarized in the chart and paragraphs below. Circle the best descriptive adjective for each factor. The distributor with the most circles is likely the one most to handle your distribution needs.

	Sell Directly Yourself	Use an Agent or Broker	Use a Wholesaler	Use a Retailer
Select the Distributor Who Best Matches Your Situation and Needs				
1. Number & Types of Customers	Few	Specialized	Hundreds	Diversified
2. Concentration of Market	Concentrated	Concentrated	Scattered	Scattered
3. Price of Product	Expensive	Less Exp.	Inexpensive	Inexpensive
4. Complexity of Product	Highly Technical	Less Technical	Simple	Simple
5. Financial Resources	Extensive	Adequate	Limited	Adequate
6. Need for Control	High	High	Low	Low

> *Distribution is all about getting products to where they are wanted; when they are wanted.*

Number & Types of Customers – If your manufacturing company deals with a few large customers, you may decide to sell directly to customers using your own sales staff. A toy manufacturer, for example, could sell direct to toy store chains, but would likely need the expertise of an agent to service independent toy stores.

Concentration of Market – Using your own distribution system is possible if your customers are concentrated in a few areas. If customers are scattered across the country, it is usually more economical to use other distributors.

Price of Product – The less expensive your product, the more likely that a distributor will be needed. Cheaper items are usually sold in large quantities to intermediaries or wholesalers who then distribute them in smaller numbers to retailers. Expensive, technological products, such as computers or industrial equipment are usually sold directly by the manufacturer or through a specialized agent.

Complexity of Product – Highly technical items are usually sold directly by the manufacturer. The producer's sales force might be able to offer pre-sale information and post-sale service, which most wholesalers cannot provide.

Financial Resources – Most new manufacturers cannot afford to establish a distribution system, grant credit or provide warehousing for completed products. It is usually more practical and economical to rely on experienced distributors who already have numerous market contacts.

> *The use of agents, brokers and reps as intermediaries are usually a must for small manufacturing businesses starting out because of their limited ability to advertise heavily.*

Need for Control – Some manufacturers want to maintain control of their product by handling distribution even though the costs are higher. They feel that they can maintain a consistent price, provide better service and maintain high performance standards by distributing directly. Most consumer products such as food, clothing or furniture are not sold directly by the producer because the control over quality of service and price maintenance is less important.

Other Factors to Consider When Choosing a Distribution Method

Not factored into the chart, but of critical importance when making a decision regarding which distribution method to use are the following five factors:

Cost of Distribution Method vs. Services Provided – Using intermediaries necessitates building a cost structure to compensate each of the channel members for the part they play in the total distribution process. Intermediaries don't work for free! When choosing a distribution method, factor in the value of the added services the intermediary provides. Agents, brokers, wholesalers, and retailers, offer different levels of service and cost. Some will do everything for you from packaging to delivery to marketing, while others will provide only a few services. Distributors and selling agencies, despite charging higher fees compared with agents, brokers and sales reps, will also stock orders, invoice and carry receivables, place regional advertising, install equipment, train their own sales staff, and provide more extensive after-sales service. The bottom line is if experience shows that your low cost distributors are unreliable or inconsistent in the quality of service they offer it may be wiser to upgrade.

Distributor Success Rate – Manufacturers trained in making products usually have less success at distributing products than intermediaries trained in marketing.

Insurance Needs – While in transit, your goods will be subject to many risks, from exposure to the elements, accidents, and damage, to outright theft. This demands that you get sufficient coverage to insure the value of your goods while you are liable. Insurance rates will vary with the mode you choose to distribute and transport your goods. A good insurance broker, besides helping you pick the insurance you need at a price you can afford, can also help identify deficiencies in packaging and even production, which can also save you money.

Storage & Warehousing Costs – If you need to store goods, for lists of U.S. warehouse facilities contact the *American Warehousemen's Association* or the *International Association of Refrigerated Warehouses (www.iawr.org)*.

Transportation & Shipping Costs – Transportation & shipping costs can range from a mere fraction of an item's selling price – as is the case of transporting grain, coal, gravel, and other bulky commodities – to as much as 40 % or more, as in the case of transporting exotic pets from distant regions. Consequently, transportation management must focus on two major objectives: (a) minimizing the costs and effort involved in physically moving a product to customers whether by land, air or water; and (b) ensuring speedy, reliable delivery. To help keep your transportation costs reasonable: ◆ have the customer negotiate shipment in cases where he or she has more leverage with the shipper ◆ ship in pieces and assemble in the market ◆ use intermodal shipping (combining 2 or more modes) ◆ investigate interlining (e.g., switching from U.S. to Canadian carriers once crossing the border) ◆ use freight forwarders or customs brokers as middlemen.

Describe and detail the manner in which your products and services will be made available to your customers. Will you sell direct, wholesale, retail, through multiple outlets, or using manufacturing reps? Will your customers purchase by direct mail, buy through catalogs, or make in-store purchases (check appropriate marketing and distribution channels below)?

- ❑ **Brokers, Sales Agents & Manufacturer's Reps–** work independently from the companies they represent. Their business activity consists of buying and selling on behalf of others, thereby earning commissions or fees.
- ❑ *Brokers* – function as intermediaries between buyer and seller, bringing together the two parties while representing either side (not both at once, of course). They find customers for products and negotiate prices.
- ❑ *Manufacturer's Reps* – represent a manufacturer, under contract, seeking distribution in a selected area and who do not have their own sales forces.
- ❑ *Sales Agents* – represent any type of business, ranging from service businesses to manufacturing & wholesaling firms while manufacturer's reps (as their name implies) represent only manufacturing firms.
- ❑ **Distributors & Selling Agencies** – unlike reps, sales agents and brokers, distributors and selling agencies are granted extensive authority over the details of prices, terms, customer selection and marketing decisions. A selling agency is often contracted to sell a manufacturing plant's entire production, and thus often maintains a sizable and effective sales force. Distributors are often charged with buying and selling part of a manufacturing plant's production in their specific marketing region. The relationship between the distributors and selling agencies and the principal is a close one.
- ❑ **Wholesalers** – sell primarily to retailers and to other wholesalers or industrial users. They do not usually sell goods to the end consumer. There are a little more than half a million wholesale establishments in the U.S. More than 2/3rd of these firms are merchant wholesalers.
- ❑ *Cash-and Carry Wholesalers* – cater to retailers who walk in, purchase needed merchandise with cash only, and take the goods out with them.
- ❑ *Drop-shippers* – supplies raw materials or bulky products of a low-unit price to industrial users. This type of intermediary, found most frequently in the coal, lumber, and metals industries, doesn't take physical possession of the merchandise at any point, or put it in a warehouse, but rather arranges for the producer to ship the goods directly to the customer.

- ❑ *General Merchandise Wholesalers* – sell a variety of different lines of goods much like a general store.
- ❑ *Industrial Distributors* – wholesale industrial products.
- ❑ *Mail Order Wholesalers* – offer retailers merchandise for resale, characteristically through the medium of printed catalogs issued periodically.
- ❑ *Merchant Wholesalers* – purchase goods in large quantities, warehouse them, and then break these quantities down into smaller shipments for distribution to their customers.
- ❑ *Rack Jobbers* – distribute a specialized line (e.g., soft-cover books and magazines, toys, health and beauty aides, novelties, household items, and the like) through supermarkets and other high-traffic outlets.
- ❑ *Single-line Wholesalers* – supply its retail clients with a complete in-depth stock in one particular line of goods, such as grocers, hardware outlets, and the like.
- ❑ *Specialty Wholesalers* – handle a small number of products within a particular merchandise line.
- ❑ *Truck Jobbers* – service retail outlets directly from a truck with fast-moving products and perishable goods (commonly encountered in the grocery trade). In addition to fresh fruits and vegetables, truck jobbers handle dairy products, cookies, frozen foods, and similar items.
- ❑ **Retailers** – like wholesalers, retailers are intermediaries in the marketing channels who forward goods form the nation's producers through to the final consumers. The retailing industry itself is a vital sector of the economy and employs more than 20 million people in approximately 1.5 million retail establishments in the U.S. (there are over 250,000 retailers in Canada). In 1997, total annual retail sales in the U.S. surpassed $2.5 trillion up from $235 billion in 1967. Retail outlets can be approached directly, especially chain outlets, or through their wholesalers and selling agents.
- ❑ **Trading Houses** –specialize in exporting, importing, and trading goods and services produced by others. They provide a wide range of specialized services to businesses who wish to export, for a fee or commission.

Back up your distribution plan with reports, rate sheets from shippers and contracts with sales representatives. Also, provide alternative methods of distribution. For example if your major shipper, Federal Express, were to go on strike, who would replace them?

Describe any special arrangements you may have with individual distributors:

List your principal distributors by name and expected sales.

Distributor	Address	Territory	Terms of Sale	Exclusive or Non-Exclusive	Total Expected Sales ($ or Units)

Describe any special arrangements you may have with key customers:

List your principal customers by name and the total amount they are expected to buy from you:

Customer	Product	Expected Purchases ($ or Units)	Share of your Sales (%)
	a.		
	b.		
	c.		
	a.		
	b.		
	c.		
	a.		
	b.		
	c.		

> *To get profit without risk, experience without danger, and reward without work, is as impossible as it is to live without being born.*
> **A. P. GOUTHEY**

Market Testing Plan

Testing is a way of buying information. It is a powerful research tool used by manufacturers, retailers, service providers and all other kinds of entrepreneurs to determine the market potential of an idea. It is an activity designed to help you discover what changes, if any, should be made to your product, service, pricing structure, service policy or advertising promotion before you head into full production or distribution.

Market Testing Strategies

Below is a collection of product, service and advertising testing strategies to help you determine the feasibility of your idea before launching a full-scale promotion.

Describe what methods you will use to test the market before going into full production with new products and services:

❑ **Alter one variable at a time.** One of the best strategies you can use to test the potential of a promotion, is to modify or change one variable of the promotion at a time to find out if that modification or change can significantly improve your results. You can alter, test, or experiment with: ✦ ad copy ✦ ad headlines ✦ ad pictures ✦ ad position ✦ prices ✦ product features ✦ promotional media ✦ seasons of the year ✦ size of ad vs. frequency of repetition ✦ subtle variations of the wording of offers ✦ use of color ✦ use of coupons ✦ use of humor.

❑ **Buy a sample of a product before you stock up on it.** Don't stock a product you haven't first seen, touched, smelled, listened to, used, tried on, handled, or tasted.

❑ **Compare classified & display advertising.** If your promotion can be sold via a classified ad or a display ad, test both media, as one may prove to be substantially more profitable than the other. Classified ads cost less, but produce less. Display ads cost more, but may also produce more, pulling in forty times more responses than a classified ad.

❑ **Compare consumer response by region.** Different regions of your city, state, country and the world can have vastly different responses to the same item. A promotion that does well in L.A. might bomb in the Deep South and vice versa. A good marketer tests the same promotion in different regions.

❑ **Compare your products with competitors' products.** Compare your product with similar items on the market. Conduct a taste test or listening test. Take pictures of your product side-by-side with the competition.

❑ **Conduct a survey.** Conduct a survey at your retail location, at stores that sell similar products, or by surveying people on the street who look like they might need your product or service. By listening and noting the responses of potential clients or buyers, you can evaluate your pricing, appearance of advertising, and other marketing strategies. Mail questionnaire surveys are less expensive than telephone surveys and personal interviews. However, telephone surveys and personal interviews will produce the most immediate response.

❑ **Distribute your product to one store only.** Ask a retailer if they will set up a display of your product in a store at no cost to them unless products are sold. Local privately owned retail outlets are more likely to agree to this than retail chains, as long as your product complements their products and have a good potential for sales.

❑ **Do a limited advertising run.** Run an ad in one and only one of your chosen advertising media. Limit your insertions until you have analyzed the response rate from this medium and have found it profitable.

❑ **Attend a trade show** (refer to page 119).

Preparing Advertising Records

Advertising records should be incorporated into your daily workflow, not to increase your administrative burden, but rather to increase your profits by giving you more accurate feedback on the results of your promotions. Outlined below are several methods for monitoring the effectiveness of advertising and promotional efforts, and keeping track of how effectively each medium pulls in customers:

Survey customers directly. To find out what kinds of advertising customers respond to, conduct a survey, or more simply, ask them directly whenever they are placing an order in person or over the phone. It makes good business sense for you to conduct regular surveys because: (1) *Surveys keeps you close to your customers.* This gives you a competitive edge. You can respond more quickly to customer likes, dislikes, and buying habits, than bigger companies. (2) *Surveys help put experience into perspective.* Surveys help you find out what kinds of information has become dated and is no longer relevant to making selling decisions.

Encourage customers to fill out a questionnaire. Questionnaires mailed to your customers or left in accessible spots in your retail locations can help you get an idea of how effective your promotions are. Questions regarding the effectiveness of a promotion can also be incorporated directly onto your order forms.

"In order to serve you better please answer the following:"

How did you hear about our product or service?

☐ referral
☐ word of mouth
☐ radio ad
☐ TV ad
☐ billboard
☐ Yellow Pages
☐ magazine
☐ newspaper
☐ direct mail
☐ newsletter
☐ other

Use what is called an *Advertising Key*. An *advertising key* is a special code, number or word added to an ad, coupon or company address, to help you keep track of your advertising effectiveness and response rates. Every time the key is spotted, it is noted and the promotional media that generated the order is traced. Mail order and direct marketing companies especially, have mastered the art of using advertising keys. To write an advertising key: ♦ add words and/or codes to an advertiser's address e.g., Studio 62, Suite 6, Room 121, Desk NW2, Dept. GH692, Box Number 512 ♦ add a suffix to your address e.g., P.O. Box 123-A, 3456-A Hornby St. ♦ use staff names or even fictitious names e.g., Attention: Pete J. Sanders (*Popular Science*, June) or Attention: Cary Grant (*Car & Driver*).

Design special coded coupons. Special codes including numbers, letters, and words can be put on order forms and coupons to indicate which magazine, newspaper, direct mail, or other promotion they come from. Usually this code includes a date of issue and an abbreviation (e.g., GH699; which means – *Good Housekeeping*, June 1999). Likewise, special stick-on labels or specially produced reply envelopes and BRC's can be used in mailings to give you keyed information.

Use "Tell Them Joe Sent You Broadcast Ads." You can monitor the effectiveness of broadcast media by asking customers at the end of your radio or TV ad to state a phrase or keyword when they enter your store (this usually works best if the phrase or keyword entitles them to a special price, discount or free gift). This technique can also help you discover exactly what areas your customers are drawn from so you can target that area more specifically with other kinds of advertising.

Use an "Advertising Cost Analysis Chart." Knowing how a customer finds out about your product or service is not easy. However, you can attempt to gauge the effectiveness of advertising costs by creating models that identify where customers see or hear ads. The "Advertising Cost Analysis" chart shown on the next page, analyzes the results of several different advertising methods. By analyzing this data, you can make better decisions about where to put your advertising dollar and how to direct your sales force. In this example, according to the "Cost per Sale" results, it is obvious that radio & television advertising is inappropriate for this particular product. The "Responses per Sale" is also a useful figure as it indicates the number of people who must be reached by the media to produce a sale

ADVERTISING COST ANALYSIS									
	Daily News	Sunday Insert	Radio 60 Sec Ad	Cable TV 30 Sec Ad	Church Bulletin	Direct Mail	Bulletin Board	Referrals	Unknown
Circulation	7,500	15,000	10,000	12,000	1,200	100	40		
type of Unit	Col. Inch	Col. Inch	minute	minute	page	letter	number		
Number of Units	8	16	1	1	1	1	1		
Total Cost	110	345	1,400	1,900	35	300	120		
Cost per Circulation	0.01	0.02	0.14	0.16	0.03	0.20	3.00		
Total Responses	190	354	590	498	138	391	97	525	1,458
Total Sales	43	76	121	124	43	66	35	48	431
Circulation per Response	39	42	17	4	9	0	0	0	0
Circulation per Sale	174	197	83	97	28	2	1	0	0
Responses per Sale	4	5	5	4	3	6	3	11	3
Cost per response	0.58	0.97	2.37	3.82	0.25	0.77	1.24	0.00	0.00
Cost per Sale	2.56	4.54	11.57	15.32	0.81	4.55	3.43	0.00	0.00
% of Total Responses	4%	8%	14%	12%	3%	9%	2%	12%	34%
% of Total Sales	4%	8%	12%	13%	4%	7%	4%	5%	44%

NOTE This above chart can also be setup using a spreadsheet program, where everything above and including total sales is inputted and everything below is computed).

Describe what kinds of strategies and methods you will use to keep track of your advertising results:

Describe your method for confirming who your customers are and how they heard about you:

Getting the Most Out of a Trade Show

One of the best ways to test the market for a product or service is at a trade show. At a trade show, you can introduce new ideas, find new partners, make new contacts, create confidence in potential customers, learn about the market, and overall, generate good public relations. Trade shows are one of the least expensive ways of making multiple sales presentations. They also offer you – and this is very important – the best chance of closing a sale. It has been estimated that each sales contact you make at a trade show has a 54% chance of success – far higher than the 15% success rate of routine sales calls. Trade shows should also be fun. Although, many attending are motivated to buy, and quite serious about researching products and services, others are attending simply to get away from the office, socialize and pick up a few good ideas. If you make your display interesting, informative and a little entertaining, great interest will be created in your display and you will meet the needs of both types of attendees. Outlined in the chart on the following page are 17 steps to help make your trade show a success:

> *If you could sell near the ladies' bathroom you were always guaranteed one of the heaviest concentrations of foot traffic at the fair.*
> **RON POPEIL**

List trade shows you plan to attend. Summarize any special strategies you have for making your exhibit stand out:

_____
_____
_____
_____
_____
_____

Pre-Show

a) *Book only national trade shows.* Only attend trade shows that have been operating for five years or more. For extensive information on trade shows, visit the *Trade Show News Network* at http://www.tsnn.com.

b) *Rent the best possible display location.* Being big is not as good as being in a good spot. Don't be the first to sign up, be well placed. Try and find out who will be next to you or better yet who you can be next to.

c) *Publicize your participation in the show to the local press a few months beforehand.* A few months before the show send a press release to all trade publications in your field. This release should describe any new products you intend to introduce at the show.

d) *Send letters to all television and radio stations in the trade show area.* Tell them some unique facts about your product and offer to appear on any of their talk shows at their convenience.

e) *Write letters or invitations to people who will be interested in your display.* The success of a trade show promotion depends upon *WHO* actually shows up to see your display. Write letters to retailers, wholesalers and sales reps who would have a lot to gain by selling your product or seeing your display.

f) *Write letters or invitations to people who might be interested in your display.* You can improve the results of your trade show promotion modestly or tremendously by writing to fringe accounts – that is people who *might* be interested in your display.

g) *Hit the local press about ten days before the show opens.* Send a press release to newspapers located in the town where the trade show is to be held.

h) *Mail reminder letters.* About a week before the show, send a reminder letter to every person you mailed to previously and remind them to visit your booth. Remember, any positive impressions you make before the show can go a long way to getting your desired result.

i) *Prepare your booth to be different.* One of the most important requirements for a successful exhibit can be summed up in two words – be different. Your booth should look like no other booth. Design your booth so that it will make as much impact as possible. If you have to make some last minute changes, do so.

Show Time

j) *Display as much promotional material as is appropriate.* Spread out your product line in as attractive a manner as your can. Have plenty of business cards, letterheads, envelopes, order forms, brochures and other material on hand to give potential buyers.

k) *Keep a detailed record of everyone who visits your booth.* Record all inquiries. Try and get as many names and addresses as possible. Make notes on casual observers who don't leave their name and even ones who walk by and have no apparent interest in your display. Overall, get as much information as you can on exactly who your target market really is or may become.

l) *Keep a sharp lookout for buyers.* Buyers for large organizations regularly attend tradeshows. Buyers may represent themselves, individual businesses, stores, production facilities, or entire chains of stores. Frequently, they will fly long distances to take advantage of the collected assortment of displayed goods relating to their industry. It will be your job to find these people and sell them on any of your ideas or products.

m) *Make a detailed study of all the other exhibitors.* Make a note of who's there, who isn't, who is selling what, which booths are getting the most attention, which products you think have potential, and especially, what the competition is up to.

n) *Approach all related businesses.* Don't hide. Circulate. Talk to other businesses at the show who might be interested in what you are promoting. Who knows, your greatest contacts may be three booths away.

o) *If the show extends over several days, consider testing your prices, redecorating your booth, or showcasing different products.* Consider using the trade show to get an idea of how response increases or decreases according to changed variables. But, don't go overboard. Test only one variable at a time.

Post-Show

p) *Follow up on all inquiries.* Otherwise, you've wasted your time. People who come to your show are not sure things, but they are highly qualified prospects.

q) *Mail thank you notes to those who came to see you.* If you mailed an invitation to someone and they came to see you, make sure you mail a thank you. This is the cheapest P/R you're ever going to get.

To Do List

Marketing Plan
*Selling
Strategies*
✓ Pricing Policies

> *In the long run, a profitable sales volume is a much better company goal than maximum sales volume.*

> *Demand-oriented pricing is usually superior to cost-orientated pricing. In the "cost approach," a pre-determined amount is added to the cost of the merchandise. In the "demand approach," prices are based on what consumers are willing to pay.*
> **PRICING TIP**

> *For most businesses, prices are determined by costs, competition, and industry pricing practices.*
> **FUNFACT**

DAY 21

Pricing Policies

Crucial to a good marketing strategy is an effective pricing policy. For the prices you charge will effect your sales volume, profit levels, and among other things, your company image. To incorporate a pricing policy into your business: (1) define your pricing objectives, (2) establish a simple yet effective pricing structure taking into consideration all your business costs, (3) choose a pricing strategy to establish a market presence, and (4) fine-tune and adapt your general pricing policy in response to trends, industry practices, and new innovative pricing strategies to help solidify your competitive position within the marketplace.

Sample Pricing Policy Statements

Product – Before (I/we) established prices for (my/our) (Product), (I/we) determined (my/our) per unit costs. (I/We) then researched the market price for similar products. At market price, it was determined that for all but (my/our) lowest sales projections, (my/our) (Product) would turn a profit in (Time Period). However, since our (Product)s offer(s) additional features, including (explain features), (I/we) feel that (I/we) can price it (XX)% above the competition.

To test this price, (I/we) conducted a survey of (100) users of (Product)s. (I/We) first questioned them about the benefits and desirability of (my/our) extra features and then asked them if (my/our) price was acceptable. (I/We) found that (50)% of those polled were interested in (my/our) product. Of this (50)%, (I/we) received (10) firm orders representing approximately (20)% of this group. A breakdown of (my/our) pricing structure is as follows: (describe pricing structure).

OR – (I/We) have determined that the market price is $(XX) per unit. If (I/we) charge this price (my/our) margin will equal (XX)%.

OR – (My/Our) unit cost has been figured at $(XX). (I/We) need a margin of (XX)% to pay overhead and earn a sufficient profit. (My/Our) selling price will be $(XX).

Service – Before (I/we) set prices for (my/our) (Service), (I/we) projected fixed and variable monthly costs to be $(XX). (I/We) then researched the market rate for similar services. At market rate, it was determined that for all but our lowest sales projections, (my/our) (Service) would turn a profit in (Time Period). However, since (my/our) service is unique and demands a high level of expertise, (I/we) feel that (I/we) need to bill higher than the competition. A breakdown of (my/our) pricing structure is as follows: (describe pricing structure).

Outline key considerations in your pricing policy:

| |
| |
| |
| |

FACTORS THAT WILL INFLUENCE PRICES	FACTORS THAT PRICE WILL INFLUENCE

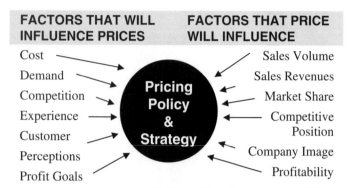

Defining Price Objectives

Price objectives must closely tie in with your overall business and marketing goals. When setting price objectives, carefully consider what impact prices will have on factors such as sales volume, sales revenue, market share, competitive position, company image, and profitability.

Writing "Price Objectives"

Price objectives are qualifying statements about what you want your pricing policy to do, such as, keep or build market share, increase profits, meet or prevent competition, introduce new products, and/or increase sales. Specific examples of price objectives include: ♦ "earn a 15% return on investment" ♦ "increase market share by 30% by end of fiscal year" ♦ "introduce new products at low prices to gain a significant market presence and once established, raise prices."

Summarize the main objectives of your pricing policy:

Check important factors that the price of your product or services will influence. Describe additional <u>*Factors that "Price" Will Influence*</u>:

❑ **Sales Volume –** Sales volume is highly dependent on prices. Usually, higher prices mean lower volume and vice-versa. Small businesses can often command higher prices because of the personalized service they can offer. It should be noted that if there is no direct relationship between pricing changes and sales volume, the sale of a product or service is relatively independent of its cost. When this is the case, it is likely that the market is saturated. This situation spells "trouble."

❑ **Sales Revenue –** Setting prices, including credit policies, is a major factor affecting total revenue. If you increase the price of your product, you can expect response to decrease by a certain percentage. However, a one-dollar item may not necessarily get twice as many sales as two dollars. It may get more, or it may get less. To maximize your revenue you must therefore test and research what consumers are willing to pay.

❑ **Market Share –** Your prices will determine to a large extent your percentage of market share compared with your competitors. Lower prices usually mean a larger percentage of the market share.

❑ **Competitive Position –** Prices will affect how your product or service stands in relation to the competition. Occasionally you might use cheaper than normal prices to introduce products or services to get consumer attention and improve your market position. However, if you set prices too low, and the competition is watching closely, you could end up in a price war (in price wars, usually the consumer wins).

❑ **Company Image –** Your prices will create an image in your consumer's mind. They will see you as a discounter, general retailer, or overpriced Rodeo Drive type operator. Discounters sell at the lowest possible price and strive for a high volume of units sold while the Rodeo Drive type operator strives for high profit per sale on a lower volume.

❑ **Profitability –** Prices will affect overall profitability. The most profitable price can be found by testing the market with different prices on the same product or service. A high price will give you more profit per sale but less sales. A low price will give you less profit per sale but more sales. Somewhere in between lies the perfect balance between profit per sale and volume of sales.

Check the most important factors that influence your pricing policy. Summarize any additional <u>Factors that Will Influence Prices</u>:

❑ **Cost Structure** – Price your product or service according to your cost structure. Above anything else, your price structure must account for all the fixed and variable costs of conducting your business, including all marketing and distribution costs. Only then, can you factor in your profit goals.

❑ *Fixed Costs* – Fixed costs generally refer to your operating expenses. They include wages, management salaries, rent, utilities, office supplies, insurance etc. and usually do not vary with your business volume.

❑ *Variable Costs* – Variable costs generally refer to your cost of goods (inventory costs) as in the case of a wholesaler or retailer and your cost of materials or supplies as in the case of a manufacturer or service provider. Variable costs increase or decrease depending upon the amount of goods, materials or supplies purchased for resale or production. They include the price paid for inventory, materials, supplies, freight charges, handling charges, commissions, etc.

❑ **Competition** – Price your product or service according to what the competition is charging. Since your products or services are competing in the market place, you must know exactly what the competition is doing before you finalize your pricing policies. To get detailed info about your competitors' pricing polices, send in a friend or go yourself to do some comparison shopping. Is there discounting? Special sales? Loss leaders? Make some "blind" phone calls.

❑ **Customer Expectations** – Price your product or service according customer expectations. Some shoppers are very price conscious; others want convenience and knowledgeable sales staff and will pay more to get it.

❑ **Demand** – Price your product or service according to how many people want it, how badly and how quickly they need it, and how much they are willing to pay for it. Obviously, if there is a large demand for your product or service and you're the only one on the block selling it, you can pretty much charge what you want.

❑ **Experience** – Price your product or service according to what people have paid for it in the past.

❑ **Final Pricing Authority** – Price your product or service according to who has final pricing authority. If you are running a franchise, you may have little say in what you charge for your goods or services. Likewise, be aware that some suppliers and manufacturers attempt to control retail prices by directly or indirectly refusing to deal with nonconforming stores.

❑ **Industry Averages** – Price your product or service according to standards and guidelines set by your industry. Research your industry to determine what its average markup percentage is and other standard pricing strategies and structures. Trade associations often have schedules for service charges.

❑ **Legal Concerns** – Price your product or service according to local and national regulations and laws. In some cases, laws may restrict how much you can charge for certain items.

❑ **Location of Business** – Price your product or service according to how good your location is. A business with a prime location can usually get away with charging more for its products or services. For example, consider two similarly equipped hotels, one with beachfront, the other overlooking a shopping mall parking lot. Which one would you pay more for?

❑ **Perceived Value to Customers** – Price your product or service according to how valuable customers perceive it to be. This will help you establish the upper limit of your price range or "what the market will bear." Perceived value is dependent upon to what extent a product or service saves money, improves the quality of life, is seen as being truly unique, is durable and made of quality parts that are generally understood to cost more, and how well it actually meets needs (if your prices are high, offer more or better service to justify your higher prices).

❑ **Physical Appearance of Business Premises** – Price your product or service according to how much money you have put into interior and exterior renovations. Clients normally expect businesses with posh surroundings to charge higher prices, while those with bare floors and simple shelving to give discounts.

❑ **Profit Goals** – Price your product or service according to your profit goals. Naturally, prices should motivate customers to buy, be competitive, and cover selling costs. But, there's no point starting a business unless you can get a decent return on your investment. Merchandise should always be priced in such a way as to maximize profit taking into account both your short-term and long-term needs.

❑ **Risk** – Price your product or service according to the risks involved in offering certain merchandise or services. For example, very fashionable clothing often carries a higher markup than basic clothing because the particular fashion may suddenly lose its appeal overnight and be replaced by a new fashion craze.

> *A fair price for oil is whatever you can get plus ten per cent.*
> **DR. ALI AHMED ATTIGA**
> Saudi Arabian Delegate to OPEC

Developing a Price Structure

Developing a systematic approach to setting prices is important to building a successful business. One way to explain and justify your pricing structure is to talk about it in terms of its "price floor" and "price ceiling." The *price floor* is the lowest cost at which you can sell a product to meet all your costs, and still make a small profit. The *price ceiling* is determined by industry practices, what the competition is charging, and the maximum cost the consumer is willing to pay based upon their perceived value of your product or service.

Calculating Retail Markup

One technique to establish a pricing structure is to markup goods sold by adding a percentage to their actual cost. Your final price is based on: (1) *the cost of acquiring the goods*, called "cost of merchandise" or "cost of goods sold" – this cost includes the actual price paid for the merchandise plus freight, import duties and any handling costs minus any quantity and cash discount given you by the wholesaler; (2) *the cost of operating the business* to sell the goods, called "operating expenses" or "overhead – this cost includes markdowns, stock shortages, theft, customer discounts, etc., and the salary of the owner; and (3) *desired profit*.

> *That which costs little is less valued.*
> **MIGUEL DE CERVANTES**

For example: A retailer (Sam's Shirt Shop) purchases a shirt at $20. Using industry averages and a desired profit of 12%, Sam calculates his markup percentage to be 40% based on **15%** for wages, **8%** for rent, **2%** for utilities, and **3%** for advertising. He adds $8 to the price of the shirt for a resale price of $28.

Cost of one shirt	**$20**
Markup amount	**$8**
Selling price per pair	**$28**
Markup percentage	**40%**

NOTE When first starting a business, it is difficult to determine how much goods should be marked up because a new business has no history of sales on which to base future sales projections. It is necessary to research industry trade journals for sales patterns and industry markup averages.

Expressing Markup as a Percentage of the Retail Price Instead of Cost – "Retail price," rather than "actual cost," is ordinarily used to express markup percentage. The reason for this is that other operating figures such as wages, advertising expenses and

Dollar amount of markup	**$8**
Retail Price	**$28**
Retail Markup **(dollar markup/retail price)**	**29%**

profit, when expressed as a percentage, are normally expressed as percentages based on retail prices rather than cost of the merchandise. For this reason, most retailers prefer to express their markup as a percentage of retail price (see "Markup Table" on next page for conversions).

> *It is not that pearls fetch a high price because men have dived for them; but on the contrary, men dive for them because they fetch a high price.*
> **BISHOP RICHARD WHATELY**

Using a Standard Markup Percentage – To maintain your desired level of profit, establish a *standard* or *average percentage of markup*. This markup percentage can be calculated using the formula on the right:

Standard Markup % Formula

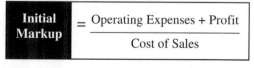

$$\text{Initial Markup} = \frac{\text{Operating Expenses} + \text{Profit}}{\text{Cost of Sales}}$$

For example, if *Sam's Shirt Warehouse* projects selling 10,000 shirts a year costing $194,000, with shipping costs of $6,000, operating expenses of $53,000, and a desired profit of $27,000, "Initial Markup" would be calculated as follows:

$$\text{Initial Markup} = \frac{(\$53,000 + \$27,00)}{(\$194,000 + \$6,000)} = 0.4 \text{ or } \mathbf{40\%}$$

NOTE A business may choose to use a standard markup % on all products, or it may have different markups for different goods. The reason for this is standard or average markup % doesn't allow for cost differences in selling different products. If product A costs more to advertise or sell than product B, a standard markup % may produce a loss on product A and a greater-than-average profit on product B.

Calculating the Cost of a Service

Services are harder to price than goods. It is more difficult for the buying public to determine a fair price for services, and comparative shopping has much less effect in service industries than it does in hard goods industries. Services are also more difficult to price because costs are harder to estimate and it is more difficult to compare prices with the competition. Nevertheless, although more complex, pricing a service is basically calculated in the same way as pricing retail goods:

Price (for a service) = *material costs + operating expenses* (which include supplies, labor and overhead) + *the desired profit*

Calculating Material Costs – *Material costs* are the cost of materials used directly in a final product, such as sparkplugs and gaskets in the repair of an engine. Supplies such as paper towels are part of overhead, not material costs. A materials costs list must always be used in preparing a bid or quoting a job. If there are shipping, handling or storage costs for materials, these must also be included in the total materials costs.

Calculating Labor Costs – Labor Cost is the cost of work *directly* applied to a service, such as a mechanic's work. Work not directly applied to the service, such as cleaning up, is an overhead cost. Direct labor costs are derived by multiplying the cost of labor per hour by the number of hours required to complete the job.

Calculating Overhead Costs – Generally speaking, overhead costs include all costs other than direct materials and direct labor. It is the *indirect cost* of the service. These costs include legal fees, supplies, insurance, taxes, rent, accounting, and the labor costs of other people on a company's payroll who perform support services that are not charged to direct labor. This cost can be expressed as either an hourly rate based on total labor hours per year or as a percentage of direct labor.

Overhead Rate in Total Direct Labor Hours – The following formula can be used in machine shops, repair shops, and design and production shops, where equip-

"Markup at Retail" & "Markup at Cost" Table

MARKUP AT	
Retail %	Cost %
30.0 =	42.9
31.0	45.0
32.0	47.1
33.0	49.3
34.0	51.5
35.0	53.9
36.0	56.3
37.0	58.8
38.0	61.3
39.0	64.0
40.0	66.7
41.0	70.0
42.0	72.4
43.0	75.5
44.0	78.5
45.0	81.8
46.0	85.2
47.0	88.7
48.0	92.3
49.0	95.9
50.0	100.0
60.0	150.0

Markup, also known as markon, is the difference between the cost of the merchandise and its selling price. It can be measured in % or $. Markup is usually figured on the basis of the retail selling price. The following table shows the equivalent percent for markup at retail and cost.

Markup Formula: To arrive at a markup at retail, let us assume that you want to sell a pair of socks that cost you $3.25 at a 40% markup. The basic markup formula is:

Cost = Retail Price - Markup

Cost = 100% - 40% = 60%

Retail Price = Dollar cost/Percentage Cost =

$3.25/60% (.60) = $5.42

Bill's Auto Shop	
Materials Cost	
Muffler	$70.00
Direct Labor Cost	
Hourly Wages (per hour)	$20.00
Fringe Benefits (30% of wage)	$6.00
Total Cost per Hour	$26.00
# of Hours	3
Direct Labor Total	$78.00
Overhead Cost (80% of direct labor)	
Total	$62.40
Total Costs	$210.40
Profit	
Profit on Materials (30%)	$21.00
Profit on Labor (25%)	$19.50
Profit on Overhead (20%)	$12.48
Total Profit	$52.98
Total Charge to Customer	$263.38

ment used is inexpensive and there is relatively little difference between skill levels and the hourly wages of employees. It can also be used for small consulting firms.

$$\text{Overhead Rate} = \frac{\text{Total overhead cost}}{\text{Total direct labor hours (per year)}} = \frac{\$40,000}{5,000 \text{ hours}} = \$8 \text{ per hour}$$

Overhead Rate as a Percentage of Direct Labor Cost – In businesses where expensive equipment is used by higher paid employees; overhead cost is more closely related to direct labor cost than to total labor hours. In this situation, overhead cost can be expressed as a percentage of direct labor.

$$\text{Overhead Rate} = \frac{\text{Total overhead cost}}{\text{Total direct labor cost}} = \frac{\$40,000}{\$50,000} = 0.8 \text{ or } \textbf{80\%}$$

EXAMPLE As shown in the example on the left, if you calculated your overhead costs to be 80% of your direct labor costs and your employee whom you pay $20 per hour worked for three hours using parts costing $70, your cost to the customer would be $263.38.

Elements of Your Selling Price: Summarize all the important elements of your selling price (refer back to the charts on page 122 and 123):

- **Manufacturing Businesses** – In manufacturing, the most important elements of the selling price are the costs of raw materials, manufacturing overhead (equip.), non-manufacturing overhead, and planned profit.

- **Wholesale Businesses** – In a wholesale business, the most important elements of the selling price are the cost of goods for resale, overhead, sales volume, competition's pricing and credit policies, and planned profit.

- **Retail Businesses** – In a retail business, the most important elements of the selling price are very similar to those of a wholesale business except, retailers are also very concerned about how prices affect their "image."

- **Service Businesses** – In a service business, the most important elements of the selling price are materials and supplies, labor and operating expenses, competition, and planned profit.

Principal Direct-Cost Elements of Your Operation

Product & Material Cost – Summarize and describe ❑ cost of goods sold including shipping costs (for retail or wholesale businesses) ❑ raw materials costs (for manufacturing businesses) ❑ material and supplies costs (for service businesses).

Labor Costs – Summarize and describe direct labor costs (for retail and wholesale operations this cost is usually factored into overhead costs):

Overhead Costs – Summarize and describe overhead costs. If you plan to operate a service business, which method will you use to calculate your overhead rate?

Other Elements of Your Selling Price

Planned Profit – Discuss typical gross and net margins for each of your product/service lines. Outline your desired profit goals:

Competition's Pricing – What are your competitors charging for similar products and/or services:

Other Important Elements of Your Selling Price – Summarize and other important elements of your selling price:

Pricing Structure

Discuss the prices you plan to charge customers (and distributors) for your product/service. Explain how your costs, profit goals, and other elements influenced your decision. If you plan to operate a retail or wholesale business, explain your markup percentage and how you arrived at this percentage? If you plan to operate a service or manufacturing business show the method you will use to calculate your prices (use worksheets on the next page):

Describe your schedule for quantity, cash, and other discounts, credit arrangements, returns policy, and other terms of sale:

Pricing Worksheet #1 – Retail or Wholesale Business

Initial Markup:

Operating Expenses for the Year (all fixed & variable operating costs)

Desired Profit for the Year

Cost of Sales (include shipping and handling charges)

A) Markup % = $\dfrac{\text{(Operating Expenses + Profit)}}{\text{(Cost of Sales)}}$ %

Direct Product Cost:

Product Unit Cost

Additional Product Unit Costs (accessories, option, etc.)

B) Total Direct Product Cost $

C) Initial Markup = (A x B) $

D) Product Price (B + C) $

Pricing Worksheet #2 – Service Quote (Contract Bid)

Materials Cost:

Description of Materials (list materials):

_____

_____

_____

_____

A) Total Materials Cost $

Direct Labor Cost:

Hourly Wages (per hour)

Fringe Benefits (30% of wage)

Total Cost per Hour

# of Hours

Other Labor Costs (specify) _____

B) Total Direct Labor Cost $

C) Overhead Cost [(yearly overhead/yearly total direct labor cost) x B] $

D) Total Direct Costs (A + B + C) $

Profit:

Profit on Materials (____%)

Profit on Labor (____%)

Profit on Overhead (____%)

E) Total Profit $

F) Other Charges $

G) Sales Tax $

H) Total Charge to Customer (D + E + F + G) $

NOTE When submitting a service quote to your customers, "Overhead Costs" and "Fringe Benefits" are factored into "Labor." Profit percentages are factored into "Materials" and "Labor" (see example on page 129).

SERVICE QUOTE

Company

Date: [ ]

Materials

Description of Materials (list materials):

_____

_____

_____

_____

A) Total Materials Charges $ [ ]

Labor

Cost per Hour

# of Hours

Other Labor Costs (specify)

_____

B) Total Labor Charges $ [ ]

Other Charges (specify)

_____

C) Total Other Charges $ [ ]

D) Sales Tax $ [ ]

E) Total Charge to Customer (A + B + C + D) $ [ ]

Notes:

_____

_____

_____

_____

The above quote is valid until **Date:** [ ]

THANK YOU for Considering our Services

Pricing Worksheet #3 – Manufacturing a Product

Direct Material Costs

Raw Material or Component Part	Description	Supplier	Landed Cost	x #/or Quantity Required Per Unit	= Cost / Unit Produced
			$		$

A) Total Direct Material Costs per Unit .... $

Direct Labor Costs

Assembly or Manufacturing Process	Estimated Labor Time Per Unit	x Hourly Rate	= Labor Cost Per Unit
		$	$

B) Total Direct Labor Costs per Unit $

C) Total Direct Manufacturing Cost per Unit (A + B) $

D) Total Estimated Packaging and Shipping Cost per Unit $

E) Total Direct Cost per Unit (C + D) $

F) Fixed Cost per Unit (Yearly Overhead/# of Units per Year) $

G) Other Variable Costs per Unit (Other V.C. /# of Units per Year) $

H) Profit per Unit [Profit Margin % x (E + F + G)] $

I) Final Product Price per Unit (E + F + G + H) $

Choosing a Price Marketing Strategy

Every industry has a favorite pricing strategy. Research your market to determine what the industry pattern is and use it as a guide. Listed on the next page are some of the most common pricing strategies.

Summarize your pricing strategy:

Check pricing strategies which reflect the objectives of your pricing policy:

❏ **Breakeven Pricing** – In breakeven pricing, you base your prices on your fixed & variable costs as well as your profit goals. The cost of merchandise (your BE point) will be at one end of your price range, while the level above which consumer will not buy your product or service will be at the other end. Much has been written on breakeven analysis as a means of determining prices. Be warned that sometimes it just doesn't work.

❏ **Buying a Market Position Pricing** – Using this form of pricing, you attempt to buy your way into the market by initially offering free samples or "heavy" discount coupons, for example 50 cents off a 99-cent purchase. This pricing strategy is usually reserved for big companies selling repeat goods and having ample cash reserves. It usually takes six months or more before this strategy starts to pay off.

❏ **Competitive Advantage Pricing** – In competitive advantage pricing, your prices are set equal to, above or below those of your competition. This strategy requires you to constantly shop your competition. A variation of this is the "we-won't-be-undersold" approach where you offer to meet or beat the prices of all your competitors.

❏ **Discount Pricing** – In discount pricing, a retail outlet offers lower prices as a trade-off for sparsely decorated interiors and fewer sales personnel. Discount stores depend on greater volume to cover operating costs. They typically work on a 35 to 38 % markup compared to 42.5 to 45 % for a department sore.

❏ **Full-cost Pricing** – In full-cost pricing, prices are calculated by adding the costs of the product or service plus a flat fee or percentage as the margin of profit. This pricing method is easy to implement.

❏ **Keystone Pricing** – Keystone pricing refers to the practice of setting the retail price at double the cost figure, or a 100 percent markup. This pricing strategy is most common with jewelry shops, high-ticket fashion shops, specialty shops, and department stores.

❏ **Loss Leader Pricing** – Loss leaders are items sold at a lower price to attract people into your store to buy other regularly priced items. A good loss leader will have a lower wholesale price than other items, look more expensive, sell at other stores at a higher price, be readily available from your suppliers, and/or be a recognized brand or item purchased frequently enough that customers recognize the savings. Loss leaders are more effective if closely associated with other items sold at the regular price.

❏ **Matching the Competition Pricing** – Using this pricing strategy, you match the prices of other businesses selling comparable products or services.

❏ **Multiple Unit Pricing** – Multiple pricing is the practice of promoting a number of units for a single price. The idea behind it is that you can increase the size of your individual sales by offering a meaningful discount for larger purchases. Example of multiple unit pricing include: ◆ bulk pricing in effect ◆ buy by the truckload ◆ buy three tires –get the fourth free ◆ buy twelve – get one free ◆ cheaper by the carton ◆ six-packs ◆ two for $1.98.

❏ **Odd Pricing** – With odd pricing you use prices that end in 5, 7 or 9 such as $2.99, $4.97, $15.95 or $69. For psychological reasons, consumers tend to round down $ figures e.g., they round $8.95 to $8 rather than up to $9.

❏ **Penetration Pricing** – In penetration pricing, you introduce your product at a substantially lower price than the competition to gain a share of the market. The purpose of this strategy is to create customer excitement and demand to help establish a strong customer base and discourage competition. However, eventually you will have to raise your prices to start making some profit, and when you do, you will learn a lot about customer loyalty.

❏ **Pre-season Pricing** – Often used by manufacturers, pre-season pricing is a strategy whereby price discounts are offered as incentives to buy early. This strategy is important to manufacturers because it is advantageous for them to be able to project production requirements and order the right amount of raw materials. This pricing strategy can also be used by retailers to even out demand and cash flow.

❏ **Price-is-no-object Pricing** – Using this pricing strategy you charge high prices to create an image of exclusivity and cater only to the cream of society (anybody with money). This strategy will only work if your product or service is: ◆ innovative ◆ in demand ◆ threatened by little or no competition ◆ within a market where price is less important than quality, service or image (i.e., Hollywood).

❏ **Price Lining** – Price lining refers to a marketing strategy where you carry products only in a specific price range e.g., a hardware store may carry hammers in good, better and best categories at $4.97, $7.97 and $9.97 and a professional model at $18.95. The theory behind this pricing strategy is that people buy products with different expectations for quality and length of useful life. This strategy also helps you meet the needs of customers who are looking a product at the price they can afford. Advantages of price lining include: ◆ ease of merchandise selection ◆ simplified buying and inventory control. One disadvantage is that by focusing too much on price, you may overlook issues of quality or consumer buying trends. It also limits your ability to meet competitor's prices.

❏ **Price Skimming** – Price skimming refers to the practice of charging high prices for the purpose of maximizing profit in the short run. It works best when: ◆ the product is unique ◆ the product targets trendsetters who are easily bored and always looking for something new ◆ you have a strong patent position. The real disadvantage of skimming is that is attracts competition like flies to horse manure. Once your competitors get wind of your profits, they will copy your product and produce "knockoffs."

❏ **Pricing Above Competitors** – Pricing above the competition is possible when non-price consideration are more important to buyers, such as: ◆ convenient or exclusive location ◆ exclusive brand or designer names ◆ free delivery ◆ helpful sales staff ◆ in-home demonstrations ◆ superior product knowledge etc.

❏ **Pricing Below Competition** – Using this pricing strategy, you beat your competitor's price. Because this strategy reduces your profit margins, it can only be effective if it greatly increases sales.

❏ **Suggested Retail Pricing** – Suggested retail pricing is the practice of selling at prices set by wholesalers & manufacturers. The advantage of this pricing strategy is that it simplifies the decision-making process and the trouble of monitoring the competition. It is also convenient because many product lines are already prepackaged and pre-priced.

Fine Tuning Your Pricing Policy

No pricing policy is complete without a few strategies to help consolidate your competitive position. Use the following strategies to expand and improve upon your basic pricing policy:

Outline any strategies you will use to fine-tune your pricing policy:

❑ **Consider allowing trade-ins as part of any purchases.** A trade-in policy is usually important for businesses that sell appliances, televisions, autos and even musical instruments. The trade-in value is almost always below what the customers could receive if they decided to sell the item themselves.

❑ **Do not lower prices without a good reason.** Dropping prices without an explanation usually means you were unable to compete at the higher price. It does not mean you are giving your buyer a bargain. Consumers catch on quickly to this and may avoid your product or service entirely being suspicious of your reasons for discounting. For example, selling books at a discount suggests that the information in them is not worth any price.

❑ **Establish a markdown policy.** A markdown is a reduction in the price of any item. Markdowns are necessary when customer demand is miscalculated, seasonal merchandise is overstocked, merchandise becomes shopworn, personal sales efforts failed, promotion, and advertising efforts failed, or the competition lowered their prices. Markdowns are used to avoid being left with old merchandise that is difficult o sell. If properly timed, markdowns can clear out merchandise quickly, thereby increasing cash flow and reducing inventory. In setting a markdown price, the original cost of the merchandise should be recovered if possible. If the original selling price was high enough, a small profit is possible. The markdown price is obtained by subtracting the dollar markdown from the previous retail price. Markdowns are generally taken early in the selling season or shortly after sales slow down.

❑ **Give discounts to distributors or customers who make large orders.** Encourage large orders with bargain bulk purchases. Discounts to distribution channels (brokers, wholesaler &retailers) may also be needed to get your products distributed to your markets.

❑ **Give discounts for early or prompt payments from credit customers.** Discounts to credit customers can improve collection rates and reduce your average accounts receivable collection period, thereby improving cash flow. Discounts are usually stated on invoices and sales orders as shown below.

❑ **Increase prices when budget projections warrant it.** Random price increases can drive away business and destroy goodwill. However, when your budget projections warrant, it is essential to make increases. Waiting too long to increase prices can destroy your business.

❑ **Issue rain checks for out of stock items.** Rain checks should be given to consumers who come in your store to buy advertised merchandise recently sold out. Not only does this improve customer relations but in some situations is required by law. Consult your lawyer or the regional Federal Trade Commission office for specific advice regarding whether rain checks are needed during advertised sales and under what circumstances.

❑ **Offer a rebate.** If you manufacture goods, overestimate demand, and hence have more goods than you can reasonably sell at present prices, consider offering a manufacturer's rebate to encourage sales. Rebates can also be used to discourage the competition from getting a foothold in the marketplace.

❑ **Re-price all in-stock quantities when your cost of a regularly stocked item goes up or down.** When this is not being done, it is usually an indication that good general business practices are not being followed.

❑ **Split an expensive price into three or four easy payments.** This is a favorite strategy among TV direct and mail order sellers as it creates the illusions of a cheaper price and allows customers to spread out their payments. A product with a list price of $59.85 can be split into 3 payments of $19.95 plus shipping, handling and taxes.

Promotion-Mixes

Wholesaler

| 25% advertising |
| 50% personal selling |
| 25% sales promotion |

Sock Manufacturer

| 33% advertising |
| 33% personal selling |
| 33% sales promotion |

Catering Service

| 75% advertising, referrals & publicity |
| 20% personal selling |
| 5% sales promotion |

Sports Shop

| 15% advertising |
| 45% personal selling |
| 35% sales promotion |

DAY 22

Promotion Plan

A *Promotion Plan* covers all phases of communication between you and your potential customers. It addresses advertising, personal selling, and sales promotion. It details, for example, how you plan to coordinate a billboard promotion to draw attention to your new spring catalog. A promotion plan is needed to: ◆ acquaint customers with new products ◆ capitalize on the seasonal nature of a product ◆ change or establish a company image ◆ emphasize quality ◆ increase store traffic ◆ inform customers of special services such as delivery or credit extension ◆ introduce new employees to the public ◆ keep your business name and location before the public ◆ promote consumer awareness of your business ◆ promote special events such as a clearance sale or grand opening ◆ stimulate sales ◆ tie in with a supplier's national promotions.

The Three Basic Components of a Promotion Plan

Although proportions vary depending on the nature of a business, there are 3 basic components of a promotion plan:

- **Advertising** – Includes newspaper, magazine, radio, television, billboard, direct mail, flyer, poster, newsletter, and directory (Yellow Pages) advertising.

- **Personal Selling** – For retail firms, personal selling begins once a shopper enters the store. For service, manufacturing and wholesale firms, customers have to be found. Prospecting outside your company in necessary.

- **Sales Promotion** – Sales promotion is a composite of activities that round out the advertising and personal selling components of your promotion plan. The primary aim of sales promotion is to assist wholesalers and retailers in moving products. Sales promotion aides include catalogs, reprints of ads, special displays, display fixtures, and banners and signs. Sales promotion activities include attending tradeshows and doing demonstrations. **Publicity** is closely linked to advertising and sales promotion, but should be considered a separate forth component (see page 139-142).

When developing your promotion plan, think in terms of blending the above 3 basic ingredients of advertising, personal selling and sales promotion, much like mixing a cocktail (refer to chart). This is called your *promotional mix.*

Outline the essential components of your promotional plan. What is your promotional mix?

	Advertising	%
	Personal selling	%
	Sales promotion	%

Selecting the Right Ad Media

Before choosing which advertising media meets your marketing needs, keep in mind that nowadays, consumers are far more sophisticated and harder to reach than ever before. They seem to have built in advertising radar and can quickly tune out *bad* advertising quicker than you can lick a stamp. You are faced with the unenviable task of becoming increasingly bold without being intrusive, irritating, or worst of all, boring. You must become more informative, innovative, and responsive to consumers needs and desires, yet at the same time, stick to your budget. Consider the following 4 strategies:

STRATEGY 1 – Choose a variety of media. Find out what types of media your target market is most often exposed to. Use common sense, practical experience and market research. Don't concentrate on one specific source.

STRATEGY 2 – Collect as much data as you can on each medium. Research and compare the following for each medium: (a) cost (b) circulation (c) resulting cost per thousand expressed as cost per M (d) error rating for the cost per M either low, medium, or high (e) market penetration.

STRATEGY 3 – Examine media from the standpoint of: ❏ *Audience* (the coverage each enjoys) – You need to know that an audience does indeed exist as well as their size and location. ❏ *Acceptance* (the impact of the medium on the audience) – The medium must be accepted in the marketplace not only by the target audience but also by potential new customers and your competitor's customers. ❏ *Frequency of Exposure* (the ability to expand its impact by being available more than once or twice in a particular time frame) – Advertising should reach potential buyers regularly, even daily. Media with a once-a-year or even once-a-month frequency deserves nothing more than a very small part of your budget.

STRATEGY 4 – Stick to your budget. Most businesses set aside anywhere between 10 to 25% of their operating budget on promotion and advertising (this amounts to 2 to 5% of projected sales revenues for retail establishments). Established word-of-mouth service businesses spend less, while mail order companies, direct-marketing companies, perfume companies, record companies, and beverage companies like Pepsi™ and Coca Cola™, spend more.

Summarizing the three the most important media in your advertising plan. Describe expected cost and impact, any unique promotional activities no one else is doing, and how your advertising will be tailored to your target market (refer to charts on the following two pages):

Outline any requirements for product/service brochures and similar descriptive material indicating expected development & production costs:

Describe other details regarding your promotional plan:

- ❑ how you are going to use publicity to reach various target markets
- ❑ whether you will use cooperative advertising
- ❑ whether commissioned sales staff, agents, pieceworkers, or independent contractors will be used
- ❑ any personal selling efforts and sales training programs you will implement

- ❑ plans you have for in-store sales promotion tools and window displays
- ❑ how you plan to measure the effectiveness of each advertising medium (include rate sheets and time lines on a first years' promotion calendar)
- ❑ what your yearly advertising budget will be
- ❑ where exactly the bulk of your advertising $ will go

Promotional Media

Media	Audience	Business	Advantages	Disadvantages
Daily Newspapers	Individual communities with some over flow.	All general retail and service industries.	Flexible timing. Reaches a large audience.	Can't pinpoint markets. Often cluttered. Short life.
Weekly Newspapers	Usually smaller community and neighborhoods.	Retailers and services located within the community.	Good local coverage.	Must be used regularly and be well timed for good results.
Magazines	Business-to-business, consumer, national, regional, special interest.	Serves known target markets. Retail, service.	Long life, shared. Aimed at special interest groups.	Long lead-time in preparation.
Radio	Usually community and area depending on size of station.	Retail & service companies. Caters to target groups: teenagers, commuters, and homemakers.	Reaches a wide market. Good for pinpointing target markets.	Somewhat limited audience.
Television National/local	Numbers vary with time of day and nature of the show.	Products, services and retail outlets with a wide appeal.	Creative and persuasive. Large market audience, can target groups i.e. children.	Short exposure. Commonly used. Most expensive.
Cable Community Channels	Varied specific interest groups.	Small retail & service businesses with cable coverage area.	Locally oriented vents and programs not covered by traditional media.	Limited audience. No statistics on viewers to measure results.
Telephone Directories & Yellow Pages	Special consumer groups, businesses.	Services, highly specialized retailers.	Low costs, long life, users are often potential buyers.	Restricted to active shoppers. Ad limited in size and content.
Billboards & Outdoor Advertising	General, drivers, passengers, pedestrians.	Adaptable to many products, services & businesses.	Flexible, repeat exposure. Builds a good corporate image.	Message must be short.
Direct mail	Advertiser's choice. Business to business, household consumer.	General services, retailers, wholesale, manufacturers.	Can be personalized. Flexible timing. Good targeting.	High disposal rate.
Printed Promotional Materials	Transit passengers, pedestrians and drivers.	Adaptable to many products, services & businesses.	Highly visible. Captive audience.	Exterior: short exposure.
Promotional Displays	Pedestrians and retail customers.	Retailers, service business owners	Helps promote impulse buying.	Requires constant restocking & upkeep.
Specialty Advertising	All kinds of customers and clients.	Retailers, service business owners, consultants.	Builds good will, fun, inexpensive.	Freebee sometimes taken for granted.

*Select from the following "**Bread'n Butter Advertising Media**":*

❑ **Business Cards** – Low cost; easily distributed; describes product or service; gives address and phone.	❑ **Local Radio** – Expensive but reaches targeted audience; advertisement can be repeated frequently.
❑ **Business Signs** – Very effective; low cost; may be subject to zoning regulations.	❑ **Shopping Bags** – Carry name and message into home.
❑ **Business Stationery** – Low cost; must be well designed.	❑ **Storefront** – Extremely effective; low cost; shows product and price.
❑ **Direct mail** – Most personalized and pinpointed of all media; tells complete story; rapid feedback; can use coupons, catalogs, letters, brochures or postcards.	❑ **Telephone Solicitation** – Low cost; effective if message is worded carefully.
❑ **Interior or POP Displays** – Attractive display of merchandise creates impulse buying; low cost.	❑ **Television** – Most expensive; reaches the masses; high visibility; instant exposure of pictures or ideas.
❑ **Local Newspapers** – Great flexibility; ad size and position can be varied; great with editorial association, such as food advertisements with cooking column.	❑ **Vehicles** – Can be effective; low cost; wide exposure.
	❑ **Yellow Pages** – Essential for small business; reaches customer who is ready to buy; wide distribution.

Preparing a Promotional Budget

A *promotional budget* attempts to answer: How much should I spend? When should I spend it? Where should I spend it? What should I spend it on? It includes, in addition to the costs of advertising, the costs of in-store displays, samples, specialty advertising, giveaways and other non-traditional media efforts (sales goals in dollars, units, or both are the basis for promotional budgets). Because promotional costs can originate from several sources, it is often a good idea to prepare one master budget broken down into several separate budgets. This way it is easier to closely monitor actual costs and results. Each product or service may also need its own promotional strategy as part of your total marketing plan.

> *You can fool all the people all of the time if the advertising is right and the budget is big enough.*
> **JOSEPH E. LEVINE**

Advertising Budget

The major portion of a firm's promotional budget is advertising. Budgeting money for advertising encourages consistent promotional efforts and prevents cash flow problems caused by sporadic and unexpected advertising endeavors. Dependable advertising channels include the Yellow Pages, DM, flyers, newspaper ads, radio ads, and business cards.

How much should you spend? In general, new retail and manufacturing businesses should be prepared to spend about 5% of projected gross revenues on advertising. An established business should budget 2 to 3%. Service businesses should budget more. In promotional budgeting, two approaches can be used:

> *Depending on the type of business you run, between 10 to 25% of your operating budget should be pumped back into your business in the form of advertising.*

- *The number of dollars considered necessary to successfully promote the sale of a given item or service at a given price will go toward advertising.* E.g., $10 of the $300 selling price for each refrigerator sold will go to advertising so that $3,000 in advertising should sell 300 units and produce $90,000 in sales.

- *A flat percentage of every anticipated revenue dollar will go toward advertising.* E.g., 3 % of an estimated $100,000 in annual sales will result in an advertising budget of $3,000.

Retail businesses prefer the second approach because it allocates advertising costs for all product lines i.e., all merchandise contributes to the cost of advertising. More than 50% of the items carried by most stores are never advertised. Their sale is the direct result of customer traffic created by other advertised items.

Comparing Your Advertising Budget with Other Companies – Check your budget allocations with those of other similar businesses. Trade associations and other organizations often gather data on advertising expenses and publish it as an *operating ratio* (expenses as a percentage of sales). If your estimated cost for advertising is substantially higher than average, take a second look. No single expense item should be allowed to get way out of line if you want to make a profit.

Check any of the following special budgeting considerations that are applicable to your business:

❑ The newer your store, the more advertising is required to make it known.

❑ If your store is in a poor location, advertising is required to attract people to go out of their way to shop there.

❑ If your store is selling highly promotional merchandise, you must spend more on advertising.

❑ In order for you to keep your share of the market, expenditures must bear some relationship to what competitors are spending. Aggressive competition usually requires aggressive advertising.

❑ If you are operating in a large community you will likely have to spend more on advertising than a merchant in a small community.

❑ Sales days, special promotional events and holidays important to your business require greater expenditures for advertising to make the event known.

❑ Funds from suppliers for media purchase and an availability of prepared ads or commercials through co-operative advertising may allow you to expand your advertising program.

Select a method for determining how much money to budget for advertising and promotions (since the cost of adverting must be paid from sales revenue, it should be expressed as a function of expected sales dollars). Detail other budget considerations. Describe how you arrived at your advertising budget and any special considerations that affected your decision:

❑ Dollar amount will vary according to individual items. ❑ Flat percentage of every anticipated revenue dollar. ❑ Other

Advertising Budget	
As a % of total sales	%
Industry %	%
Budget in $	$

Preparing an Advertising Budget

	Plan				**Allocation**					
Year	Total Sales in % per month	Projected Sales in $ per month	Ad Budget in % of Total Sales / month	Advertising Budget in $ per month	Media 1 ___% of total	Media 2 ___% of total	Media 3 ___% of total	Media 4 ___% of total	Media 5 ___% of total	Reserve Fund (10%)
JAN										
FEB										
MAR										
APR										
MAY										
JUN										
JUL										
AUG										
SEP										
OCT										
NOV										
DEC										
TOTAL	100%									

Media	Audience Size	Schedule	Frequency of Use	x	Cost of a Single Occasion	=	Estimated Cost
					$		$
					$		$
					$		$
					$		$
				Total Estimated Cost			$

Indicate the trade shows you plan to attend to exhibit your product or service (of particular importance to manufacturing firms):

Trade Show	Location	Timing	Estimated Cost
			$
		Total Estimated Cost	$

Describe any repair, informational, support, or value-added services you plan to provide and their anticipated costs:

Service	Estimated Cost
	$
	$
	$

Describe any other sales promotion activity:

Choosing an Advertising Design Theme

Advertising always works better if designed around a central focus or theme. For example, an *Advertorial or News Ad* is a type of ad that announces a new product, something new about an existing product, or states a position on a social, business, or consumer issue. Statements are backed with engaging evidence, an analysis, and most importantly, a product solution. Typically, this type of ad uses a newspaper type headline and a newspaper editorial format. This ad format is especially useful in reaching a segment of the population that shares attitudes or ideologies similar to your own (see online GB 📖 #55 for 52 ad design themes).

Describe suitable themes for your advertising promotions:

> *There are a million definitions of public relations. I have found it to be the craft of arranging the truth so that people will like you.*
> **ALAN HARRINGTON**

Publicity Plan

Publicity is news about you, your product or your service that appears in a public medium. *Publicists* are people you hire to attempt to control, manipulate, or use to your advantage, public media coverage.

Writing a NEWS RELEASE

The most important form of publicity a small business operator can generate is by writing a *news release*, also called a *press release* or *media release*. A news release can be used to generate positive publicity, inform the world of new products, or update everyone on important newsworthy events regarding your company. A video can accompany a news release targeted towards TV broadcasting stations. Outlined below are the major parts of a news release:

- ❑ **Title of News Release** – If there is to be a title, and titles are entirely optional, it should come between the address block and the body of the release, flush left. Typically, the title does not extend beyond the address block by more than a few characters, which usually means that it will be stacked (broken into two lines on top of each other). The title should be in all caps, single-spaced, with the last line underlined (a subtitle below the title is also optional).

- ❑ **"Release Date" Block** – When submitting a news release, provide the editor with exact information concerning the appropriate timing for the release (release dates and times). This information should appear below the title, flush right.

- ❑ **Releases with no Specific Time Frame** – By far the most common type of release. Usually designated by, "For Immediate Release."

- ❑ **Releases with Specific Date** – An example would be, "For Release January 23 or Thereafter."

- ❑ **Identifying Block** – The identifying block is placed below the address block, title and release date block. It should include the date the news release was sent, name of the contact person (usually the person who wrote the release), and a phone #. It is especially important to include nighttime as well as a daytime number. Newspapers don't shut down at night and if an editor needs further or clarifying information and can't reach you, the release may get dumped.

- ❑ **Body Copy Format** – The body of the release begins about one-third of the way down the page allowing some white space for comments, or notes from the editor. The body of the news release is double-spaced – never single-space a news release. Paragraphs are usually indented with normal spacing between graphs. Often the city of origin of the news release begins the copy (some companies prefer no indention and triple-spacing between paragraphs, but the standard is indented).

- ❑ **Releases More than Two Pages** – If the release runs more than a page, the word "more" is placed in brackets or within dashes at the bottom of the page. Following pages are identified by a slug-line followed by several dashes and the page number at the top of the page, usually either flush left or right.

- ❑ **End of Release** – The end of the release is designated in one of several ways: use the word "end," the number "30" either in quotation marks or within dashes, or the symbol #####.

- ❑ **Photos** – Photos should be glossy, black and white, and 8 by 10 inches. Color is better, but expensive. To save money, take both color and black and white, then mail out the black and white and write color photos available upon request at the end of the release.

Describe any special news release strategies you have:

Describe any additional plans to obtain free publicity:

A media kit, which can be sent to newspapers and magazines, sometimes accompanies a news release. Check which items you will include:

MEDIA KIT

- ❑ backgrounder (additional facts & information about product)
- ❑ biography (or biographies) and accompanying photos of key personnel in you company
- ❑ cover letter explaining what the kit is about
- ❑ feature story or sidebar, if appropriate to the subject matter
- ❑ T of C or list of what is in the kit
- ❑ brochures of product and its uses
- ❑ annual reports

- ❑ basic facts sheet outlining the participants at the press conference
- ❑ clipsheet of illustrations, company logos and illustrations that can be used by the advertising medium
- ❑ color product photos (with captions)
- ❑ color photos of other products made from the manufactured material (with captions)
- ❑ company magazines or newsletter
- ❑ cover letter for TV stations
- ❑ hard copy of the product presentation speeches

- ❑ in-house magazine article tear sheets on the product
- ❑ magazine ad folder with sample return order card
- ❑ press release describing another application of the material
- ❑ press release on new materials being developed
- ❑ press release on the product's content (the material used to manufacture the product)
- ❑ radio and TV scripts
- ❑ storyboard for TV spot

Study the following sample of a news release:

Company Name & Address
Telephone Number

NEWS RELEASE

Date: *Jan 12, 1998*   Contact: *Your Name*
                              Days: *Phone*
For Immediate Release   Evening: *Phone*

"New Technology Saves Water in Seconds"

Now every homeowner can save gallons of water, every time they use Cromdale's new shower adapter, the Water Miser.

The Water Miser takes only seconds to install and saves gallons of water every time you take a shower.

The portable adapter is about the size of a small grapefruit and fits easily over any standard showerhead, with little fuss and no tools, using a new patented leakproof technology.

"You can take it to a friends house," says Walter Cromdale, president of Cromdale Innovations. "It's that fast and easy. Plus, turn up the hot water, vary the flow to a fine mist, and PRESTO!" he adds. "You have a steam bath."

Priced at $19.95, the Water Miser is available at hardware stores coast to coast. For further information, phone Cromdale Innovations at (555) 555-5555.

-end-

Company Name & Address
Telephone Number

COVER LETTER

Date: *Jan 12, 1998*

Dear Member of the Media:

Cromdale Innovations of Vancouver, British Columbia, has recently introduced a brand new product, Cromdale's Water Miser Showerhead, which allows any homeowner to save gallons of water while taking a shower.

Until now, these types of adapters required tedious installation procedures. But now, with the Water Miser, even a child can complete installation in less than 10 seconds.

Because I am convinced that consumers will want to know more about this convenient new device, I am sending you a packet of information and a free sample.

Please call me if you have any questions or if I can be of any help.

Sincerely,

Walter Cromdale

Walter Cromdale
President

Writing a News Release Summary

(Use Letterhead: which includes company name, address, phone, email and URL)

NEWS RELEASE

Date: 12/27/98

For Immediate Release . . .

Contact: Your Name; Company Name; (404) 555-5555; Email; URL

Headline

Type a descriptive, clever and catchy headline in capital letters and center it. Lure the editor to read more. Then space down four lines and get into the body of the release.

Issue or problem

The lead paragraph is designed to invite the largest number of people to read the article. It must have broad appeal; make it interesting. The release should be ***issue oriented***; write about the ***problem***, not the product or service. The release should begin by stating the problem and telling why this is an important subject. Make it provocative.

Development

Write a second paragraph to develop the message. Put the most interesting information first to keep the reader reading. Recite the most important items in descending order so that if some are cut from the end, the most important will remain. Provide interesting facts and statistics.

How the product or service solves a problem

Now move from a ***what*** orientation to a ***how*** orientation. Tell how your product or service solves a problem. Continue with some background on your product or service and show why it is unique, useful and timely. Recite benefits. Describe key features. Don't use fluffy language to try and promote your product or service. Editors won't like it. Don't sell. Inform! Keep in mind that anyone who has read this far will be interested.

Company information

Write a paragraph about your company. Outline its history. Describe important events.

Ordering information

Include the price of your product or service and mention where it is available and in which stores. List your address so readers will know where to send inquiries. Code your address so you can keep track of inquiries.

End the release with the newspaper termination sign: -30-

News Release Worksheet

Company Name, Address, Phone, URL and Email

NEWS RELEASE

Date:

For Immediate Release . . .

Contact: Company: Phone :   Email:

Headline

Lead Paragraph (Attract Readers – *State Problem*):

Development (Explain the *What*):

How the Product/Service Solves the Problem (Explain the *How*):

Company Information (*History & Interesting Facts*):

Ordering Information (Include *Address & Price*):

*Packaging is a
competitive tool to
help influence your
customer's buying
decisions. It helps
make your product
stand out from
others and acts as
a silent sales-
person to all those
who pass by.*
BUSINESS TIP

*Your product
should have a Uni-
versal Product
Code (UPC)
printed on its pack-
age. The UPC
symbol is about
1.5 inches long
and consists of 30
vertical dark lines
with 29 spaces
and a 10 digit se-
ries of numbers.
The first 5 num-
bers designate the
manufacturer; the
second 5 identify
the product and
package size.*
FUNFACT

DAY 23

Packaging Concept

Successful packaging is the result of feedback and input from marketing managers, salespeople, manufacturing reps, distributors, graphic and product designers, and customers. In developing your *packaging concept*, explain how your packaging better positions your product in the minds of your target customers. Show how you have considered their tastes. Talk about its size, shape, color, material, wording, and how your packaging meets or exceeds FDA and FTC regulations.

7 Steps to Designing the "Perfect Package"

Putting a widget in a box, covering the box with a few pictures and labels, and calling it *packaging,* is DANGEROUS. Packaging is more than that. Packaging has protective, distributive, and promotional functions. It makes products convenient to use, safe to use, and easy to ship. It also performs an integral role in all advertising and marketing efforts, and more than any other single factor is responsible for creating a company's image. In fact, some people prefer to think of packaging as an exact science. Consider the following 7 steps to package design:

STEP 1 – **Gather information.** To create a package that is unique, aesthetically pleasing, and meets the needs of your company, consumers, and distributors, shop the competition, and gather as much information as you can. In-store research can be useful, along with information gleaned from books, periodicals, and brochures.

STEP 2 – **Develop a preliminary concept.** Make at least 10 to 25 sketches. Indicate typestyles and logos. Make sure sketches are neat and clear and keep them in your portfolio for future reference and for use as presentation material.

STEP 3 – **Prepare a "comprehensive."** Plan the structural design of the package, taking into account potential production and manufacturing problems. Its size and shape should make it easy for employees, distributors, and customers to handle it. The construction material used must protect its contents during shipping.

STEP 4 – **Design a box cover.** Use markers to prepare a layout showing what you want the final box cover to look like. Construct a mock-up of this layout and take a Polaroid of it. Do several variations if needed. When satisfied, have a pre-production meeting with your photographer. At this meeting: present your layout; describe your ideas about the set, lighting, mood, and the appearance of models (if required); and review your budget. Once the photo shoot is under way, let the photographer shoot as many rolls of film as needed to cover every possible situation and angle. After processing the film and choosing the best results, scan the photos into a computer. Here, words, logos and other information can be added, as well as images retouched and imperfections removed.

STEP 5 – **Construct a prototype.** Build a prototype or mock-up as close as possible to the final design. Use the prototype to further test the viability of the design.

STEP 6 – **Test the prototype.** Test the package from an engineering, visual, dealer, consumer, and cost effective point of view. If the packaging is not durable enough, appealing enough to attract customers, or too expensive, make the necessary changes to improve it or scrap it entirely and start all over again.

STEP 7 – **Prepare a production mechanical.** A production mechanical incorporates all final art, photographs, illustrations and type onto one sheet, which will later be attached to the cardboard, glass or plastic container.

Describe the key factors that have influenced your package design. Check factors that apply below:

❑ **Art & Beauty Needs** – Beauty of package design is essential. People buy what they like the looks of.

❑ **Budget** – For most products, packaging should not add more that 5% to the total cost of your product.

❑ **Company Needs** – You must connect your company to the buying public or market in a way that attracts customers and keeps them coming back.

❑ **Competitive Pressures** – 75% of all goods purchased by consumers in the United States are distributed in packages, all of them vying for consumer attention. How will your package stand out?

❑ **Consumer Needs** – Package design is molded by the needs, preferences, tastes, purchasing power and buying habits of your consumers.

❑ **Distribution & Shipping needs** – Design packages so they can fit on top of each other to allow for more compact shipping. Design packaging to be as light as possible to reduce shipping costs. This is especially necessary if the product is to be mailed.

❑ **Environmental Concerns** – More than 20 million tons of plastic a year is produced in the U.S. alone. The cubic volume of plastics has surpassed that of steel, copper and aluminum combined. All the plastic material currently in use will take up to five centuries to degrade. With this in mind, it is no wonder that more and more companies are seriously looking at how their packaging is disposed, whether it's biodegradable, reusable or environmentally green. They also debate about whether they should use recycled paper or switch to biodegradable protective filler (like popcorn) instead of using environmentally hazardous Styrofoam chips.

❑ **Future Trends in Marketing** – Consider new production and distribution techniques, as well as, new marketing techniques and procedures.

❑ **Government Regulations** – Packaging attracts a great deal of government attention. Regulatory agencies such as the Food and Drug Administration (FDA), have strict procedures for the labeling of items falling within its jurisdiction. The Federal Trade Commission (FTC) through its *Fair Packaging and Labeling Act*, also regularly enforce strict safety and strength standards on all packaging. In Canada, consider: The *Food and Drug Act, Consumer Packaging and Labeling Act,* and the *Hazardous Product Act*.

❑ **Industry Standards** – Government regulations and industry standards and are designed to protect users of a carton. There are laws pertaining to shipment method, such as rail, airfreight, truck and regular parcel post. Common tests involve subjecting packaging materials to drops, jolts, shock, and vibration.

❑ **Input from Professional Package Designers** – A package designer can help you with graphic and structural design concerns as well as package production, printing and the modeling process.

❑ **Labeling Requirements** – On your principle display panel (which should be more than 40% of the total front display area), include the product's name, manufacturer, and packer or distributor. The manufacturer's name and address, may appear anywhere on the package. Quantity statements, descriptions of contents and safety warnings must also appear somewhere within the lower 30% of the label, be parallel to the base of the package and be separated above and below from other printed matter. If multiple products are further packaged in a corrugated shipping box, this box must include a *Box Certificate* specifying weight, paper content, puncture and bursting test strength, and gross width.

❑ **Marketing Needs** – Package design must also be tied in effectively with newspaper, magazine and television advertising so that consumers can easily identify a product by its packaging.

❑ **Message Desired** – Packaging can deliver messages about your product, brand, product category, target market, or benefits offered by the product. It can also project uniqueness, create and image, and even send subliminal messages (e.g., color, shape, size and texture can be used to suggest luxury).

❑ **Packaging Equipment & Production Techniques** – What packaging and filling equipment do you have or have access to in your area?

❑ **Product Needs** – Size, weight, shape and fragility, are obvious design concerns. You wouldn't put perfume in a plastic container if you could afford glass, and you wouldn't shrink wrap expensive china.

❑ **Wholesaler & Retailer Needs** – Consider the needs of the people who will sell and distribute your products. You may need special promotional materials to complement your packaging design for supermarkets, department stores, boutiques and so on.

Sample Packaging Concept

The competitive advantage of *Bradley's Whole-wheat Mini-Buns* is that they are an all-natural product that appeals to the health-conscious. Because of their quality, customers must see the mini-buns through the package. Therefore, *Bradley's Whole-wheat Mini-Buns* will be boxed in clear material. The positioning statements, "For real bun eaters who know the difference" and "It's all natural" will appear on the face of the package. Across the left corner of the package will be a red slash that reads, "Keep the goodness. Keep us in the fridge."

Summarize your packaging concept. Explain how your packaging and product design will better position your product in the consumer's mind:

Describe product packaging requirements and estimated costs for development and use:

Personal Selling Program

Putting together your own sales force is not recommended for businesses just starting out. It is better to use established intermediaries. It may be appropriate however, if you are planning to create a network marketing (MLM) sales force.

Outline your personal selling program – the number and type of people in your sales force and how they will be paid:

Previous Marketing Methods

Describe marketing methods you and other companies have found effective in the past. What was the cost per customer or unit of sale? What percentage of your budget was allocated to this program?

Describe past marketing methods:

Services & Products Mix

If you plan to sell both products and services, each should complement each other to increase over all sales. For example, a beauty salon, in addition to providing hairstyling services, may also find it profitable to retail hair care products.

Describe how and which of your products and services will complement each other to increase over all sales:

Timing of Market Entry

A company can be started any time. However, the *act* of entering the marketplace (e.g., opening your doors or introducing new products) must be carefully timed. Having your products & services available at the right time is dependent upon industry conditions and the buying habits of potential customers. It should NOT be a decision based on your internal planning schedule. It must be *market driven*.

Tell when you plan to enter the market and how you arrived at this decision. Describe any special buying trends or patterns:

Warranty Policies

A *warranty* tells customers you will correct any problems arising within a specified time frame following the performance of a service or sale of a product at no charge. Warranties build trust and promote repeat business. A typical *service* warranty might be 30 days on parts and 90 days on labor.

Describe your product and service guarantee or warranty strategy:

Write your warranty policy:

> *Most business activities including advertising are dedicated to solving the firm's problems. Success, however, is more likely if you dedicate your activities exclusively to solving your customer's problems.*
> **SBA**

Marketing Approach

One final area of your *Marketing Plan* that deserves special attention is a summary description of your marketing approach. Your *Marketing Approach* describes how you ultimately plan to satisfy the needs of your target market by combining your marketing research, competitive analysis and marketing strategies. It acts like a mission statement for your marketing plan.

Comparing the "Old" Marketing Approach with the "New"

There are two specific ways in which the "old" classic, or "sales" approach to market planning differs from the "new" marketing approach:

First, in the "old" marketing approach, management tells designers and engineers to create a product, which once produced, is given to salespeople, who are then told to find customers to buy the product. In the "new" marketing approach, management *first* determines what customers really need or want then pass that information on to designers and engineers who develop and produce a suitable product. When sales staff are given the finished merchandise, they already have leads on potential customers. The "old" marketing approach *ends* with the customer, while the "new" marketing approach, *begins* and *ends* with the customer.

> *Under the "old" marketing approach the customer exists for the business, while under the "new" marketing approach, the business exists for the customer.*

The **second** major difference between the "old" marketing approach and the "new" is the *focus* of management. The "old" marketing approach focuses on *volume* and *sales* while the "new" marketing approach focuses on *profit*.

The two above distinctions can be simplified into two marketing approach rules of thumb. Your marketing approach should:

- **Focus on the *needs* of your customers, not products.** All company policies and activities should be aimed at satisfying customer needs.

- **Focus on making a *profit*, not increasing *sales volume*.** Profitable sales volume is a better company goal than maximum sales volume.

Getting the Most Out of Your Marketing Approach

To further develop your marketing approach: ◆ identify specific markets you now serve ◆ determine the needs and wants of your present customers ◆ determine what you are doing now to satisfy those needs and wants ◆ prepare a marketing plan to meet customer needs you are presently not meeting ◆ find out which advertising is the most effective at reaching old and new customers ◆ test to see if your new strategies are yielding results ◆ periodically analyze your firm's competitive advantage to find out what you do best ◆ capitalize on this strength.

Describe your marketing approach. Show how your company has been able to focus on needs & profits rather than products & sales volume:

Begin this section with a half or full-page summary addressing all the key areas of your financial plan.

DAY 24
FINANCIAL PLAN

- Capitalization Plan (Financial Needs)
- Uses of Funds Statement
- Pro Forma Statements
- Current Financial Statements
- Business Financial History
- Profit Planning
- Risk Assessment
- Closing Statement

IN THIS section, the fourth major section of your business plan, detail all aspects of your *Financial Plan*. Show your past, current, and projected financial needs. Prepare both pro forma (projected) and current financial statements. In this section, also provide a business financial history statement, outline a profit plan, assess the risks investors and lenders face, show how you plan to lessen those risks, and make closing statements to summarize your business plan.

List which financial documents you will include in this section (ones already checked must be included, others are optional):

☑ Capital Required (Start-up Costs)	☑ Pro forma Balance Sheet	❑ Deviation Analysis
❑ Uses of Funds Statement	☑ Pro forma Income Statement	❑ Market-value Balance Sheet
☑ Asset Sheet	☑ Breakeven Analysis	❑ Balance sheets and income statements for past 3 years
☑ Income Projection	☑ Cash Flow Projection	❑ Historical financial reports
-1st year detailed by months	- 1st year detailed by month	❑ Tax returns
-2nd and 3rd year detailed by 1/4s	- 2nd and 3rd year detailed 1/4s	
-Three-year Summary		

Capitalization Plan

A *Capitalization Plan* is used to summarize all your capital requirements and financial needs, whether you need a loan, investment capital or not. Specifically, it tells your potential lenders or investors how much money you're trying to raise, what collateral you offer, loan repayment schedules, and what percentage of the company they will own in return for their investment.

Summary of Financial Needs

This is a brief outline usually in the form of chart indicating why you are applying for a loan and how much you need. This summary should be used if you are applying for a loan and should be placed at the front of your capitalization plan.

Summarize capital requirements. If a loan is required, state amount needed, main reason you need the loan, and collateral offered:

Capital Required (Start-up Costs)

Describe your capital requirements by detailing your initial start-up costs and estimated monthly operating expenses. Describe cost of facilities, equipment, and materials. Include relevant estimates and quotes from contractors and suppliers

INITIAL STARTUP COSTS (estimated one-time financial requirements)

Item	Total Cost	Cash Needed	Balance	How Financed
Land	$	$	$	
Building				
Improvements (mechanical, electrical)				
Repairs & Remodeling (construction)				
Machinery & Equip. (include installation costs)				
Shop Tools & Supplies				
Fixtures & Equipment (shelves, wall brackets, tables, chairs, cabinets, etc.)				
Office Supplies (include stationary costs.)				
Vehicles (include cars, trucks, vans etc.)				
Opening Inventory (include any materials needed for the manufacturing of products)				
Utility Hookup & Installation Fees				
Licenses & Permits (include association & membership fees)				
Pre-opening Legal & Professional Fees				
Pre-opening Promotions & Advertising				
Security Deposits (advance money required for rent, utilities, telephones, leased equip.)				
Accounts Payable				

Cash reserve	$
OTHER Initial Start-Up Costs	$
Total Estimated Initial Start-Up Costs	$

NOTES – *Initial Start-Up Costs:*

❑ **Pre-opening Legal & Professional Fees** – Include money spent regarding incorporation, the writing up of partnership contracts, review of lease agreements or purchase contracts, and the setting up of an accounting system. ❑ **Pre-opening Promotion Costs** (include Yellow Pages listing, business cards, flyers, newspaper ads, catalogues, brochures, newsletters, signage and any other advertising costs)	❑ **Repairs, Remodeling & Decorating of Business Site** (include electrical rewiring, ventilation, air conditioning, partitioning, painting, carpeting, and other expenditures which improve the operating site but are not considered removable) ❑ **Other Initial Start-up Costs & Services** (include any miscellaneous pre-opening expenditures entered nowhere else, such as training of staff, travel to suppliers, logo design etc.)

ESTIMATED MONTHLY START-UP OPERATING EXPENSES for _____ *Months (it is recommended that you include at least three months of operating expenses in your start-up capital projections):*

Item	Estimate of Monthly Expense	x Number of Months* Before Breakeven (3)	= Total Cash Required
Fixed Operating Costs **Wages of Owner**	$		$
Employees' Salaries, Wages, & Benefits			
Rent or Lease Payments *(building)*			
Rent or Lease Payments *(computers or any other piece of leased or rented equipment)*			
Insurance *(include home owner's, fire, life, theft, personal, & product liability coverage)*			
Office Supplies & Postage *(include supplies used up and in need of replacing)*			
Operating Loan Payments *(include monthly payments on outstanding loans)*			
Membership Fees *(include association dues)*			
Phone			
Subscriptions *(to business periodicals)*			
Utilities *(include power, water, gas and installation and hookup charges)*			
Variable Operating Costs **Advertising & Promotions**			
Auto & Travel			
Building & Equipment Maintenance			
Interest			
Legal & Professional Fees			
Operating Inventory *(includes inventory purchases required to meet supply demands)*			
OTHER Supplies/Purchases *(include purchases planned once business is underway)*			
OTHER Monthly Operating Expenses			

Total Cash Required to Cover Monthly Operating Expenses	$
Plus: total Initial Start-Up Costs (from Previous table)	$
Total Cash Required for Start-Up	$
Recommended Start-up Capital Required (add 25%)	$

NOTES – *Estimated Monthly Start-Up Operating Expenses:*

❑ **Recommended Start-up Capital Required (add 25%)** Start-up costs can fluctuate considerably depending on the size and scope of your business, the length of time it will take to produce marketable products or services, competition pressures, and a great many other variable factors such as unforeseen expenses, delays, inflation, strikes, supplier bankruptcies, and even personal emergencies. For this reason, it is recommended by many financial advisers that in addition to whatever calculation you have come up with, that you add 25 percent to protect yourself from the unexpected.

❑ **Wages of Owner** (Personal living expenses are one of the most important and often overlooked expense items. Normally it is figured as the salary you pay yourself; don't forget withdrawals during prep-start-up time)

Summarize any important considerations when making your start-up capital estimations:

Renting, Leasing, Buying & Financing Options

Every business eventually finds itself in a situation where it has to choose between renting, leasing, buying or financing capital acquisitions such as: automobile, buildings, computers, equipment, machinery, and land. As can be expected, your decision will depend upon the particulars of your situation and the pros and cons of each form of capital acquisition.

What is a rental or a lease? A *rental* is a short-term agreement or contract under which capital property is rented from one person to another on an hourly, daily, weekly or monthly basis with rates tending to decrease the longer the rental period. On the other hand, a *lease* is a long-term agreement or contract, under which capital property is rented from one person to another for a fixed period of time (usually one year or more) at a specified rate. Rentals and leases of any equipment can often be obtained from the company that sells the equipment.

Why Rent or Lease? In general, *rent* for convenience, flexibility, to "try before you buy" and to avoid locking yourself into a long-term lease. *Lease* because it's cheaper than renting, doesn't require a big down payment, and helps control your cash flow. *Rent* or *lease* because its easier than getting financing, you lack the funds to buy, to avoid taxing your cash reserves, to avoid maintenance and repair responsibilities, to avoid obsolescence and depreciation, to improve asset liquidity, and to get immediate tax deduction benefits.

> *Lease because it's cheaper than renting, doesn't require a big down payment, and helps control your cash flow.*

State reasons for choosing to rent or lease equipment, land etc., rather than buy or finance:

Compare the costs of renting, leasing, financing & purchasing a major capital acquisition such as land, a building, a vehicle, or equipment:

Description of Item:				
	Renting	Leasing	Financing	Purchasing
Length of Lease or Loan:				
Interest Rate Charged:				
Down Payment/Deposit:				
Cost per Month:				
Cost per Year:				
Cost for Three Years:				
Total Cost:				
% of Costs Tax Deductible:				

Present Financial Structure (Capital Sources)

Describe how much capital you have available to capitalize your business and the sources of these funds. Detail the amount of your initial investment and the investment of others. Bankers and investors like to know exactly what you and other owners have at risk. Your chances of raising money are better if you can show a considerable personal level of commitment to financing your business.

Provide an overview of the current financial structure of your business and the proportion of your total start-up requirements obtained to date:

Detail the amount of your initial investment and the investment of others to fund your company:

Source of Funds	$ Amount	Debt or Equity	Repayment Schedule
Self (savings)			
Friends, neighbors, relatives			
Banks, credit unions, and other financial institutions			
Mortgage and insurance companies			
Credit from suppliers			
Government grants and loans			

> *Banks are here to help the people who want to come up in the world.*
> **DAVID ROCKEFELLER**
> Investment Banker

Loans Required

State the amount of loans or additional funds required (if any), when they are required, and your preferred terms. Support the amount requested with information such as purchase orders, estimates from suppliers, advertising rate sheets, and marketing results. If necessary, include more detailed information in your *Supporting Documents* section. Also provide details about collateral offered, credit rating, present and previous financing, and your repayment schedule.

NOTE Be thorough in your presentation of financial needs. If you need a loan, the more details supplied to support your case, the more likely you will earn the lender's favor. Bankers prefer dealing with people who *plan* their financial needs.

Amount Required – State the amount of loans required (if any), when they are required, and your preferred terms:

Collateral Offered – List all collateral (assets and possessions), to be offered as loan security. Include your estimate of the present market value of each item and other important information about owners and supporters and their collective ability to pay back any loans:

Credit Rating – If you are asking for a loan, you may want to outline your personal history at repaying debts. To do this accurately, purchase a copy of your personal credit record from a local credit bureau. Explain why you would be a good credit risk:

Present & Previous Financing – List present and previous financing (if applicable). Include terms loans outstanding (balance owing, repayment terms purpose, security held); lines of credit applied for (security offered); and you current operating line of credit (amount, security held). Include letters of credit in supporting documents:

Repayment Schedule – Write a statement indicating how the loan funds are to be repaid. Include repayment sources and time required, copies of cash flow schedules, budgets, and other appropriate information (in your "repayment schedule" many investors like to see at least two different sources of repayment):

Type of Loan Required – Check one of the following: ❑ "operating loan" – provides funds to look after day-to-day operating requirements of a business ❑ "working capital loan" – used to meet fluctuating needs that must be repaid in cash during the business's next full operating cycle ❑ "equity capital loan" – raised from investors who will take the risk in return for some combination of dividends, capital gains, or share of the business ❑ "growth capital loan" – used to meet needs that are to be repaid with profits over a period of a few years, usually not more than 7:

Finding Capital

Many businesses never blossom into mature ventures due to one serious but common problem: *lack of capital*. It is many a would be entrepreneur's plight to scrounge up enough funds to meet not only basic start-up costs but also to cover operating costs needed to keep the business going long enough to establish itself. To make matters worse, banks and investors typically want nothing to do with a new business unless its owners can personally guarantee their loan with collateral of equal or greater value. An "I'll pay you back as soon as I can," along with a "cross my heart and hope to die" is not good enough for them (see online Guidebook 📖 #81 for a list of over 50 possible sources of capital):

Outline what kinds of capital you will use to finance your business. Explain any important factors regarding your decision:

❑ Credit Capital (vendor financing)   ❑ Debt Financing   ❑ Equity Financing   ❑ Cash Capital (personal financing)

❑ **Credit Capital (vendor financing)** – Credit capital, also called trade credit or vendor financing, can be obtained from suppliers or credit card companies who give you a grace period before payment is due or interest charged. Many suppliers, if convinced of the soundness of your venture, will strongly consider granting you credit in their own efforts to find new customers and expand their business. Credit capital is often overlooked as a means of financing a start-up.

❑ **Debt Financing** – Debt financing is a direct obligation to pay interest to someone (an investor or lender), in exchange for having lent you the money. The biggest advantage of debt financing is that it allows you to retain, for the most part, control of your company. You're entitled to all company profits and have ultimate decision-making authority. After you have repaid the borrowed money, the lender has no further claim on your business. On the other hand, the biggest disadvantage of debt financing is making those monthly loan payments. If you miss a payment or are late, the lender may impose severe penalties, such as additional fees, a poorer credit rating or the possibility of calling the loan due.

❑ **Equity Financing** – Equity financing requires selling a partial interest in your company. In effect, all new equity investors become new business partners. The advantage of equity financing is that there is no monthly loan payments and no direct obligation to pay back any funds (i.e., there is no debt!). Also, you will likely have more freedom for trying new ideas with a potential equity investor than with a debt investor. On the other hand, the biggest drawback, besides the fact you have to share the profits, is the loss of control over your business. Quite often, your equity investors won't agree with your short- or long-term plans, and since you have given them a share in your business, you will have to listen to their point of view. Another drawback is that equity financing tends to be very complicated and invariably will require the advice of attorneys and accountants.

❑ **Cash Capital (personal financing)** – Cash capital is capital that you have to pay no interest on and you have ready access to. It is derived from personal savings, cashed in equity or borrowing from future cash contracts. Using cash capital is certainly the easiest, if not the best way to finance your business.

What Investors Look for When You Apply for Capital

Banks favor emerging and developing businesses that have a proven track record and need additional capital for expansion, NOT start-up operations. The reason for this is simple: many start-up operations fail. Why should they take the risk?

Check factors on the next page that should make investors look favorably upon your loan application. Summarize any additional factors:

❑ **Ability to Serve a Debt** – Banks and investors want to know how well you can service a debt – that is carry interest charges and eventually be able to repay the loan in full. They need reassurance and proof that earnings will cover interest payments and the principal covered by the liquidation of whatever it is the money is going to be used for.

❑ **Adequate Owner Investment** – Most proposals will be rejected flat-out unless the owner has risked a substantial amount of the businesses capital needs. Investors and banks want to know that you have a serious level of commitment to the success of your business and that you too are sharing the risk. There is no fixed percentage for this equity contribution, but most lenders require at least 25 percent of the total amount needed to establish the business.

❑ **Attractive Return on Investment** – Investors can obtain returns of up to and sometimes exceeding 10% with relatively safe investments in mortgages and bonds. For them to consider investing in your enterprise, which probably carries a greater degree of risk than mortgages, your business must promise better financial returns. Since equity investors usually take a greater risk, they also expect to earn more on their investment than do debt investors.

❑ **Collateral** – Anything of value that is owned by your company or owed to you and contributes to the worth of your business is an asset and can be pledged as collateral for a loan, property, or equipment purchase. Common types of collateral include accounts receivable, real estate, equipment and inventory. On the other hand, soft assets which include such intangibles as good will, patents, formulas, and capitalized research and development (R&D) are not always accepted as collateral; they are, in fact, thought to distort a business's value and are regarded by investors as a danger signal if given to high a value.

❑ **Company Stability** – Bankers and investors like to think your company will be around for a while. They prefer public companies that issue stock purchasable on the stock market and have a life of their own. Public companies provide excellent liquidity and the greatest opportunity for obtaining equity capital since their shares can be sold to anyone. Bankers and investors will also look at your retained earnings; company profits; equity; and dividend payments in order to determine your overall stability.

❑ **Equity Position** – Bankers will review the current and projected equity position of a business. The important aspect of equity is not so much the dollar amount but the ratio of equity to assets or debt. A growing business usually shows an equity position of 30 to 50 percent in relation to total assets i.e., the owners own 30 to 50 percent of the company.

❑ **Financial Ratios** – Financial ratios are used by bankers and investors to determine the relative health of a business. The basic data for ratio analysis is contained in your company's *Balance Sheet* and *Income Statement*. One of the most important ratios is your total debt to total assets ratio (calculated by dividing total debt/liabilities by total assets), also known as your equity position. This ratio looks at the ability of a business to repay long-term debt. It is given special focus in the American Bankers Association guidelines for evaluating a business.

❑ **Industry Performance** – Bankers and investors will also examine the current state of the industry, including its past, recent and future performance.

❑ **Liquidity of Company Assets** – Banks and investors need to know how quickly your current assets such as inventory and receivables (used as collateral for short term loans), as well as your fixed assets such as land, buildings and equipment (used for collateral for long term loans) can be converted into cash, in case your business goes bankrupt.

❑ **Management Experience** – A vital ingredient of every startup loan application is management expertise. It has been proven that lack of management expertise is the single biggest cause of business failures. Loan officers and investors will also look at your reputation and integrity (have you kept your promises in the past), your proven ability and experience (have you previously managed or owned a successful business), as well as the reputation and experience of all key individuals in your company.

❑ **Potential for Involvement in Key Decisions** – Although, this is not always the case, many investors want to be involved in key management decisions and may also want to function as directors or officers of the company.

❑ **Potential Growth** – Banks and investors will also analyze your expected rate of growth. They don't like to see companies growing too slow or too fast.

❑ **Proven Credit Rating** – Banks and investors like to invest in companies with solid credit ratings – they need to know you will pay interest and principal payments on time. Records and references for loans previously paid provide excellent proof. In addition to your company's credit rating, banks and investors may also want to know your personal credit history.

❑ **Regular Financial Reporting** – Banks and investors usually want to see tight financial controls in place and prompt financial reporting. They like to have for example cash flow budgets updated monthly and a list of aged receivables and payables, all preferably prepared by outside accountants. They also like to be informed of any major changes before they happen; new and large order anticipated; plans for expansion; and whether your payment is going to be late.

Loan Application

When you are interested in obtaining a business loan, the institution considering the loan will supply you with an application. The format may vary slightly, but will usually ask for the information shown below:

Check which kinds of information you already have and what kinds of information you need to complete your loan application:

❑ *Assets, Liabilities and Net worth* – These can be found on your balance sheet.

❑ *Contingent Liabilities* – These are debts you may come to owe in the future.

❑ *Inventory Details* – Summarize your inventory status, current policies and methods of evaluation.

❑ *Income Statements* – You may need to compile several *years* of information on to one sheet.

❑ *Real Estate Holdings, Stocks and Bonds* –

❑ *Sole Proprietorship, Partnership or Cooperation Information* – There are generally three separate schedules on the financial history, one for each form of legal structure.

❑ *Audit Information* – You may be asked about other prospective lenders you are seeking credit from and when your books were last audited.

❑ *Insurance Coverage* – Banks are very interested in seeing that you have covered key insurance risks.

Outline any loan application forms you plan to fill out and include:

Loan Application Summary – *Check the following factors that speak positively and negatively about any loan application you wish to make:*

Factors Your Lender May Use to Evaluate Your Application:

❑ Your character, integrity and overall management skills

❑ Your company's track record i.e. its sales and profits

❑ Your product and its relative importance to the market

❑ Your financial statements preferably accompanied by a CPA's statement

❑ A description of the purpose of the loan

❑ Your company's ability to provide data to the bank both accurately and timely.

❑ The primary and alternative sources of repayment.

Factors Your Lender May Look Negatively on In Approving Your Loan:

❑ Accounts receivable past due, indicating that cash is coming too slowly.

❑ Accounts payable abnormally extended.

❑ Poor inventory operation, such as low turnover and large back orders.

❑ High debt-equity ratio, signifying large outstanding loans.

❑ Large withdrawals of profits by company owners.

❑ Attempts to borrow short-term fund to meet long-term needs.

❑ Insufficient financial data.

❑ Poor credit rating for principal business owners/officers.

❑ Personal problems of executives.

Uses of Funds Statement

If the main reason for writing your business plan is to obtain a loan, include a *Uses of Funds Statement* (also called a *Uses of Loan Funds*). This statement is brief and specific and describes: how loan funds will be distributed among your fixed assets and working capital, how the purchases and expenditures will help increase production and sales (back up these statements), and how you plan to pay the loan back. Give valid reasons for all purchases and expenditures. This is especially important your reasons will ultimately make it easier to repay back loans. Make sure all supporting data and research is easy to locate in your *Supporting Documents*. If this information is not well organized and retrievable, a loan officer examining your application may refuse it for the simple reason that your backup material could not be found. You may also want to outline any backup plans you have, in case you are not able to secure the full amount of the loans requested.

Sample Uses of Funds Statements

The money invested in (Company Name) will be used for the following purposes:

❑ Inventory; raw materials – ($115,000)	❑ Computer equipment – 4 IBM Aptiva's Pentium/266 MHz – ($6,000)
❑ Purchase of (Machine), Model # 627899 including installation – ($50,000)	❑ Start-up costs – legal fees, filing fees – ($5,000)
❑ Working capital – ($30,000)	❑ Initial office expenses, lease deposits, phone, fax, office furniture – ($2,000).
❑ Leasehold improvements – (est. $25,000)	
❑ Delivery truck (Ford Ranger, $13,000)	❑ Computer software – 4 Order Entry, 1 MS Office 97, 1 Quickbooks – ($1,500)
❑ Office equipment and supplies – ($1,000).	

The above cash outlays, totaling $248,500, will allow us to purchase the above items outright rather than lease or finance them. This will enable us to lower our overhead and meet our conservative sales projections for the first year.

Describe any major purchases or expenditures you plan to make. Explain your reasons:

USES OF LOAN FUNDS

1. Funds Required

a. HPS Inc. will need an anticipated $25,000 in loan funds to purchase three new pieces of equipment.

2. Dispersal of Loan Funds

b. The equipment needed is as follows:

1) Swanson G-34 Blender – $14,000

2) Atlas Juice Press J-3 – $4,000

3) G.E. Mixer S12 – $5,500

c. The remaining $1,500 will be used to market the new product & contribute to the 1st monthly installment.

3. Backup Statement

d. The equipment will result in a 20% increase in sales, at a projected $40,000 a year, and a net profit increase sufficient to repay the loan and interest within three years with a profit margin of 15%.

DAY 25
Pro Forma Financial Statements

The purpose of preparing pro forma financial projection statements is to show lenders and investors that you have researched your market and profit potential in relation to your costs. Since a new business does not have a track record, this analysis must be thorough, critical, logical and probable – not just possible. Any inconsistencies will be quickly spotted leaving a bad impression on lenders who may lose faith in your entire proposal no matter what its merits. The following five statements belong in every business plan and are by far the statements most lenders want to see (refer to GB📖 #80). They should be presented in the order shown below (from left to right) as each one builds on the one done previously:

| ❑ **Twelve-month Income Projection** – Summarizes profit & loss projections for the next 12 months. Also referred to as a Pro Forma Profit & Loss Statement. | ❑ **Three-year Income Projection** – Summarizes your profit & loss projections for the next 3 years. | ❑ **Cash Flow Statement** – Summarizes cash flow projections for the next year of operation and annually for another 2 years. | ❑ **Breakeven Analysis** – Projects the amount of revenues your company needs to breakeven. | ❑ **Pro Forma Balance Sheet** – Summarizes balance sheet projections annually for each of the next 3 to 5 years. |

Basic Budgeting Terminology

The ability to know your cash flow status at any particular moment in time, as well as make accurate income projections on a regular basis is the only way to be sure that you will not come to work one day and discover that your company is flat broke and creditors are threatening to repossess your desk. In this section, to help you gain a better understanding of budgeting, the following terminology is explained: ◆ Budget ◆ Income Projection ◆ Cash Flow ◆ Cash Flow Statement ◆ Working Capital ◆ Working Capital Cycle ◆ Cash Capital Conversion Cycle.

What is a Budget?

A budget is a forecast of all cash sources and expenditures. It usually follows an income statement type format covering a 12-month period, month by month. At year's end, the projected income and expense figures are compared to the actual performance of the business as recorded in the financial statements. The two most important budgeting tools are the *Cash Flow Statement* and the *Income Projection*.

What is an Income Projection?

An *Income Projection* takes a look at all revenues & expenses (including depreciation & mortgages) and attempts to determine the monthly and yearly profitability of a venture.

What is Cash Flow?

The term *Cash Flow* refers to the amount of funds actually available to make purchases and pay current bills. Over a specific period, it is the difference between cash receipts (the money you take in) and cash disbursements (the money you spend).

> *The largest determining factor of the size and content of this year's budget is last year's budget.*
> **AARON WILDAVSKY**
> Political Scientist

What is a Cash Flow Statement?

A *Cash Flow Statement* (also known as a *Cash Flow Projection*) refers to an estimate of anticipated cash sales as well as anticipated cash payments of bills. These estimates are usually scheduled on a weekly, monthly, or quarterly basis and are frequently used to help project the amount of money required to finance your operations on a yearly or even day-to-day basis.

NOTE *Cash Flow* and *Income Projection Statements* are not the same. The difference between the two results from how principal payments and depreciation are recorded. Loan principal payments are included as cash outflow in a cash flow statement but are not recorded on the income statement. On the other hand, depreciation is included as a business expense on the income statement but not as cash outflow on the cash flow statement. Many financial experts like to define cash flow as net income exclusive of depreciation.

What is a Breakeven Analysis?

A *Breakeven Analysis* determines at what point your income matches your expenses and overhead. This information can help you project the profit potential of your venture as well as point out the necessity for controlling your costs.

What is Working Capital?

Working Capital is the difference between a business' current assets and its current liabilities. Working capital includes: ◆ cash ◆ marketable securities ◆ accounts receivable ◆ inventories ◆ accounts payable ◆ accrued wages and taxes.

Working capital management, like cash flow management, is primarily concerned with the day-to-day operations of a business rather than long-term business decisions. Working capital policies deal with decisions related to types and amounts of current assets and the means of financing them. These decisions involve: ◆ the management of cash and inventories ◆ credit policy and collection of A/Rs ◆ short-term borrowing and other financing opportunities such as trade credit ◆ inventory financing ◆ A/Rs financing. Since the average firm has about 40% of its capital tied up in current assets, decisions regarding working capital greatly impact the success of a business. This is especially true for smaller businesses, which often minimize their investment in fixed assets by leasing rather than buying, but which cannot avoid investing in inventories, cash and receivables.

What is the Working Capital Cycle?

The *Working Capital Cycle* involves the steps a business takes from the time it makes the first cash commitment toward providing a product or a service, to the point when it receives cash payment for its sales (accounts receivable). An individual cycle ends when the full cash amount for the sale is received.

Calculating the Working Capital Cycle – The Working Capital Cycle may be calculated by using the following formula:

$$WCC = ICP + RCP$$

ICP – (Inventory Conversion Period) refers to the length of time between purchase of raw material, production of the goods or service, and the sale of the finished product.

RCP – (Receivable Conversion Period) refers to the time between the sale of the final product on credit and cash receipts for the accounts receivable.

What is the Capital Cash Conversion Cycle?

The *Capital Cash Conversion Cycle*, also referred to as the *Cash Flow Cycle*, is defined as the length of time between the payment of what a business owes (payables), and the collection of what a business is owed (receivables). During this cycle, a business' funds are unavailable for other purposes. Cash has been paid for purchases but cash has not been collected from sales.

Calculating the Capital Cash Conversion Cycle – The *Capital Cash Conversion Cycle* may be calculated by using the following formula:

$$\textbf{CCC = ICP + RCP - PDP}$$

ICP – (Inventory Conversion Period) refers to the length of time between purchase of raw material, production of the goods or service, and the sale of the finished product.

RCP – (Receivable Conversion Period) refers to the time between the sale of the final product on credit and cash receipts for the accounts receivable.

PDP – (Payable Deferral Period) refers to the time between the purchase of raw material on credit and cash payments for the resulting accounts payable.

For example, if it takes 35 days after orders are placed to receive and process the raw material into finished product, the ICP is 35 days. Assuming that 25 days after the arrival of raw material, the firm pays for them, the PDP is 25 days. Finally, if the firm receives cash payment for the sale of it product or service in 30 days, the RCP is 30 days. The **CCC** is 35 + 30 - 25, or **40** days.

Reducing the Capital Cash Conversion Cycle – Since there is always a cost to such financing, a goal of any business should be to minimize the length of time funds are "tied-up" in order to reduce the amount of working capital needed for operations. A few strategies include: ◆ reducing the ICP – e.g., processing the raw material and producing the goods as quickly as possible ◆ reducing the RCP – e.g., speeding up collection ◆ lengthening the PCP – e.g., slowing payments.

Twelve-month Income Projection

A *Twelve-month Income Projection* shows sales & receipts, cost of sales, gross profit, expenses, and net profit for the entire year, all of which can be expressed as a % of sales. This statement looks at ALL expenses & revenues, not just cash-based ones.

Sample Sales and Income Projections & Assumptions

Sales have been forecast at the following growth rates:

	Year 2	Year 3
(Product/Service) 1:	(XX)%	(XX)%
(Product/Service) 2:	(XX)%	(XX)%

Returns and discounts are estimated at 5% of total sales. This rate is based on operating ratios from (Source). We are offering a range of quantity discounts, plus an early payment discount to A/Rs customers.

Cost of goods sold will increase at 0.25% per month or 3% per year. This rate is equivalent to this year's projected inflation rate (Source).

Freight will be paid by customers.

When making financial projections, one never has all the necessary information. Assumptions have to be made. In developing your projection statements, make sure to state all the assumptions including those directed towards the inflation rate, cost of living increases, cost of goods increases, rent increases, and prime interest rate fluctuations.
FINANCE TIP

State any assumptions made when projecting your income or expenses:

Preparing a Twelve-month Income Projection

A *Twelve-month Income Projection* is valuable as both a planning and management tool to help control and monitor business operations. It allows you to make projections of income generated each month and for the business year, based on reasonable predictions of monthly levels of sales, costs and expenses. It looks similar to a cash flow projection, but it keeps track of **ALL** expenses and revenues (not just cash based ones), and also factors in depreciation. The real value of an income projection becomes more apparent when your projected values are compared with actual operating results. This comparison will allow you to make more accurate projections in the future and take steps to correct any serious problems. To use the "Twelve-month Income Projection" shown on page 163, follow the steps shown below:

a. **Find out industry percentages.** Industry figures serve as a useful benchmark against which to compare your cost and expense estimates. These percentages can be obtained from trade associations, accountants or banks. Also, your reference librarian might be able to refer you to documents that contain these percentage figures. These figures are derived by dividing:

$$\text{Ind. \%} = \left[\frac{(\text{Cost} + \text{Expense Items})}{\text{Total Net Sales}}\right] \times 100\%$$

Making Twelve-month Projections
XYZ Supply Company Inc.

Sales	523,063	100%
Cost of Goods	366,144	70%
Gross Profit Margin	156,919	30%
Operating Expenses:		
Advertising	3,605	0.7%
Depreciation	4,000	0.8%
Insurance	2,900	0.6%
Legal and accounting expenses	4,412	0.8%
Office expenses	2,995	0.6%
Rent	24,000	4.6%
Repair & maintenance	437	0.1%
Salaries	34,650	6.6%
Telephone and utilities	6,683	1.3%
Miscellaneous	8,507	1.6%
Total operating expenses	91,919	17.6%
Net profit	65,000	12.4%

b. **Determine your total net sales (revenues).** Estimate your total number of units of products or services that you realistically expect to sell each month at the prices you expect to get. Make sure to consider returns and markdowns.

c. **Calculate your cost of sales.** Determine how much you paid for your products (cost of goods sold). Don't forget to include transportation costs and direct labor. The cost of goods sold is often expressed as a percentage of sales. Check with your trade association to get the operating ratios for your business.

d. **Calculate your gross profit.** Subtract the total cost of sales from the total net sales to arrive at your gross profit. For example, with a cost of sales operating ratio of 59.4%, and revenues of $100,000, your gross profit would be $40,6000.

e. **Calculate your gross profit margin.** The gross profit is expressed as a % of total sales (revenues). It is calculated by dividing gross profits by total net sales.

f. **Estimate your controllable (variable) and fixed expenses.**

Include all and non-cash expense items such as depreciation as well.

NOTE You should depreciate any individual item of equipment, furniture, fixtures, vehicles etc., costing over $100. To do this, divide the cost of each fixed asset item by the number of months over which it will be depreciated. For more info on allowances for depreciation, request free publications and assistance from your local IRS office.

g. **Calculate your net profit before taxes.** Subtract your total expenses from your gross profit.

i. **Estimate your tax payments.** Include inventory and sales taxes (if not taken off in your cost of goods sold calculations), excise tax, real estate tax etc.

j. **Calculate your net profit after taxes.** Subtract taxes from net profit.

k. **Total your monthly columns.** Add each of the monthly sales and expense items across the table.

l. **Calculate your annual percentage.** Compare this figure to the industry percentage in the first column. Use the following formula:

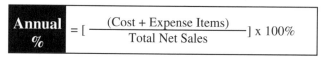

$$\textbf{Annual } \% = [\frac{(\text{Cost} + \text{Expense Items})}{\text{Total Net Sales}}] \times 100\%$$

m. **Compare your *projected* 12-month Income Statement with *actual* sales and expenses.** On a regular monthly basis, fill out a second 12-month income statement using actual results. This final step is the most important step of the entire process. As a business owner, any reliable feedback you can get is as good as gold.

Three-year Income Projection

A *Three-year Income Projection Statement* shows your income and deductible expense projections (such as depreciation), for the next three years of your business's operations (see page 164). It does not show all sources of cash and cash to be paid out (such as owner drawings), as in a cash flow statement. To prepare your three-year income projection statement, use your income projection for your first year's figures. Base your second and third year's figures on economic and industry trends that you have researched.

Estimate sales and receipts, cost of sales, gross margin, expenses, and net profit for the next 3 years. State any assumptions made:

SAMPLE 3-YEAR INCOME PROJECTION (YEAR 1)		
3 Year Projection FOR: *Sam's Auto Supply Shop* **As OF:** Dec. 31, 1997		
	YEAR 1	
GROSS SALES (less returns and allowances)	$450,000	
ADD OTHER INCOME:	50,000	
LESS Cost of Goods Sold	350,000	
GROSS PROFIT	$150,000	
LESS VARIABLE Expenses (controllable) (selling)	25,000	
LESS FIXED Expenses (overhead) (administrative)	85,000	
TOTAL Operating Expenses (fixed + variable)	110,000	
NET INCOME (Before Taxes)	$40,000	
LESS Estimated Tax Payments	17,000	
NET INCOME (After Taxes)	$23,000	

Twelve-month Income Record or Projection

	Industry %	Jan	Feb	Mar	Apr	Jun	Jul	Aug	Sep	Oct	Nov	Dec	Annual Total	Annual %
Total Net Sales (revenues)														
Cost of Sales														
Gross Profit														
Gross Profit Margin														
Controllable Expenses														
Salaries/Wages														
Payroll Expenses														
Legal /Accounting														
Advertising														
Automobile														
Office Supplies														
Dues/Subscriptions														
Utilities														
Miscellaneous														
Total Controllable Expenses														
Fixed Expenses														
Rent														
Depreciation														
Utilities														
Insurance														
Licenses/Permits														
Loan Payments														
Miscellaneous														
Total Fixed Expenses														
Total Expenses														
Net Profit (loss) Before Taxes														
Taxes														
Net Profit (loss) After Taxes														

THREE-YEAR INCOME PROJECTION

Three Year Projection FOR: **As OF:**

	YEAR 1	YEAR 2	YEAR 3
GROSS SALES	$		
LESS Returns and Allowances			
LESS Sales Tax (if included in sales)			
ADD OTHER INCOME:			
Royalties and Dividends on Stock			
Interest from Bank Accounts			
Gains from Sale of Fixed Assets			
Other Income			
GROSS INCOME	$		
LESS COST OF GOODS SOLD:			
Inventory at Beginning of Fiscal Period			
ADD Cost of Goods Purchased During Fiscal Period			
ADD Freight & Delivery Charges			
LESS Purchased Returns			
LESS Inventory at the End of the Fiscal Period			
TOTAL Cost of Goods Sold			
GROSS PROFIT	$		
LESS VARIABLE Controllable Selling Expenses			
Accounting & Legal Fees			
Advertising			
Business Tax, Fees, Licenses, Dues & Subscriptions			
Interest Charges (Debt Expenses)			
Maintenance & Repairs			
Meals & Entertainment			
Motor Vehicle Expenses (except Deprec. Allowance)			
Office Supplies			
Sales Salaries & Wages			
Other Variable Expenses			
LESS FIXED Overhead Administrative Expenses			
Administrative Salaries & Wages			
Bad Debts			
Depreciation			
Insurance			
Mortgage / Rent Payments			
Payroll Expenses & Taxes			
Property Taxes			
Telephone & Utilities (Heat, Hydro)			
Other Fixed Expenses			
TOTAL Operating Expenses (fixed + variable)			
NET INCOME (Before Taxes)	$		
LESS Estimated Tax Payments			
NET INCOME (After Taxes)	$		

Cash Flow Statement

A *Cash Flow Statement*, also called a *Cash Flow Budget*, is a key part of every business plan. It is the only tool you have to assure that you can meet your financial obligations and show lenders you have sufficient cash to carry a loan. A cash flow statement identifies when cash is expected, how much cash will be received, when cash must be paid out, and exactly how much cash is needed to pay expenses. Overall, it helps present a clearer picture of your cash inflow and outflow on a monthly basis for the next year of operation and assess profits after taxes.

Preparing a Cash Flow Statement

The primary concern of all *Cash Flow* projections is to help anticipate cash receipts and cash expenditures so that at the end of each month you will have a good idea of how much money you have or won't have to pay your bills. Three basic steps for preparing a *Cash Flow Statement* are:

FIRST, estimate sales and all incoming revenue on a monthly basis. Sales from previous years of similar companies can be used as a guide. Be sure to also consider seasonal trends that may affect your sales volume at different months (use the "Sources of Cash Worksheet" below).

SECOND, after you have projected cash receipts from all sources, estimate the expenses necessary to achieve your anticipated sales. Operating expenses can be expressed in dollars or as an operating ratio in the form of a % of sales. Industry operating ratios can be found at your trade association and can be used as a guide (use the "Cash to be Paid Out Worksheet" on page 166).

THIRD, subtract projected cash expenditures from sales. The remaining sum will indicate a negative or positive cash flow. A positive cash flow at the end of the year is good, especially if occurring in all twelve months and generating a profit. But, this is unlikely. Most start-up companies will have a negative cash flow initially, with a breakeven point occurring at some point in the future (hopefully within a few months). A negative cash flow after one year is not good, unless you have ample financial reserves and substantial evidence that this will change in the future.

NOTE A cash flow statement deals *only* with cash transactions. All sales and expenditures listed are actual *cash sales* and *cash expenditures*. A cash flow statement does not consider depreciation, amortization of goodwill, or other non-cash expense items. Prepaid items, such as insurance and supplies contracts, affect cash flow only in the period they are actually paid. A/Rs and A/Ps are not included unless cash is actually received or paid out during the period.

Sources of Cash Worksheet
Cash Flowing INTO Your Business

Cash on Hand

Sales & Revenues

Sales

Service Income

Deposits on Sales or Services

A/R Collections

Other Income

Interest Income

Sale of Long-term Assets

Liabilities

Loans Received

Equity

Owner Investments (sole-p or part.)

Contributed Capital (corp.)

Sale of Stock (corp.)

Venture Capital

Other Cash Sources

TOTAL CASH AVAILABLE

Preparing a Twelve-month Cash Flow Budget

Cash flow projections are best made on a spreadsheet. Not only does this allow you to change variables and projections and have the results automatically calculated, but it lessens the need to list similar expenditures repeatedly. The sample cash flow statement on page 170 can be used as a guide to set up a spreadsheet, or as a worksheet to customize your own personalized cash flow statement. Follow the steps outlined below (it is recommended that you do separate cash flow budgets for worse, average, and best case scenarios).

1a. Projected ☐ – Check this box if you are preparing a projected cash flow statement.

1b. Actual ☐ – Check this box if you are preparing a cash flow statement based on actual results. Preparing this kind of statement is a good way to sharpen future projections.

1c. Type – State whether projection is a worst, average, or best case scenario.

2. Beginning CASH BALANCE – Start with the first month of your business cycle. Enter your start-up capital or cash on hand balance from the previous month's end (also referred to as your opening cash balance, surplus cash, or total cash in the bank at the first of the month). If you don't know this exact figure, estimate it.

NOTE If your business is new, you will have to base your projections on your market research and industry trends. If you have an established business, you can use previous financial statements.

3. CASH IN – Estimate all cash revenues your company expects to take in during the month (use industry operating ratios).

3a. Cash Sales – Estimate all the cash revenues your company expects to take in specifically from the sale of your goods or services. Include cleared checks and credit card slips. Omit accounts receivable sales unless cash is actually received. Also omit orders taken and invoices sent out where no cash has been received. If necessary, divide this section into several categories, e.g., sales of widgets, sales of shoes, etc., depending on how useful you think this information is.

NOTE The primary source of cash revenue in your business will be from sales, but sales will vary from month to month due to seasonal patterns and other factors. It is thus necessary to project whether monthly sales will produce enough income to pay each month's bills. Bear in mind that it is much easier and more accurate to project expenditures than to project sales; sales projections are critical to the success of your company but often wildly inaccurate. Serious research and extra precautions should be evident and reflected in your final projections.

Cash to be Paid Out Worksheet
Cash Flowing OUT OF Your Business

Start-up Capital Expenditures
Business License (annual expense)
DBA Filing Fee (one-time cost)
Other Start-up Costs:

Inventory
Cash Out for Items for Resale
Raw Materials Purchases
Total Start-up Expenses
Variable Expenses (controllable)
Advertising
Car & Travel
Shipping & Delivery
General Supplies
Legal & Accounting Fees
Outside Labor & Services
Packaging Costs
Payroll Expenses
Repairs & Maintenance
Sales Salaries
Miscellaneous Direct Expenses
Total Variable Expenses
Fixed Expenses (overhead)
Administrative Salaries
Insurance
Interest Charges
Licenses & Permits
Rent Payments
Telephone
Utilities
Miscellaneous Indirect Expenses
Total Fixed Expenses
Long-term Asset Purchases
Fixed Asset Payments
Liability Payments
Debts, Loans and A/Ps
Federal Income Tax
Other Taxes
Owner Equity
Owner's Withdrawal
TOTAL CASH to be PAID OUT

Start with your 12-month income projection statement. Then, develop your cash flow statement.

3b. *A/R Collections* – Estimate the amount your company expects to collect from its sales on account. Some cash flow statements further break down this category into (a) collections from last month's sales, (b) collections of sales from 2 months ago, and (c) collection from sales more than 2 months ago. This is a good idea if the majority of your sales will be credit sales.

3c. *Interest Income* – Estimate interest from investments, marketable securities and bank accounts.

3d. *Sale of Fixed Assets* – If you plan to sell any fixed asset your company owns such as a car, building, piece of office furniture, estimate the amount you expect to receive.

3e. *Loans Received* – Project any borrowed amounts you expect to take possession of during the month.

3f. *Other Cash Sources* – Estimate all other sources of cash that you expect to receive during the month. Include items like rent income, capital gains on shares sold, and dividends received from investments.

4. CASH OUT – Project all fixed and controllable expenses for the month. Include any amounts that will be written by check, bearing in mind that if you write a check in January for the full years' insurance, the full amount of the check is put in the January column and nothing else is entered for the rest of the year (this procedure is quite different when you post the payment to your accounting records). Some of the expense items listed in this cash flow statement may not be applicable to your business, and some may be missing. Add and subtract where necessary. Try and make all categories as appropriate to your situation as possible and reflect your bookkeeping system.

NOTE A purchase order placed with a supplier, a bill, or even a mailed check is not a cash expenditure. A check that clears your bank account is a cash expenditure. By keeping all of the above in mind you can forecast cash flow in a reasonably intelligent manner. Depreciation of machinery, buildings and other equipment and furniture should not be included in a cash flow statement.

4a. *Inventory & Raw Material Purchases* – Estimate inventory purchases intended to be resold to the public, that you expect to make during the month. Also, include any parts and materials used to manufacture goods intended for sale. You may find it useful to further break down this section to keep track of key items and further control costs.

4b. *Staff Salaries & Wages* – Estimate all base salaries and wages as well as overtime or bonuses paid. You may want to further breakdown this category to keep track of administrative, manufacturing and selling labor costs.

4c. *Payroll Expenses* – Estimate payroll expenses including paid vacations, paid sick leave, health insurance, unemployment insurance, security taxes and other payroll taxes. This figure is usually between 10% to 45% of the amount for "Staff Salaries & Wages."

4d. *Outside Labor & Services* – Estimate amounts if any expected to be paid for outside labor or temporary services for specialized or overflow work, as well as subcontracting and consulting services.

4e. *General Supplies* – Estimate amounts expected to be paid for office and operating supplies (supplies are items purchased for use in the business but are not for resale).

4f. *Repairs & Maintenance* – Estimate amounts needed for periodic expenditures such as painting or decorating.

4g. *Advertising* – Estimate amount needed for marketing your products or services. Amount should be adequate to maintain sales volume.

4h. *Car & Travel* – Estimate amount for use of personal car if any, as well as, freight, postage and shipping charges. Include parking charges.

4i. *Shipping & Delivery* – Estimate shipping, delivery, postage and freight costs.

4j. *Legal & Accounting Fees* – Estimate legal and bookkeeping services.

A cash flow projection is a management and planning tool that can eliminate much of the anxiety that can plague you when starting out and further down the road during lean periods.

4k. Rent Payments – Estimate rent or leasehold payments only used in your business. Enter rent and lease payments only when you pay them. If you pay in three-month chunks, enter payments every three months. Do not split them up as you would when you enter them in your accounting books.

4l. Telephone – Estimate phone charges, including long-distance and modem charges.

4m. Utilities – Estimate water heat, light and power consumption charges.

4n. Insurance – Estimate amounts needed for coverage on business property and products including fire and liability, as well as worker's compensation. Exclude executive life insurance. This should be included in owner's withdrawal.

4o. Licenses & Permits – Estimate amount needed for licenses & permits.

4p. Interest Charges – Estimate interest charges on loans, bank overdrafts, and lines of credit (accounts payable). Bear in mind that if the purpose of your cash flow statement is to help you figure out how much money your want to borrow, this interest figure may be very difficult to estimate. Consequently, you may decide to leave the line blank for now. If it is likely to be a small amount, you may decide to omit it altogether.

4q. Federal Income Tax – Enter estimated quarterly payments you will make to the IRS. Note that if yours is a new business, no quarterly payments may be necessary until after your first fiscal year, since the IRS has no information to calculate your payments. Nevertheless, funds should be set aside to meet these payments.

4r. Other Taxes – Estimate real estate taxes, inventory taxes, sales tax, and excise tax.

4s. Other Operating Expenses – Estimate any other operating expenses for which separate accounts would not be practical such as dues & subscriptions, packaging costs and miscellaneous expenses incurred prior to first month projections and paid for after start-up.

4t. Loan Principle Payments – Estimate the monthly amount to be paid if you are paying off a mortgage on any buildings or property, an operating loan or loan for a vehicle. For example, if you borrow $43,000 to purchase a half-ton truck and monthly payments are $1,000 with the first payment due in March, then $1,000 will be entered in line 19 for each month beginning in March (you may want to include interest in this column to simplify calculations).

4u. Fixed Asset Payments – Estimate amounts if you are renting, leasing or financing equipment.

4v. Capital Expenditures & Start-up Costs – Enter your start-up costs here. As well, estimate money, if any, spent for the purchase of a fixed asset such as a vehicle, equipment, building, leasehold improvements, shelving, computer or a filing cabinet. List the amount for the month when the check was written.

4w. Owner's Withdrawal – Estimate here the amount of money you need to live on, the amount of money you pay yourself, or the amount you expect to withdraw from the company bank account for whatever reason. Include payments for such things as owner's income tax, social security, health insurance, executive life insurance premiums, as well as cash dividends paid to stockholders.

5. **Total CASH OUT –** Total all cash payments for the month.

6. **CASH FLOW –** Cash flow is calculated by subtracting *Total CASH IN* by *Total CASH OUT*. If the result is a loss, put it in brackets, use a red pen (black for a gain), or use a negative sign. If the *deficit* is large, an operating loan will be required or increased to cover the deficit. If the *surplus* is large, excess funds should be applied to any operating existing loans.

   NOTE Some owner-managers also like to include a *Cumulative Cash Flow* entry. *Cumulative Cash Flow* adds the previous months total to the new months total.

7. **CASH Balance –** Your *Cash Balance*, also referred to as your closing cash balance or cash position, is calculated by adding your *Beginning Cash Balance* and your *Cash Flow*. This result is then automatically posted to the next

When preparing your financial statements, you have the option of dividing costs and expenses into **fixed costs** *or expenses (also known as "overhead" or "administrative" costs) and* **variable costs** *or expenses (also known as "controllable" or "selling" costs). Your decision should be based on whichever method you consider more appropriate, convenient, and better able to help you understand your financial situation so you can make better financial decisions.*
BUSINESS TIP

> *Even though work stops, expenses run on.*
> **CATO THE ELDER**

month as your beginning or opening cash balance.

8. **Essential OPERATING DATA** – The following data totals are not part of a cash flow statement but they do provide important information for management decision-making. It is from these figures that the complete cash flow projection can be evolved and shown in the above form.

8a. *Sales Volume* – This is a very important figure and should be estimated carefully, taking into account size of facility and employee output as well as realistic anticipated sales (do not include orders received. This figure includes all sales on account.

8b. *Accounts Receivable* – This figure includes previous unpaid credit sales plus current month's credit sales, less amounts received current month. Don't forget to deduct you anticipated bad debts.

> *Cash flow problems can result from poorly adjusted mark-ups, pilferage, and incorrect tax reporting.*

8c. *Bad Debts* – Your bad debts ratio can be projected using industry standards as a percentage of your total accounts receivable. Bad debts should be subtracted from 8b in the month anticipated.

8d. *Inventory on Hand* – This figure is estimated by taking your estimated last month's inventory plus merchandise received and/or manufactured in the current month minus the amount sold in the current month.

8e. *Accounts Payable* – This figure is estimated by taking your previous estimated accounts payable plus current month's payable minus amount paid during month.

8f. *Depreciation* – This figure is established by your accountant, or can be estimated by taking the value of all your equipment and dividing it by its useful life (in months) as allowed by Internal Revenue Service.

> *Cash flow is actually quite easy to understand: if your business spends more than it takes in, soon you will be out of business.*

Sample Cash Flow Assumptions

(I/We) project that we will be able to generate sufficient revenues from operations to meet our initial needs after receiving the loan of $(XXX). A positive cash flow is anticipated after 5 months of operation. However, our projections are in industries that have never been fully addressed and are based upon our experience and present buying conditions. Should sales not meet our initial projections, adjustments will be made to inventory levels and other long-term commitments decreased or postponed.

Summarize important details regarding your cash flow statement. When will your company become profitable? If your business has a negative cash flow position for more than several months, how will you handle this? Will you be able to make loan payments? Describe any assumptions made when preparing your cash flow statement:

CASH FLOW STATEMENT

Name of Business: _____   Projected ☐ Actual ☐   Type: _____   Date: _____

	Jan	Feb	Mar	Apr	May	Jun	Jul	Aug	Sep	Oct	Nov	Dec	T
										FIRST OF MONTH			
Beginning Cash Balance													

CASH IN

	Jan	Feb	Mar	Apr	May	Jun	Jul	Aug	Sep	Oct	Nov	Dec	T
Cash Sales													
A/R Collections													
Interest Income													
Sale of Fixed Assets													
Loans Received													
Other Cash Sources													
Total CASH IN													

CASH OUT

	Jan	Feb	Mar	Apr	May	Jun	Jul	Aug	Sep	Oct	Nov	Dec	T
Inventory & Raw Mater.													
Staff Salaries & Wages													
Payroll Expenses													
Outside Labor & Serv.													
General Supplies													
Repairs & Maintenance													
Advertising													
Car, Delivery & Travel													
Legal & Account. Fees													
Rent / Lease Payments													
Rented / Leased Equip.													
Telephone													
Utilities													
Insurance													
Licenses & Permits													
Interest Charges													
Federal Income Tax													
Other Taxes													
Other Operating Exp.													
Loan Repayments													
Payments on Fixed Assets													
Capital Expenditures													
Owner's Withdrawal													
Total CASH OUT													

	Jan	Feb	Mar	Apr	May	Jun	Jul	Aug	Sep	Oct	Nov	Dec	T
										END OF MONTH			
CASH FLOW													
CASH Balance													
(non-cash flow info)										**OPERATING DATA**			
Sales Volume													
Accounts Receivable													
Bad Debts													
Inventory on Hand													
Accounts Payable													
Depreciation													
Loan Required													

Quarterly Cash Flow Budget						
For three months: from _____ to _____	Budget	Actual	Budget	Actual	Budget	Actual
Expected Cash Receipts	**1**		**2**		**3**	
1. Cash sales						
2. Collection on accounts receivable						
3. Other income						
4. Total cash receipts						
Expected Cash Payments						
5. Raw materials/inventory						
6. Payroll						
7. Other factory expenses (including maintenance)						
8. Advertising						
9. Selling Expense						
10. Admin. Expense (incl. salary of owner-manager)						
11. New plant and equipment						
12. Other payments (taxes, estimated income tax; repayment of loans; interest)						
13. Total cash payments						
14. Expected cash balance at beginning of the month						
15. Cash increase or decrease (4 – 13)						
16. Expected cash balance at end of month (14 + 15)						
17. Desired working cash balance						
18. Short-term loans needed (17 – 16, if 17 is larger)						
19. Cash available for dividends, capital cash expenditures, and/or short investments (16 – 17, if 16 is larger)						
Capital Cash:						
20. Cash available (item 19 after deducting dividends etc.)						
21. Desired capital cash (item 11, new plant equipment)						
22. Long-term loans needed (21 – 20, if 21 is larger).						

DAY 26

Breakeven Analysis

A *breakeven point* occurs when a company's expenses exactly match its income generated from sales; there is neither profit nor loss. This point can be expressed in total dollars or revenue offset by total expenses or total units of production (cost of which exactly equals the income produced from its sales). This analysis can be shown both mathematically and graphically.

Preparing a Breakeven Analysis

Once you have determined all the fixed and variable operating costs of your business, you can use this information to prepare a *Breakeven Analysis*. Several methods for preparing breakeven analyses for retail, manufacturing and service-related businesses are explained below.

NOTE When preparing a *Breakeven Analysis*, you will need to make several assumptions. These assumptions include: ◆ selling prices do not change ◆ total fixed expenses remain the same ◆ variable expenses increase and decrease in direct proportion to sales.

Using the "Basic" Breakeven Formula

All B.E. formulas are derived from the following *Basic B.E. Formula*:

Basic Breakeven Formula

$$\text{Sales - Cost} = 0$$

> *Most of the figures needed for a B.E. analysis can be derived from cash flow and three-year income projection statements.*

EXAMPLE #1 – Clara Shoemaker plans to start a widget manufacturing company with $40,000 in start-up capital. Presently, her competitors are selling similarly featured widgets at a price of $140 per widget. Clara calculates that each widget will cost her $80 to manufacture including materials and labor. She also estimates that additional variable costs for each widget (W), including delivery, storage and returns, to be $10 per widget. Estimating her annual fixed operating expenses to be $10,000 (not including her own salary), she calculates her breakeven point to be:

$$140W - \$10,000 - 90W = 0$$
$$50W = \$10,000$$
$$\mathbf{W = 200}$$

Clara needs to sell 200 widgets to breakeven. However, if she wants to make a salary of $30,000 to equal her the salary of her old job and a profit of $6,000 (15%) on her start-up investment of $40,000, she must sell an additional 720 widgets.

$$140W - \$10,000 - 90W = \$36,000$$
$$50W = \$46,000$$
$$\mathbf{W = 920}$$

If, on the other hand, Clara finds out from her market research that is nearly impossible to sell 920 widgets annually and that a more realistic volume would be 800 widgets, and if she still wants to maintain her profit and salary level, then she has to either increase her selling price or find ways of reducing her variable and fixed costs. To solve this problem, she might decide to make the following four changes: ◆ increase her selling price to $147 per widget ◆ decrease her variable costs by $8 per unit by locating cheaper suppliers ◆ add an extended warranty service to justify her higher prices at a cost of $5 per widget ◆ increase her advertising budget by $2,000. The result would look like this:

$$147W - \$12,000 - 87W = \$36,000$$
$$60W = \$48,000$$
$$\mathbf{W = 800}$$

Calculating the B.E. Point for a Retail Business

The basic B.E. formula says that for any business, it B.E. point occurs when sales minus costs equal zero. For a retail business, this formula can be rearranged as follows.

> The basic B.E. formula says that for any business, its B.E. point occurs when sales minus costs equal zero.

$$\boxed{\mathbf{Sales = FC + VC}}$$

S = Sales in dollars at B.E. point
FC = Fixed Costs or operating expenses
VC = Variable Costs or cost of goods

This formula looks harmless enough. But substituting values directly into it is impractical, being that for a retail business, variable costs (cost of goods sold) cannot be known until the end of the year when inventory levels are taken (CGS = inventory at beginning of a period + purchases during the period - inventory at end of period).

To calculate a breakeven point for your business, you must instead use a variation of this formula that asks you to first calculate your gross profit, change this value to your gross margin (also known as the contribution margin), and then substitute this value back into the original breakeven formula. By calculating your gross margin in this way for all merchandise sold, the price structure that generates a level of revenue to purchase goods, pay operating expenses and make a profit for you, can easily be determined. Our new simple more practical retail breakeven formula can be derived as follows:

Since, gross profit (GP) is equal to sales (S) minus the cost of sales (VC).

$$GP = S - VC \quad or \quad \mathbf{VC = S - GP}$$

And, gross margin (GM) is equal to Gross Profit (GP) divided by sales (S).

$$GM = GP/S \quad or \quad \mathbf{GP = GM \times S}$$

And, sales (S) must equal FC plus VC, according to our original B.E. formula.

$$S = FC + VC$$

Then, by substituting the second formula into the first and the first into the third, the following equality results:

$$S = FC + [S - (GM \times S)]$$

Simplifying this equation leaves us with: FC = GM x S   *or*   S = FC/GM

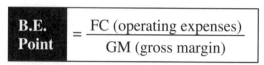

| B.E. Point | = | $\dfrac{\text{FC (operating expenses)}}{\text{GM (gross margin)}}$ |

EXAMPLE #2 – To get a feel for this formula, let's look at the following example. Suppose Jane Bundy opens up a shoe store and sells shoes for $40 a pair. If her cost is $25 per pair then her gross margin per pair is $15 or 37.5% of the total.

> Selling price = $40 or **100%**
> Cost of shoes = $25 or **62.5 %**
> Gross Margin = $15 or **37.5%**

If she calculates her operating expenses (fixed costs) to be $75,000 per year, her breakeven point would be:

FC ($75,000) / GM (37.5%) = **$200,000**

Sales of $200,000 means Jane must sell 5,000 pairs of shoes at $40 per pair to breakeven. However, she projects that this is unlikely. Instead, she decides to raise her price, which will in turn raise her gross margin. The question is how much will she have to raise her price to breakeven?

Determining that she can sell shoes for $50 a pair, she calculates her new breakeven point as follows:

> Selling price = $50 or **100%**
> Cost of shoes = $25 or **50 %**
> Gross Margin = $25 or **50%**

With operating expenses of $75,000 the sales volume to breakeven is:

FC (75,000) / GM (50%) = **$150,000**

At a price of $50 per pair, Jane now has to sell 3,000 pairs of shoes to break-even. She is confident she can sell this volume, however she will not make a profit selling at $50 a pair. Therefore, she has to again rethink her strategy. She decides she would like to realize a profit of 10 percent on her operating or fixed costs ($75,000 x 10% = $7,500). To calculate the volume of sales required to earn this profit, she adds the profit to the fixed costs. If she holds the price at $50 for a gross margin of 50%, the sales needed to realize this profit are:

FC + profit ($75,000 + $7,500) / GM (50%) = **$165,000**

To generate $165,000 in sales, she must sell 3,300 pairs of shoes at $50 per pair. This level of sales will cover her variable expenses (cost of goods), her fixed expenses (operating expenses), and generate a profit of $7,500. However, if she is still not confident she can sell this volume of merchandise, and realizes that she has little or no competition, then she may instead decide to raise her gross margin to 55%. She would then calculate her new pricing strategy as follows:

> Unit selling price = Unit Costs of Shoes/VC% =
> ($25) / VC% (.45) = $55.56 or **$56** selling price

If your plan is not workable, it is better to learn it now than to realize six months down the road that you are pouring money into a losing venture.

Unit selling price = 100 % = **$56**
Variable cost = 45% = **$25**
Gross margin = 55% = **$31**

With total sales of $165,000 and cost of sales of $67,500, her gross margin is $82,500. With fixed costs of $75,000, her profit margin is $7,500.

Calculating the B.E. Point Using Markup Percentage

The formula used in the above example can be easily modified to use markup % instead of gross margin as one of the unknown variables. Since markup % is virtually the same as gross margin, the breakeven point is determined as follows:

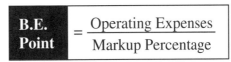

$$\text{B.E. Point} = \frac{\text{Operating Expenses}}{\text{Markup Percentage}}$$

EXAMPLE #3 – If your operating expenses are $50,000 and your average markup is 30% then your required sales to breakeven would be would be $166,667

Calculating the B.E. Point for a Service Provider

Another variation of the *Basic B.E. Formula* is shown below. This formula can be used to calculate a B.E. point in terms of total sales required for a service business to breakeven.

EXAMPLE #4 – Jan London plans to open a beauty salon. She estimates her fixed costs to be $17,000/year and variable costs to be $3,500 for every $8,500 of sales. To calculate the *Volume of Sales* she needs to B.E., she uses the following formula:

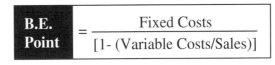

$$\text{B.E. Point} = \frac{\text{Fixed Costs}}{[1 - (\text{Variable Costs/Sales})]}$$

B.E. Point = volume of sales to breakeven
Fixed Costs = fixed expenses, depreciation etc.
Variable Costs = cost of sales & variable expenses
Sales = the corresponding sales volume or income from the sale of goods & services over the same specified period as used to determine your variable costs

B.E. Point =
$17,000 / [1 - ($3,500/$8,500)] =
$17,000 / (1 - 0.41) =
$17,000 / 0.59 =
$28,813

Calculating the B.E. Point for a Manufacturer

In this last example, using still another variation of the *Basic B.E. Formula,* a manufacturer can calculate the number of product sales required to breakeven.

EXAMPLE #5 – James Billings plans to start a tennis racquet manufacturing company. He calculates his fixed costs to be $80,000 per year and his variable costs

By calculating your B.E. point using markup percentage and knowing each product's contribution to overhead, it is also quite easy to figure breakeven points for individual products or services, so you know which products to promote or discontinue (assign floor space to etc.).
BREAKEVEN TIP

per racquet to be $40 per unit. His selling price to suppliers and retailers is $90.

To calculate the *Number of Units* volume of sales he needs to breakeven, he uses the following formula:

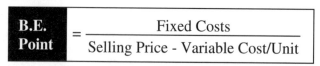

$$\text{B.E. Point} = \frac{\text{Fixed Costs}}{\text{Selling Price - Variable Cost/Unit}}$$

B.E. Point = # of units to breakeven
Fixed Costs = fixed expenses, depreciation, etc
Variable Cost/Unit = your costs per unit
Selling Price = what you charge suppliers

B.E. Point =
$80,000/ $90 - $50 =
$80,000/ $40 =
2,000 units

What to Do With Your Results?

Once you have figured out your B.E. point, stop and evaluate how realistic it is. If it's too high, review your cost figures and breakdown of yearly expenses on your *Twelve-month Income Projection*. Compare them with industry operating ratios. If any of your cost items are too low or too high, change them. With your revised figures, work out a new breakeven analysis.

> *The engine which drives Enterprise is not Thrift, but Profit.*
> **KEYNES**

If it still doesn't look right, think about ways of decreasing your variable & fixed costs, as well as, whether you can raise your per unit selling prices (as long as it won't drastically affect sales volume). If it looks better, don't pat yourself on the back just yet. Get a contact person at the SBA or other advisor on the subject to take a good look at your figures. They may be able to see something you've missed. The bottom line is don't back your start-up plan with your life's savings until your B.E. point is reachable.

Drawing a Breakeven Graph

Use graph paper to graph the results of your breakeven analysis (or use the worksheet on page 178). Use the horizontal axis to represent sales volume in dollars (or number of units sold), and the vertical axis to represent expenses and revenues in dollars (refer to graphs #1 and #2).

EXAMPLE – In example #4 on page 175, Jan London knows her fixed costs are $17,000 per year and variable costs are $3,500 for every $8,500 of sales. To draw a breakeven graph:

First, draw a straight line to represent the dollar value of all fixed costs.

Second, starting from "0" draw a sloping line to a point towards the end of the graph where total sales equals total revenues and expenses (e.g., $45,000 in "total sales" = $45,000 of "total revenues"). This line represents your total revenues.

Third, starting from your fixed expense line, draw a sloping line to a point where you know your variable expenses derived from a certain amount of sales (e.g., for

$34,000 in sales yields $17,000 + $14,000 = $31,000 in expenses). This line represents your total expenses. The intersection of lines 2 and 3 is your breakeven point and should agree with your mathematical calculations. The shaded triangular area below that point represents company losses, while the shaded triangular area above represents potential profits.

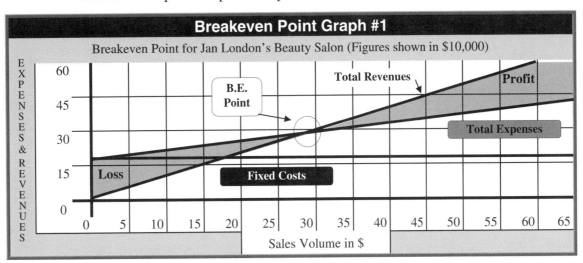

Breakeven Point Graph #1

Breakeven Point for Jan London's Beauty Salon (Figures shown in $10,000)

Sample Paragraphs for a Breakeven Statement

The following chart shows our breakeven point:

Profit	Revenue	Fixed Costs	Variable Costs
$0	$45,000.00	$11,400.00	$33,600.00

It is projected that (Company Name) will be profitable in the (1st, 2nd, 3rd, 4th Quarter) of (199X, 200X).

Indicate the minimum level of sales you will require to cover all fixed and variable costs to breakeven. Explain any assumptions made:

Breakeven Point (in *Sales Dollars* or *Units*) = [Total Fixed Operating Expenses (found in 12-month Income Projection Statement)] / [1 - (Variable costs/Sales)] or [GM] or [Selling price - Variable Cost/unit]

B. E. Point =

=

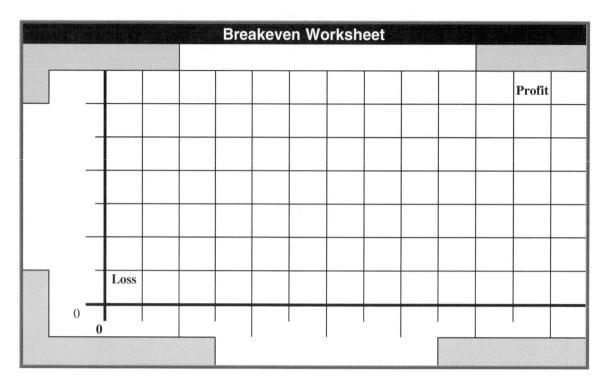

Breakeven Worksheet

Using a GM, BE, ROI & Projected Profit Sheet

A GM, BE, ROI & Projected Profit Sheet as shown on page 179 can be used to determine your B. E. for a single item. Follow steps 1 to 34. Explanations of key terms are provided below. Use the results to draw a graph.

> **Line 11** – Make sure you include return charges and losses usually a factor of .05 to .03 x total sales (i.e., 3 to 5% of total sales).

> **Line 22** – To determine your total variable costs accurately, anticipate other costs of doing business including: ◆ future markdowns for goods that do not sell quickly enough ◆ shrinkage (theft or disappearance) ◆ miscellaneous transportation and delivery costs ◆ cost of doing any alterations that may be requested by your customer.

> **Line 23** – Calculating your total variable costs is pretty much the same as calculating your cost of goods sold except that the former is used to calculate the costs for one individual item while the later is used to calculate the costs of your entire inventory.

> **Line 28** – Collectively referred to as gross profit, GM (gross margin) is the difference between sales income and the cost of the goods sold before any fixed expenses have been taken out for an individual item. GP (gross profit) is the term used to refer to the total of all gross margins. GP = Sales - Cost of Goods Sold. GM = Total Selling Price - Total Variable Costs.

> **Line 29** – A list of fixed operating costs can be found on an income projection.

> **Line 30** – The breakeven point is equal to your overhead or fixed operating costs (O) divided by the difference of your unit sales price (P) minus your unit variable costs (V). B.E. = O/(P - V).

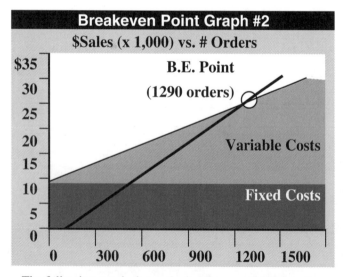

Breakeven Point Graph #2

$Sales (x 1,000) vs. # Orders

B.E. Point

(1290 orders)

Variable Costs

Fixed Costs

The following graph shows the breakeven point for mailing 6,000 brochures for Jack's Jewelry Warehouse promoting a gold chain that sells for $22.95. Fixed costs are $12,500. Gross Margin is $9.69/unit (B.E. = FC/GM = 1290).

Line 31-32 – ROI refers to your Return on Investment or your Net Income = Revenues - Expenses. In the graph #2 shown on page 178, Jack's Jewelry Warehouse would have to sell 2580 units to have a 100 percent return (net income) on an investment of $12,500.

If your business is based on marketing a single KEY product, fill in the following breakeven worksheet:

	GM, BE, ROI & PROJECTED PROFIT SHEET			
PROMOTION:			**Date:**	
Item #	**Description**	**Formula**	**Subtotal**	**Total**
	Variable Costs (per unit) & Fixed Operating Costs			
1	Selling Price of Product or Service (do not include sales tax)			
2	ADD Other Charges (postage & handling etc.)			
3	TOTAL PRICE OF PRODUCT OR SERVICE	1 + 2		
4	Owner's Cost of Product or Service			
5	Handling Expense & Order Processing			
6	Package Expenses (mailing carton, tape, etc.)			
7	Shipping (postage or UPS charges)			
8	*Premium* Costs Including Handling (if premium offered)			
9	Special Business Sales, Hidden or Use Tax, if any	3 x ( ) %		
10	TOTAL COSTS OF FILLING THE ORDER	add 4 TO 9		
11	Estimated % of Returns (expressed as a decimal)			
12	Postage & Handling of Returns	5 + 7		
13	Refurbishing Returned Merchandise	10% of 3		
14	Total Costs of Handling Returns	12 +13		
15	CHARGEABLE COSTS OF HANDLING RETURNS	11 x 13		
16	Estimated % of bad debts (expressed as a decimal)			
17	CHARGEABLE COSTS OF BAD DEBTS	3 x 16		
18	Estimated % of Sales via Credit Cards (as a decimal)			
19	Credit Card Processing Charge	( ) % OF 3		
20	CHARGEABLE COST OF CREDIT	18 x 19		
21	ADMINISTRATIVE OVERHEAD PER UNIT			
22	OTHER COSTS PER UNIT			
23	**TOTAL VARIABLE COSTS**	10 + 15 + 17 + 20 + 21 + 22		
24	Unit Profit After Variable Costs	3 - 23		
25	% of Final Sales (expressed as a decimal)	1.0 - (11)		
26	Net Unit Profit	24 x 25		
27	Credit for Returned Merchandise	4 x 11		
28	**GROSS MARGIN** (NET PROFIT PER ORDER)	26 + 27	$	
29	**TOTAL FIXED OPERATING COSTS** (Mailing, Advertising etc.)		$	
	Profit Calculations			
30	**NUMBER OF ORDERS TO BREAKEVEN**	29 / 28		
31	NUMBER OF ORDERS TO OBTAIN 50% ROI	1.5 x 30		
32	NUMBER OF ORDERS TO OBTAIN 100% ROI	2.0 x 30		
33	PROJECTED PROFIT IF ? # OF ORDERS RECEIVED	(# of orders x 28) - (29)		$
34	PROJECTED PROFIT IF (XX) # OF ORDERS RECEIVED	(# of orders x 28) - (29)		$

COMMENTS :

Even if you plan to spread the purchase of some assets through the year, for the purposes of your pro forma balance sheet, assume that all assets will be provided at start-up.

Pro Forma Balance Sheet

Worthy of inclusion in a business plan is a *Pro Forma Balance Sheet* reflecting sources and uses of equity funds (and borrowed funds) before your company begins operations. A summary statement of your balance sheet should also be included (see sample below). Pro forma balance sheets come in a variety of formats. If requesting a loan, you may find it prudent to ask your banker for the form they use. It will make it easier for them to evaluate the health of your business using a form they are familiar with.

Sample Pro Forma Balance Sheet Summary

Initially, (Company Name) books will be maintained manually, using (an Expense Journal and an Income Journal). At a future point, (I/we) will seek out a computerized accounting package to help us more effectively monitor our financial performance. Information for financial statements will be compiled monthly and reviewed against our pro forma statements. If we find that we are consistently over budget, appropriate actions will be taken to adjust costs and other budget projections. Our next step will be to recheck our cost structure (and reevaluate our markup on our products) to make certain we are obtaining the best possible prices.

PRO FORMA BALANCE SHEET

Balance Sheet FOR:	As OF: A	$
Current Assets		
A/Rs (LESS allowance for bad debts)	_____	
Cash in Bank	_____	
Cash on Hand (includes Petty Cash)	_____	
Inventories (Merchandise)	_____	
Prepaid Expenses	_____	
Short-term Investments	_____	
Long-term Investments	_____	
Supplies	_____	
Other Current Assets	_____	
Total Current Assets	A	$
Fixed Assets		
Buildings	_____	
Land	_____	
Furniture & Fixtures	_____	
Leasehold Improvements	_____	
Materials & Equipment	_____	
Motor Vehicles	_____	
Other Fixed Assets	_____	
Total Current Assets	B	$
Total Assets (C = A + B)	C	$
Current Liabilities		
Accounts Payable	_____	
Interest Payable	_____	
Taxes Payable	_____	
Short Term Loans Payable	_____	
Other Current Liabilities	_____	
Total Current Liabilities	D	$
Long Term Liabilities		
Long Term Loans Payable	_____	
Mortgages	_____	
Other Long Term Liabilities	_____	
Total Long Term Liabilities	E	$
Total Liabilities (F = D + E)	F	$
Total Net Worth (G = C - F)	G	$
Total Liabilities & Net Worth (H = F + G)	H	$

Outline any assumptions or estimations made, as well as, procedures followed in preparing your pro forma balance sheet and future financial statements. Also, estimate sources and uses of both equity and borrowed funds (provide proof of equity):

DAY 27

Current Financial Statements

If your business has already been in operation for a year or more, include actual performance statements reflecting your business activities. Specifically, include a current (1) *Income Statement*; (2) *Balance Sheet*; and (3) *Asset Sheet*. You might also consider adding a *Deviation Analysis* and *Market Value Balance Sheet*.

How Detailed Should Financial Statements Be?

Income statements and balance sheets should be limited to one page each. For large companies with many accounts, financial schedules can be used to provide greater details for any summary accounts used. These schedules can be added to your *Supporting Documents* section. For income statements, financial schedules can breakdown in greater detail selling expenses, general and administrative expenses, and cost of goods sold. For balance sheets, they can breakdown asset and liabilities accounts such as Property Owned and Loans Payable.

Accepted Income Statement &
Balance Sheet Formats

INCOME STATEMENT

INCOME
    a. *Net Sales* (gross sales - returns and allowances)
    b. *Cost of Goods Sold*
    c. *Gross Profit* [a - b]

EXPENSES (expenses do not have to be split)
    a. *Selling Expenses* (direct, controllable, variable)
    b. *Administrative Expenses* (indirect, fixed, office overhead)

INCOME from OPERATIONS
(gross profit - total expenses)
    a. *Other Income* (interest income)
    b. *Other Expenses* (interest expense)

NET PROFIT (loss) Before Income Taxes

    a. *Taxes* (federal & state)

NET PROFIT (loss) After Income Taxes

BALANCE SHEET

ASSETS
    a. *Current Assets*
    b. *Long-term Investments*
    c. *Fixed Assets*

LIABILITIES
    a. *Current Liabilities*
    b. *Long-term Liabilities*

NET WORTH (Assets - Liabilities)
    In the case of a *Proprietorship or Partnership*, net worth is equal to the owner's original investment plus earnings after withdrawals. In the case of a *Corporation*, net worth is equal to the sum of contributions by owners or stockholders plus earnings retained after paying dividends.

Current Income Statement

The *Income Statement* – also referred to as a *Profit & Loss Statement*, an *Income & Expense Statement*, or an *Operating Statement* – summarizes the results of all business activity for a specified period of time. It is the most important financial statement you will prepare each year, as its totals are used to determine your tax liability. It shows the income sources for your business, your expenses incurred in obtaining the income, and the profit or loss resulting. It can also help reveal things like whether you're paying too much rent, whether you need to schedule work so your truck fleet can be used more efficiently, whether mail should be used instead of telephones, or whether you need to reduce inventory supplies. Analyzing your income statements can also help you pick out strengths and weaknesses of ad campaigns and inventory management practices (see page 185).

Allocating Depreciation Costs to the Period of Time Covering the Statement – One difficulty in developing an income statement is in properly allocating *depreciation costs* to the period of time covering the statement. Since fixed assets, such as equipment and building costs, cannot be included under *expenses*, to allocate these costs properly, their purchase price must be divided by the expected life in years or months, whichever corresponds to the period covered by the income statement. Using the straight-line method of calculating depreciation, their purchase price is charged uniformly over the life of the asset.

If your business has already been in operation for sometime, provide income statements and balance sheets for your current year and the last three in your supporting documents section.

Current Balance Sheet

The *Balance Sheet* summarizes the financial position of a business at the time of the report (usually the ending of an accounting cycle). It looks at assets, liabilities, and net worth (owner's equity). If your business possesses more assets than it owes to creditors, your net worth is *positive*. If you owe more money to creditors than you possess in assets, your net worth is *negative*. The balance sheet is useful for purposes of control, management direction, and decision-making. To fill out the balance sheet provided on page 186, use the following 8 steps:

NOTE Figures used to compile your balance sheet are taken from previous balance sheets as well as your current income statement.

1) **Title the balance sheet.** At the top of the page fill in the legal name of your company and the day the balance sheet was prepared.

2) **List all current assets.** List anything of value that is owned or legally due your business and can be converted into cash within 12 months of the date of the balance sheet (or during one established cycle of operations).

● *Inventory* – When listing your inventory, include raw materials on hand, work in progress and all finished goods either manufactured or purchased for resale.

● *Short-term Investments* – When listing your short-term investments, list them at either cost or market value, whichever is less.

3) **List all long-term investments.** These include all long-term assets such as stocks and bonds that you intend to keep for longer than a year.

4) **List all fixed assets.** Fixed assets are listed at cost less depreciation. This is called their net value. However, land is listed at its original purchase price irrespective of its market value.

● *Accumulated Depreciation* – Instead of listing their fixed assets at their "net value," some balance sheets list them at their "original value." However, an additional Accumulated Depreciation account must be added to this kind of balance sheet. The total here is then subtracted from the total of the fixed assets.

● *Leased Fixed Assets* – If any of your fixed assets are leased, depending on the leasing arrangement, both the value and the liability of the leased property may need to be listed on your balance sheet.

An "Income Statement" is like a moving picture showing what happened to your business over a period of time.

5) **List all current liabilities.** This includes all debts, monetary obligations and claims payable within 12 months or one cycle of operations.

● *Short-term Loans Payables* – When listing your short-term loans payables, list the balance of principal due on all short-term debt and the current amount due of total balance on notes or loans whose terms exceed 12 months.

● *Taxes Payable* – These amounts are estimated by your accountant to have been incurred during the accounting period. On the balance sheet found in many SBA booklets, this account is split up into federal income tax, state income tax, self-employment tax, sales tax, and Property tax.

6) **List all long-term liabilities.** All long term liabilities such as loans payable, contracts payable and mortgages are listed at their outstanding balance less the current portion due (which is listed in short term loans payable).

7) **List your net worth.** In a proprietorship or partnership, *net worth* is each owner's original investment plus any earnings after withdrawals. In a corporation, *net worth* is reflected in a capital stock account, surplus paid in (retained earnings as of) and retained earnings.

8) **Compare your total liabilities and net worth.** The sum of these two amounts must always match that for total assets.

A "Balance Sheet" is like a snapshot of your business at an exact moment in time.

> *It sounds extraordinary but it's a fact that balance sheets can make fascinating reading.*
> **MARY ARCHER**

Current Asset Sheet

A *Current Asset Sheet* lists all assets currently in use by your business, how much investment each required, and the source of funds used to capitalize them (see example on page 184).

Other Financial Statements

Other financial statements you may want to include in your *Financial Plan* include: ❑ capital expenditure projections ❑ quarterly, annual, or three years sales projections (sales volume should be indicated in units and dollars if possible) ❑ detailed business expenses (projected, actual, and budgeted) ❑ cost of sales (outlines production, marketing costs, pro-rated expenses, and administrative costs) ❑ expected taxation liabilities.

Three other statements worthy of inclusion are explained below:

- **Deviation Analysis** – A *Deviation Analysis* compares actual income and expenses to projected income and expenses on a month-to-month basis. It helps you spot strengths and weaknesses in your projections and budgeting.

- **Market-value Balance Sheet** – One of the problems in a growing business is that the existing equity or collateral position can be artificially low because of accelerated deprecation. Using accelerated depreciation results in a *Book-value Balance Sheet* that has less equity or collateral than a market-value balance sheet. The former shows assets at their depreciated value whereas the latter shows the assets at their current market value. To develop a *Market-value Balance Sheet*, present your current book-value balance sheet with an additional column for the market value. Documentation of market value can be provided through appraisals or advertisement that includes prices on similar equipment or assets. The market-value balance sheet usually increases the equity dollar amounts and the equity-to-assets ratio. This should result in a banker's willingness to a loan a larger amount for growth activities.

- **Statement of Change in Financial Position** – This document shows how changes in working capital occurred over a specific time period. It is not a requirement of the *Tax Act* but management is increasingly using it as a tool to better profits and cash flow. Accountants and bankers are also placing increasing emphasis on this statement.

Discuss both positive and negative aspects of your current income statements. List any assumptions or special concerns, as well as, areas of critical importance (this is no place to try and hide from the facts):

Discuss both positive and negative aspects of your current balance sheets. List any assumptions or special concerns:

Sources and Costs of Assets – List all current assets. Include value: EXAMPLES:

Asset	Cost	Source of Funds	Asset	Cost	Source of Funds
			Cash	$4,500	Personal Savings
			Accounts Receivable	5,000	From Profits
			Inventory	4,000	Vendor Credit
			Pickup Truck	6,000	Previously Owned
			Packaging Machine	12,000	Installment Purchase
			Office Desk & Chair	600	Previously Owned
			Calculator	80	Personal Cash
			Personal Computer	3,000	Personal Savings

List other financial statements you will include and why they are relevant:

INCOME STATEMENT

Statement of Income for: **As of:**

	GROSS SALES	
LESS Returns and Allowances	_____	
LESS Sales Tax (if included in sales)	_____	
ADD OTHER INCOME:		
Royalties and Dividends on Stock	_____	
Interest from Bank Accounts	_____	
Gains from Sale of Fixed Assets	_____	
Other Income	_____	
	GROSS INCOME	$
LESS COST OF GOODS SOLD:		
Inventory at Beginning of Fiscal Period	_____	
ADD Cost of Goods Purchased During Fiscal Period	_____	
ADD Freight & Delivery Charges	_____	
LESS Purchased Returns	_____	
LESS Inventory at the End of the Fiscal Period	_____	
TOTAL Cost of Goods Sold	_____	
	GROSS PROFIT	$
LESS OPERATING EXPENSES:		
Accounting, Legal & Professional Fees	_____	
Advertising	_____	
Bad Debts	_____	
Car & Truck Expenses (except depreciation allowance)	_____	
Commissions & Fees	_____	
Depreciation (Capital Cost Allowance)	_____	
Employee Benefit Programs	_____	
Insurance	_____	
Interest Charges (Debt Expenses)	_____	
Mortgage Payments	_____	
Office Expenses	_____	
Payroll Taxes	_____	
Pension and Profit Sharing Plans	_____	
Property Taxes	_____	
Rent or Lease	_____	
Repairs & Maintenance	_____	
Salaries & Wages	_____	
Supplies	_____	
Taxes, Fees, Licenses, Dues & Subscriptions	_____	
Telephone	_____	
Travel, Meals & Entertainment	_____	
Utilities (Heat, Hydro)	_____	
Other Operating Expenses:	_____	
TOTAL Operating Expenses	_____	
	NET INCOME (Before Taxes)	$
LESS Estimated Tax Payments	_____	
	NET INCOME (After Taxes)	$

BALANCE SHEET

Balance Sheet FOR: **As OF:**

Current Assets

Accounts Receivable (LESS allowance for bad debts)   _____

Cash in Bank   _____

Cash on Hand (includes Petty Cash)   _____

Inventories (Merchandise)   _____

Prepaid Expenses   _____

Short-term Investments   _____

Supplies   _____

Other Current Assets   _____

Long-Term Investments

_____

Fixed Assets

Buildings   _____

Land   _____

Furniture & Fixtures   _____

Leasehold Improvements   _____

Materials & Equipment   _____

Motor Vehicles   _____

Other Fixed Assets   _____

TOTAL ASSETS $ _____

Current Liabilities

Accounts Payable   _____

Interest Payable   _____

Income Tax Payable   _____

Wages & Salaries Payable   _____

Short Term Loans Payable   _____

Other Current Liabilities   _____

Long Term Liabilities

Long Term Loans Payable   _____

Mortgages   _____

Bonds Payable (applies to corporations)   _____

Other Long Term Liabilities   _____

TOTAL LIABILITIES $ _____

Owner's Equity

Proprietorship or Partnership Equity   _____

Capital Stock   _____

Retained Earnings as of: _____

Earnings Retained (Net Income) for: _____

Total Owner's or Stockholder's Equity = **NET WORTH** $ _____

TOTAL LIABILITIES & NET WORTH $ _____

Business Financial History

Your business financial history is a summary of financial information about your company from its start to the present. Of particular importance in this section, is the calculation of key financial and operating ratios useful for making projections and analyzing the financial health of a business. This section is also of great interest to bankers and investors. A *Personal Net Worth* and *Personal Income* statement may also be included in this section (see page 207 and 208).

Summarize financial information about your company from start to the present:

Corporate Capitalization Info		S-Prop. Capitalization Info	
Number of Shares Authorized		Product revenues of	$
Number of Shares Authorized		Product revenues of	$
Number of Shares of Stock Outstanding		Product net income of	$
Par Value of Stock	$	Number of customers and clients developed	
Owner(s) Number of Shares of Stock Owned		Markets Developed	
Date Acquired Capital Contributions		Market Share Secured	%
		Categories Market Share Secured in	

Financial & Operating Ratios

> *I don't have any experience in running up a $4 trillion debt.*
> **H. ROSS PEROT**
> After President Bush's stress on experience on the 1992 presidential election debates

The relationships between amounts of invested capital, levels of sales, various cost categories, inventory turnover, and other items, form what bankers and investors like to refer to as *Financial Ratios*. Financial ratios are used by bankers and investors to determine the relative health of a business. They can also be used by management to provide valuable checkpoints allowing you to better control key aspects of your business before it's too late to make adjustments. The basic data for ratio analysis is contained in your balance sheet and income statement.

Financial and operating ratios can be found in the various publications listed on page 189 as well as in trade journals particular to your industry. The publications on page 189 should be available at your public library. You may also be able to find them at local business centers and SBA offices. Each publication provides various ratios useful for making projections for various types of businesses.

Sample Statement of Compiled Operating Ratios

(I/We) have included financial standards as compiled Dun & Bradstreet, Robert Morris Associates, and *Business and Industrial Financial Ratios* (1996 edition).

Review the financial ratios outlined below. Select those that best show the financial condition of your business:

The three financial ratios shown below play an important role in the granting or denial of loan request. Small businesses should calculate and monitor these financial ratios as part of their working capital management policy:

$\dfrac{Current}{Ratio} = \dfrac{\text{Current Assets}}{\text{Current Liabilities}}$	$\dfrac{Quick \ or}{Acid \ Ratio} = \dfrac{\text{(Current Assets - Inventories)}}{\text{Current Liabilities}}$	$\dfrac{Debt \ to \ Total}{Assets \ Ratio} = \dfrac{\text{Total Debt}}{\text{Total Assets}}$

- **Cost of Sales to Total Inventory** – This ratio is used to assess how well your company has used the resources at its command. It is calculated by dividing the total cost of sales by total inventory.

- **Current Assets to Current Liabilities** * – This ratio is used to assess your company's solvency i.e., its ability to pay off debts promptly. A high current ratio is looked upon favorably and means that you have more than enough cash on hand – and short-term assets such as inventory that can be quickly converted into cash – to meet all debts falling due within a year's time. As a general rule, this ratio should be two to one. It is calculated by dividing current assets by current liabilities.

- **Net Income to Total Sales** – This ratio, also called the Profit Margin ratio, is used to determine how profitable your company is. It is calculated by dividing net income by total sales. In this case, the larger the ratio, the better.

- **Net Sales to Tangible Net Worth** – This ratio shows how actively invested capital is being put to work by indicating the number of times it turns over during a period. It is calculated by dividing net sales by tangible net worth (equity). Tangible net worth is the true worth of a business (assets - liabilities) minus intangible assets such as good will or incorporation costs.

- **Profits to Tangible Net Worth** – This ratio is a measure of return on investment and is considered one of the best criteria for profitability. It is calculated by dividing Net profits (after taxes) by tangible net worth (equity).

- **Quick or Acid-test Ratio** * – This ratio is calculated by dividing current assets less inventory, by the amount of current liabilities. It measures liquidity and reveals whether a firm can meet its maturing obligations.

- **Return On Assets** – This ratio is similar in function to the Profits to Tangible Net Worth ratio and is calculated by dividing your companies net income by total assets.

- **Sales to Fixed Assets** – This ratio shows what sales are generated by each dollar invested in plant & equipment. It is calculated by dividing total sales by total assets. For example, if sales are $400,000 and assets $150,000, your sales to fixed asset ratio would be 2.76. This means that $2.76 of revenue is generated from $1 of assets.

- **Sales to Inventory** – This ratio gives the average turnover of inventory for your company and is useful for comparing your company's performance with others within the industry. It is calculated by dividing annual sales by current inventory. For example, if annual sales are $400,000 and current inventory $100,000, your sales to inventory ratio would be 4. This means that you inventory turnovers four times each year.

- **Sales to Receivables** – This ratio is used to find the number of days money is tied up in receivables to determine the average collection period. It will tell you (and your banker) how much it will cost to run your business for the amount of days you're A/Rs are tied up, and thus how much money you need to have on hand-or to borrow. As a general rule, the greater you're A/Rs (what customers owe) the more capitalization you will need to tide your business over until those accounts are paid. This ratio is calculated by dividing A/Rs by daily sales. For example, if annual sales are $400,000 of which $100,000 is A/Rs, and your business was open for 300 days, making your average daily sales $1,333, then your sales to A/Rs ratio would be 75 days.

- **Times Interest Earned Ratio** – This ratio measures the long-term solvency of your company. It is calculated by dividing your net income before interest and income tax expenses by the amount of interest expense.

- **Total Debt to Current Debt** – This ratio shows the proportion of a company's debts within the present operating year. It further shows whether the company might be exposed to unusual financial strains from debts maturing during the current year. It is calculated by dividing your companies total debts by its current debts.

- **Total Debt to Total Assets** * – This ratio looks at the ability of a business to repay long-term debt. It is given special focus in the American Bankers Association guidelines for evaluating a business. It is calculated by dividing total liabilities by total assets. For example, if you owe $100,000 and have total assets of $200,000, then your debt to asset ratio would by 1:2 or 50%. This means that the assets are twice as large as the debts. Your company presents a healthy financial picture.

<u>**Where to Find FINANCIAL & OPERATING RATIOS**</u> – *Visit your library and consult the publications listed below. List the source you will use to make projections and other estimations.*

❏ **Dun & Bradstreet Information Services** – *Industry Norms & Key Business Ratios*. Desktop Edition. New York (annual), also available on diskette. Gives balance sheet and income statement statistics, as well as, financial ratios for over 800 lines of business. Arranged by 4-digit SIC industries. D&B also publishes *Key Business Ratios*, which contains over 700 pages of British financial ratios for some 378 SIC, industries in the U.K.

❏ **Financial Research Associates** – *Financial Studies of the Small Business*, P.O. Box 7708, Winterhaven, FL 33883-7708 (annual). Contains financial & operating ratios for about 50 lines of small business (those with capitalization under $1 million – retail, wholesale, services, contractors & professional services, and manufacturers – by asset size categories).

❏ **Robert Morris Associates** – *Annual Statement Studies*, One Liberty Place, Philadelphia, PA 19103. Contains financial and operating ratios for more than 360 lines of business (by 4-digit SIC number). Includes manufacturers, wholesalers, retailers, services, and contractors.

❏ **Tryo, Leo Ph.D** – *Almanac of Business & Industrial Financial Ratios*, Englewood Cliffs, NJ: Prentice-Hall (annual). Lists operating ratios for about 160 industries arranged by a 4-digit industry classification similar to SIC. Features IRS data on 3.7 million U.S. corporations.

❏ **U.S. Bureau of the Census** – *Quarterly Financial Report for Manufacturing, Mining, and Trade Corporations*, Washington, DC: U.S. Government Printing Office. Contains quarterly income statement & balance sheet data as well as selected financial & operating ratios classified by industry (22 industries) and asset size.

Research financial & operating ratios for your industry and list them here:

<u>Selected Operating Ratios for Small Businesses</u> – *(Source: compiled from "Almanac of Business and Industrial Financial Ratios" 1996 edition; available at most libraries).*

Type of Business	Cost of Sales	Gross Profit	Operating Expenses	Operating Profit
MANUFACTURING				
Electronic Components	62.1	37.9	34.4	3.5%
Bread & bakery products	59.4	40.6	37.9	2.7
Sporting and athletic	56.7	43.3	34.5	8.7
Jewelry, precious metals	61.1	38.9	32.5	6.5
Women's dresses	61.4	38.6	33.8	4.8
Commercial Printing	59.6	40.4	35.6	4.7
WHOLESALERS				
Stationary supplies	66.5	33.5	31.2	2.3
General groceries	77.0	23.0	21.1	1.9
Jewelry	70.1	29.9	26.1	3.8
Sporting goods & toys	68.5	31.5	29.2	2.3
Fresh fruit & vegetables	78.2	21.8	19.3	2.5
RETAILERS				
Jewelry	54.0	46.0	41.2	4.8
Books and stationary	61.5	38.5	36.7	1.8
Women's ready to wear	59.3	40.7	37.7	3
Gasoline service stations	77.7	22.3	19.6	2.7
Groceries and meats	76.3	23.7	21.7	2.0
Sporting goods & bikes	66.2	33.8	30.1	3.7
SERVICES				
Travel agencies			98	2
Accounting			86.5	13.5
Leasing equipment			90.8	9.2
Motels and hotels			96.5	3.5
Computer programming			95.7	4.3
YOUR BUSINESS				

<u>Detailed Operating Ratios for Book, Greeting Cards & Miscellaneous Publishing Businesses</u> *(Source: "Almanac of Business and Industrial Financial Ratios" 1996 edition; available at most libraries).*

Performance Indicator (%)	All	$100,000 to $250,000 in Assets	
Cost of Operations	39.5	30.0	
Rent	2.3	3.4	
Taxes Paid	3.0	2.4	
Interest Paid	4.4	1.1	
Depreciation, Amortization	4.1	3.4	
Pension and Other Benefits	2.5	1.4	
Other	42.3	41.6	
Operating Margin	1.9	16.7	
In Thousands of Dollars:			
Average Total Revenues	$2,952	$527	
Net Receivables	$672	$10	
Inventories	$309	$31	
Total Assets	$3,494	$176	
Notes and Loans Payable	$1,157	$54	
Selected Financial Ratios:			
Current Ratio	1.2	1.5	
Quick Ratio	0.6	0.7	
Net Sales to Working Capital	14.6	22.5	
Inventory Turnover	3.5	5.2	
Receivables Turnover	4.1	–	
Total Liabilities to Net worth	2.2	1.2	
Financial Factors (%):			
Debt Ratio	68.9	53.7	
Return on Assets	7.9	18.5	
Profit Margin Before Income Tax	5.5	5.1	
Profit Margin After Income Tax	4.0	4.9	
# of Enterprises Compared	10,864	1644	

To Do List

Financial Plan
Profit Planning

✓ Cost Reducing
   Measures
✓ Retirement Plan
✓ Investment Plan
✓ Tax Planning

A man is the richest whose pleasures are the cheapest.
HENRY D. THOREAU

Getting money is like digging with a needle; spending it is like water soaking into sand.
JAPANESE PROVERB

Every increased possession loads us with a new weariness.
RUSKIN

Beware of little expenses: A small leak will sink a ship.
BENJAMIN FRANKLIN

Most of the money a businessman calls profit is merely money that has not been wasted.
JOSEPH COSSMAN

DAY 28
Profit Planning

A *Profit Plan* starts with finding ways to reduce costs, in particular, your tax burden. It blossoms when you develop goals and strategies for investing profits or leftover cash in short and long term investments, as well as, developing personal and company retirement plans to secure profits. Cash should never be idle. Your profits must work for you as hard as you did to earn them.

Cost Reducing Measures

There is one cardinal rule known to every successful entrepreneur:

"The quickest way to increase profits is to lower overhead."

To generate profits and increase the amount of cash you have available for investment purposes, implement cost-cutting strategies to control & reduce your expenses. Consider for example the following: If you're operating at a 10 % profit ratio, for every $100 you spend, an additional $1,000 is needed in increased sales to balance these expenditures. Remember, overhead *kills* profits.

All Time Biggest Money Wasters

To start you off on the road to reducing your business and personal overhead, browse through the following checklist of *All Time Biggest Money Wasters*. How many have you fell victim to? ❑ buying a new car every few years ❑ buying anything new & improved without asking yourself if it *really is* new & improved ❑ buying anything on sale that you don't really need ❑ buying designer clothing ❑ buying life insurance for children ❑ driving to work alone ❑ eating in fancy restaurants ❑ keeping money in low interest savings accounts ❑ playing the lottery ❑ taking credit card loans ❑ taking expensive vacations ❑ using a *gold card* because it makes you feel successful.

33 Scrooge Strategies

Anyone can spend a million dollars (large corporations do it all the time). But it takes patience, determination, planning, and research, to spend it wisely, and even more, not spend it at all. The "33 Scrooge Strategies" on the following page are aimed at helping you reduce your business and living expenses.

NOTE Reducing business overhead costs, such as rent, utilities, and interest, immediately lowers your breakeven point. When your breakeven point is lowered, you can reach profitability sooner.

Outline how you plan to reduce costs and overhead in your business:

Check strategies below you will use to lower your business and living overhead. Add some "Scrooge Strategies" of your own:

33 Scrooge Strategies

❏ Always think of ways NOT to spend your money.

❏ Attend free IRS sponsored workshops to reduce taxes.

❏ Avoid buying convenience foods. Convenience and junk foods not only cost more, but in the long run are bad for your health (and contribute to higher medical bills).

❏ Be wary of get-rich-quick seminars. Much of the advice get-rich-quick schemers have to offer is simplistic, deceptive, wrong and quite often harmful. Stay away from no money down real estate courses.

❏ Buy a used car. With new cars depreciating by 20% after one year, and 50% after three years, should you be spending $15,000 to $20,000 on a new car?

❏ Buy in small quantities at first. You can always reorder.

❏ Buy inventory & supplies in larger quantities to get volume discounts, once you have a clear understanding of your markets.

❏ Buy only the clothes you need and when you do buy, buy quality. The wealthy can't afford to waste time buying cheap things over and over again. Why should you?

❏ Buy quality to save in the long run. Cheap equipment and furniture wear out faster and become obsolete quicker.

❏ Carefully consider all new technology before spending any money on it.

❏ Clean with natural products. Use baking soda, ammonia, boric acid, vinegar, and lemon juice. Not only is this cheaper but it's better for the environment.

❏ Cut down or give up tobacco and alcohol. Cutting down on tobacco and alcohol can save the average heavy drinker and smoker over $3,000 a year.

❏ Develop a good relationship with your suppliers and service providers. Not only can good contacts lead to discounts, buy suppliers and service providers are often your best link to keeping up with the latest trends.

❏ Don't buy more furniture than you need. The less you have, the more spacious your rooms will look.

❏ Drastically reduce the amount you spend on beauty products. The best-kept beauty secrets are almost free.

❏ Enter contests in which you have a good chance of winning. Many promotional contests run by various companies offer excellent chances of winning. Some people even claim to make a living doing so.

❏ Follow the 80/20 rule. Your profits lie in the 20% of your customers who give you 80% of your business.

❏ Follow the two-thirds rule. Always put two-thirds of your energy into reducing costs and one-third into increasing income.

❏ Get rid of your second car. Cutting out that extra car payment, as well as insurance and maintenance costs, could easily save you $300 to $600 a month.

❏ Join a local, state/provincial or national barter exchange and swap for items you need to run your business.

❏ Keep all warranties and bills of major purchases. You never know when clock radios, hair dryers and the like will suddenly expire for no good reason.

❏ Lower your thermostat. Heat is money. For each Fahrenheit degree above 68 degrees Fahrenheit, your fuel consumption goes up an average of 2.5 percent. If you permanently lower your thermostat from 72 degrees to 68 degrees you will save 10 percent on your annual fuel consumption.

❏ Make all your holidays, partially tax deductible as business trips.

❏ Make it a habit of reviewing newspaper ads, newsletters, and supplier circulars for special discounts.

❏ Minimize transportation costs. Driving to and from your business is a daily expense. If you drive less, you can save on gas, parking, maintenance, and repairs.

❏ Reduce meals out. If you're like most people, you spend about $5 a day on lunch and snacks. Preparing yourself a lunch from home could quite easily save you $50 to $100 a month.

❏ Reduce personal long distance calls. Write letters instead, Fax or better yet, send E-mail.

❏ Send faxes after 11 P.M. Rates are as much as 60 % lower.

❏ Settle for a smaller house to keep your mortgage payments reasonable.

❏ Stay at budget motels on business trips.

❏ Take in borders or rent a basement suite.

❏ When first staring out, try not to hire. Do most of the work yourself, especially if your business is small or home-based.

❏ Yearly reassess your own insurance needs and deductibles to see if you can't reduce these costs.

Retirement Plan

The *first* part of your retirement plan is to take advantage of the federal government's deferred tax sheltered savings plan by opening an individual retirement account. This is an essential strategy for reducing your taxes and increasing your net worth. In fact, the sooner your start contributing, the more rewards you will reap in the future. Compounding is the key (see charts below). In America, open an IRA (Individual Retirement Arrangement). In Canada, open an RRSP (Registered Retirement Savings Plan). The *second* part of your retirement plan is to start a company pension plan for both yourself and your employees.

NOTE A *deferred tax sheltered savings plan*, also referred to as a *fixed annuity*, is the long-term investment most favored by financial planners. It offers safety, interest reinvestment, and tax deferment. It can easily make you a millionaire if you start early enough. Of course due to inflation, $1 million may not buy as much when you're ready to retire, but you will still be way ahead of the game.

The IRA Plan for USA

In the U.S., you can set up and contribute to an IRA if you received taxable compensation during the year and will not reach age $70\frac{1}{2}$ by the year's end. Compensation includes taxable wages, salaries, commissions, bonuses, tips, professional fees, self-employment income, and taxable alimony. You can have an IRA whether or not you are covered by any other retirement plan. The most you can contribute for any year is the lesser of $2,000 or your taxable compensation.

The RRSP Plan for Canada

In Canada . . . the long-term policy of Canadian policy-makers is to pull back, over the coming years, from the burden of public responsibility for retirees. The government would much rather have Canadians look after themselves. The maximum RRSP contribution is the lesser of 18% of your earned income or $13,500 (1998 budget). However, if you did not use your entire RRSP deduction limit for previous year, you may be able to carry forward those amounts.

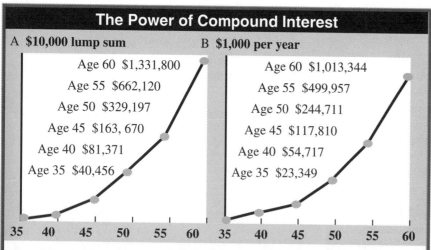

The Power of Compound Interest

A $10,000 lump sum

Age 60	$1,331,800
Age 55	$662,120
Age 50	$329,197
Age 45	$163,670
Age 40	$81,371
Age 35	$40,456

B $1,000 per year

Age 60	$1,013,344
Age 55	$499,957
Age 50	$244,711
Age 45	$117,810
Age 40	$54,717
Age 35	$23,349

Example A shows a 25 year-old man or woman investing a lump sum of $10,000 in an IRA or RRSP and getting an annual rate of return of 15%.

Example B shows the same 25 year-old investing $1,000 each year for 30 years and also getting an annual rate of return of 15% (if, in the first example, you invest an additional $2,000 at the end of each year, by age 65 you will have over $8 million dollars!).

Tax Sheltered Growth

Years in Plan	5%	10%	15%
10	13,207	17,531	23,349
20	34,719	63,002	117,810
30	69,761	180,943	499,957

Note: Tax sheltered growth of a $10,000 lump sum.

Company Retirement Plans for USA

Company retirement plans are savings plans that offer you tax advantages to set aside money for your own and your employees' retirement. They can be funded entirely by your contribution or by a mix of your contributions and employee contributions. Your contributions as an employer to an employer-sponsored retirement plan are generally deductible within certain limits. You can set up either a *qualified plan* (which includes defined contribution plans and defined benefit plans) or an *unqualified plan*.

❏ **Defined Contribution Plan** – There are five types of defined contribution plans:

❏ *The Keogh (HR-10) Plan* – A Keogh plan is a tax-deferred pension plan that can be set up by either full-time or part-time sole proprietors or partnerships. To set up a Keogh plan, it is not necessary to have employees, as a self-employed person is considered both an employer and an employee. Under this plan your deduction for contributions to a profit-sharing plan cannot exceed 15% of the yearly compensation from the business paid to any common-law employees participating in the plan. In the case of a money purchase pension plan, contributions cannot exceed 25%. On the other hand, personal contributions are limited to the smaller of $30,000 or 13.0435% of your net earnings for a profit-sharing plan and 20% for a money purchase pension plan.

After age 59, half of your Keogh plan savings can be withdrawn as a lump sum and taxed using five-year forward averaging. This is one advantage of Keogh plans over IRA plans – the latter does not have five-year forward averaging available. All paperwork for your Keogh plan must be completed by December 31 of each year, though the actual money need not be paid into the fund until tax-filing time April 15 of the following year.

❏ *Profit Sharing Plan* – This is a plan that lets your employees or their beneficiaries share in the profits of your business. The plan must have a definite formula for allocating the contributions to the plan among the participating employees and for distributing the funds.

❏ *Money Purchase Pension Plan* – Under this plan, your contributions are a stated amount, or are based on a stated formula that is not subject to your discretion. For example, your formula could be 10% of each employee's compensation. Your contributions to the plan are not based on your profits.

❏ *Stock Bonus Plan* – This plan is similar to a profit-sharing plan, but only a Corporation can set it up. Benefits are payable in the form of the company's stock.

❏ *The Simplified Employee Pension (SEP)* – A SEP is an ideal plan for small to medium-sized businesses. It is easy to establish and understand, with minimal record-keeping and government reporting. Corporations, proprietorships and partnerships can setup a SEP. Under a SEP, you make deductible contributions to an IRA which is owned by you or your common-law employees. Under this plan, yearly contributions cannot exceed the smaller of 15% of the employee's compensation (or your net earnings) or $30,000. This limit does not include employee contributions. Employees can also make contributions of up to $2,000 per year. Mutual funds can be an excellent investment for your SEP.

SEP contributions can lower your taxable income. If your taxable income is $250,000, and your corporate tax rate is 34%, a $50,000 contribution will lower your taxable income to $200,000. Instead of paying $85,000, you will pay $68,000, saving $17,000. A $50,000 SEP contribution thus costs only $33,000.

❏ **Defined Benefit Plans** – A qualified defined benefit plan must provide for set benefits. Your contributions to the plan are based on actuarial assumptions. To set up such a plan you will likely need professional help, as the IRS must approve the plan. It may be easier for you to adopt an existing IRS-approved master or prototype retirement plan than to set up your own original plan. Master and prototype plans can be provided by trade or professional organizations, banks, insurance companies and mutual fund organizations.

❏ **Unqualified Plans** – You can deduct contributions made to a non-exempt trust, or premiums paid under a non-qualified annuity plan. Your employees include the contributions or premiums in their gross income.

Company Retirement Plans for Canada

Retirement plans in Canada offer similar tax advantages as those in the U.S. The most important being that employer contributions are tax deductible. The two most important types of Canadian retirement plans are the *RPP* and the *DPSP*:

❑ **Registered Pension Plans –** RPPs are formal savings plans run by employers voluntarily or as a result of contract negotiations with unions. They are not required by law, but once set up face stringent provincial and federal regulations. An RPP may be contributory or non-contributory.– In a contributory RPP, contributions are required by employees members. In a non-contributory RPP, the employer pays the full cost of the plan.

Defined Benefit Plan – The most common form of an RPP is the "defined benefit plan." In this plan, the employer promises a set amount of retirement income, usually based on years of service and average income. This type of RPP is often used for government employees and those who work for large corporations. If you have employees, they must be included in your company pension plan, if they work at least 1,000 hours a year and have been with the company for a minimum of two years. Part-time employees who work less than an average of 20 hours a week or who are employed for only a short while need not be included.

❑ **The Deferred Profit Savings Plan –** A DPSP is an employer-sponsored plan, registered with Revenue Canada, in which the employer shares the profits of a business with all the employees or a designated group of employees. A DPSP is similar to a defined contribution RPP in that an employee's pension amount is not known until the end of their career. It differs in that employees do not contribute.

DPSPs are not as widespread as other retirement plans and are generally offered in addition to one or more other types of retirement plans. To their advantage: ◆ A DPSP can focus employee attention on your bottom line. ◆ The allocation of funds to member accounts can be highly structured or arbitrary. ◆ The annual information return is not complicated. ◆ No contributions need to be made in years which you had no profit. You may contribute an amount no greater than 9% of your employee's earnings for the current year to a maximum of $6,750 (half of the RPP maximum). The minimum contribution is 1% of payroll, or 1% profit, or $100 per member.

*Detail your **personal** retirement plan, including your planned monthly contributions (percentages or amounts):*

*Detail your **company** retirement plan, including your planned monthly contributions (percentages or amounts):*

Investment Plan

Any profits left over after you've paid your business expenses, covered your living expenses, and contributed to your retirement plan, should immediately be invested in one or a combination of the following investment products:

❑ *Cash Investments* ❑ *Bonds & Debt Instruments* ❑ *Equities* ❑ *Mutual Funds*

The investment vehicle you choose will likely depend upon liquidity needed, rates of return desired, and risk involved (see charts on page 196).

The Four Major Categories of Investments

Summarized below are the four major types of financial investment vehicles available to you to help build your investment portfolio:

Cash Investments – Savings accounts, money market certificates, term deposits, short-term investment certificates, and T-Bills are generally seen as very low risk investments. Except for term deposits and investment certificates, which are usually cashable after 3 months to five years, cash investments are very liquid (cashable), but offer low rates of return (4% to 8%). Having part of your portfolio in cash gives you the flexibility to react quickly to investment opportunities or emergencies and makes your portfolio less exposed to market volatility.

Bonds & Debt Instruments – Debt instruments are contracts between someone who wants to borrow and someone who has money to lend. They include investments such as bonds, debentures, mortgages and personal loans. The contracts involve the borrower paying certain amounts of money in the form of principal and interest at certain times in the future, once the loan has been made. Debt instruments usually earn interest at a predictable rate (5% to 9% or more). However, if you sell them prior to maturity, there is the potential for capital gains or losses. If interest rates go up, your contract is valued less by the market. If interest rates go down, your contract, with its higher rate of interest, becomes more attractive. Bonds are usually purchased at a $25,000 minimum in multiples of $1,000.

Equity Investments (Stocks) – Equities are shares of a company or organization that increase or decrease in value depending on the market's perception of the company's future earnings prospects. This group includes stocks, equity, and shares of private companies. It also includes real properties and collectibles. Equity investments are expected to grow in value over time and may even provide some income in the form of regular dividends. Historically, they have achieved the best returns but are also the most risky, because their value is based on market demand.

Mutual Fund Investments – Mutual funds pool resources to invest solely or in a combination of cash investments, debt instruments or equities. The variety of mutual funds available to investors is almost limitless. To find top mutual funds visit:

http://www.findafund.com

http://www.stockmaster.com

1996 Investment Return Rate for $100 Invested in 1950

	Value	Rate
Consumer Price index (cost of Living)	$728	(4.4%)
90-Day Canada Treasury Bills	$1,889	(6.5%)
Scotia McLeod Long Term Bond index	$2,395	(7.1%)
5 year Guaranteed Investment Certificates	$3,511	(8.0%)
Toronto Stock Exchange 300 Total Return Index	$11,291	(10.7%)
U.S. Stock Total Return Index in Cdn. $	$30,179	(13.1%)
U.S. Small Stock Total Return Index in Cdn $	$51,296	(14.4%)

$100 $1,000 $10,000 $20,000 $30,000 $40,000 $50,000 $60,000

1950   **1996**

RETURN RATE for a $100 INVESTMENT (value quoted in Cdn$) The following chart shows how much an $100 investment made in 1950 would have grown if it was invested any one of the above 7 investment vehicles.
Source: Canadian Government Document

Four Ways to Save $100,000

Monthly Deposit required to accumulate **$100,000** (with an average return of 10%)		
Monthly Deposit	**# of Years**	**Total Invested**
$44.24	30 years	$15,926.40
$131.69	20 years	$31,605,60
$488.17	10 years	$58,580.40
$1,291.37	5 years	$77,482.20

Investment Risk vs. Returns

Asset	Volatility	Return	RISK
Cash Investments	Low	Low	**Low** (but may not earn more than inflation)
Debt Investments (*Bonds*)	Mod.	Mod.	**Moderate** (but may not beat inflation; or interest rates may rise creating capital losses)
Equities (*Stocks*)	High	High	**High** (market may fall)
Mutual Funds	Low to High	Low to High	**Low to High** (depends on type of mutual fund)

Choosing the Best Investment Mix for Your Age

	20 + years	15-20	10-15	5-10	0-5 (retirement)
Short-term Investments	10%	10%	10%	15%	15%
Income	15%	20%	30%	40%	55%
Growth Income	15%	20%	30%	25%	20%
Growth	60%	50%	30%	20%	10%

There are essentially five different kinds of portfolio mixes to choose from, depending on your age to retirement. The above are recommended guidelines, which factor in the need for capital conservation and appreciation.

Choosing the Right Investment: Investment Strategy Summary Chart

Investment	Strategy	Average Yearly Return
No-load mutual funds	Money movement	**12-15%** Passive
Mutual funds margin accounts	Leverage	**25%** Passive
RRSP accounts	Self-directed accounts	**15-20%** Passive
Your own home	Leverage & personal use	**20%** Passive
Asset Management Checking accounts	Legal float and debit card	**8-14%** Active
Employer's pension plan	Money movement and payroll deducted	**20%** Passive
Discounted mortgages	Guaranteed interest tax deferral	**30%** Active
Investment real estate	Leverage & equity growth capital gains	**30%** Active

Outline your investment goals and strategies. Describe investment vehicles and your reasons for choosing them:

Tax Plan

The tax levy imposed by each governmental entity is the single most important impediment impacting upon your financial goals. To make matters worse, it seems governmental agencies purposely write confusing tax laws to keep you from getting what you legally deserve. It's as if they're counting on the fact that

Making decisions about foreign operations is complex and requires an intimate knowledge of a country's commercial climate, with a realization that the climate can change overnight. **ERNST & YOUNG** International Business Series

you are too easily intimidated by the complexity of tax laws to do anything at all to reduce your tax liability. However, with knowledge and careful planning, you can legally save tens of thousands, if not hundreds of thousands of dollars over your lifetime. A tax planning strategy is your first step to beating the taxman.

Tax Liabilities in the U.S.

The tax collection agency of the U.S. government employs more than 100,000 people and annually siphons off about $2 trillion from the more than $8 trillion in annual gross national income. Dozens of manuals and films on every conceivable tax problem are available, often at no charge, at local IRS field offices or in the Freedom of Information Reading Room. Some are for sale at prices ranging from less than $5 to more than $100. The due date for individual and partnership returns is the 15th day of the 4th month after the end of the tax year. The due date for filing returns for corporations and S-corporations is the 15th day of the 3rd month after the end of the tax year. If the 15th day of the month falls on a Saturday, Sunday, or a legal holiday, the due date is the next day that is not a Saturday, Sunday, or legal holiday (visit http://cpaexpert.com/chou_cowley/ for tax tips).

❑ **Income Tax** – All businesses except partnerships must file an annual income tax return. Partnerships file an information return. Which form you use depends on how your business is organized. Partners are taxed personally on their share of the business income. Corporations are taxed separately from its shareholders. Proprietorships and partnerships can generally deduct the same expenses as corporations from taxable income, i.e., those expenses incurred in pursuit of earning business income.

The Federal income tax must be paid as you earn or receive income during the year. This means, paying an estimated tax. For sole proprietorships, partners in a partnership, or shareholders of an S-corporation, installments must be made by the 15th day of the 4th, 6th, 9th and 12th month. Generally, each installment must equal 25% of the required annual estimated tax. If a corporation or an individual fails to pay a correct installment of estimated tax in full by the due date, they may be subject to a penalty.

❑ **Self-Employment Tax** – The SE tax is a social security and Medicare tax for individuals who work for themselves. It provides business owners with retirement benefits, disability benefits and medical insurance benefits. The SE tax rate on net earnings for 1996 was 15.3% of which 12.4% is for social security (old-age, survivors, and disability insurance), and 2.9% for Medicare (hospital insurance). The maximum amount subject to social security tax for 1996 was $62,700.

❑ **Employment Taxes** – Business owners who are employers must pay employment taxes. These taxes include social security, Medicare taxes, and Federal unemployment (FUTA) taxes.

Social Security and Medicare Taxes – Social security and Medicare taxes pay for benefits the workers and their families receive under the Federal Insurance Contributions Act (FICA). This act requires the employer and employee to each pay 6.2% for social security and 1.45% for Medicare of the employee's income (1996).

Federal Unemployment Tax – Federal unemployment tax systems, along with state systems, provide unemployment payments to workers who have lost their jobs. The gross FUTA tax rate is 6.2%. The maximum amount of wages subject to FUTA tax is $7,000 (1996).

❑ **Excise Taxes** – An excise tax is a tax imposed on the selling price of particular types of goods manufactured or produced in the U.S., such as luxury cars, coal, and gas. You may have to pay this tax if you manufacture or sell certain products, operate certain kinds of businesses or use various kinds of equipment, facilities or products.

❑ **Alternative Minimum Tax (AMT)** – Tax laws give special treatment to certain kinds of income and allow special deductions for certain kinds of expenses. So that taxpayers who benefit from these laws will pay at least a minimum amount of tax, a special tax was enacted, the "alternative minimum tax (AMT)" for corporations and individuals. The AMT rate for corporations is 20%.

Tax Liabilities in Canada

In Canada, the federal, provincial, and municipal governing bodies have distinct responsibilities and taxing authority. The federal government has general taxing powers and levies income tax, capital tax, excise tax, sales tax and customs duties. The provinces have given additional taxation powers, which also allow revenue from income tax, sales tax and resource royalties, permits and licensing levies. Some provincial responsibilities have been delegated to municipalities, which levy taxes upon real estate and business, usually on the basis of the value of the property occupied and the type of business conducted. All individuals and corporations resident in Canada must pay income taxes from all sources of income received or receivable during the taxation year, less certain deductions.

❑ **Corporate Income Tax** – Unlike individuals, corporations may have a taxation year-end other than the calendar year-end. The corporation calculates and pays its tax on the basis of this period. A corporation must pay at the end of each month of its fiscal period either one-twelfth of its estimated tax for the year or one-twelfth of the tax paid in the previous taxation year. After the year-end, the corporation calculates its actual tax for the year and within two months of the year-end, pays any balance owing in addition to the installments. If there is no tax owing, the corporation has up to six months after the fiscal year to file its return. Corporate tax returns must be filed both federally and provincially.

❑ **Proprietorships & Partnerships Income Tax** – Proprietors and partnerships must remit quarterly tax payments on all business income in advance, after making allowances for approved deductions (partners are taxed personally on their share of the business income). Four installments must be made – one on March 31, June 30, September 30 and December 31. Each installment must be equal to one-quarter of either the taxpayer's estimate of his or her tax for the year or his or her tax for the previous year. The taxpayer calculates his or her actual tax for the year on or before April 30 of the following year and pays any amount he or she owes in excess of the installment or claims a refund.

❑ **G.S.T.** – In December of 1990, after considerable debate, the federal government passed legislation to bring the Goods and Services Tax (G.S.T.) into law. As of January 1, 1991, this broad-based, value added tax replaced the Manufacturer's Sales tax. The responsibility and obligation to both collect and remit the G.S.T. has been passed onto the business community by the federal government. As the implications, which flow from this taxation process, are significant, it is strongly recommended that all business owners carefully assess the impact of the G.S.T. on all aspects of their operation.

❑ **Excise Tax** – Excise tax is a tax that is applied on the selling price of particular types of goods manufactured or produced in Canada such as jewelry, cigarettes, tobacco, wines and watches. Manufacturers and producers of excisable goods must operate under a manufacturer's excise tax license.

❑ **Municipal Taxes** – Property taxes are levied on the local level on the owners of businesses. There is an assessment of 65% on buildings and land based on market value in the base year of general assessment in the municipality. The amount of tax payable depends upon the mill rate of the municipality. Some municipalities also levy a local business tax. For further information regarding property taxes, contact the local municipal authority or council for the area in which you locate.

How Long Should You Keep Your Records?

Retain Indefinitely – ❑ audit reports and financial statements ❑ canceled checks for taxes, capital purchases, and important contracts ❑ capital stock and bond records ❑ income and sales journals ❑ contracts and leases that are current ❑ copyright, patents, and trademark registrations ❑ corporation charters, minute books of meetings (if incorporated), and bylaws ❑ correspondence on legal and tax matters ❑ deed, mortgages, easements, and other property records ❑ general and private ledger sheets ❑ general journals if they are essential to the understanding of the general ledger entries ❑ insurance records ❑ property appraisals ❑ share records ❑ special contracts and agreements ❑ tax returns, including supporting records, and work papers.

Retain 7 Years – ❑ accounts payables and receivables ledgers ❑ all canceled checks indicating outlays of money ❑ all operating expenses, such as rent and advertising ❑ asset records ❑ bad debt deduction ❑ capital expenditures ❑ charitable donations ❑ employee disability benefits records ❑ employee taxes and withholding statements ❑ inventory records ❑ invoices and sales records ❑ monthly trail balances ❑ old contracts and leases ❑ payroll records and time sheets ❑ purchase orders ❑ remittances of unemployment insurance premiums and pension plan contributions where applicable ❑ vouchers for payments to vendors, employees, and so on.

Retain 3 Years – ❑ bank reconciliations ❑ expired insurance policies (no cash value) ❑ personnel files on departed employees ❑ petty cash vouchers.

Retain 2 Years – ❑ general correspondence ❑ requisitions.

"Personal" Tax at a Glance for the U.S. and Canada:

U.S.	
Income Tax Rate	39.6%
Capital Gains Tax Rate	28% (a)
Estate and Gift Tax Rate	55%

a) Tax rate on long-term gains. The maximum rate of tax on short-term gains is 39.6%.

CANADA	
Income Tax Rate	52.92% (a)
Capital Gains Tax Rate	36.69% (b)
Estate and Gift Tax Rate	0

a) This is a combined rate for 1996 in Ontario, which consists of a federal component of 31.32% and a provincial component of 21.60%.

b) 75% is included in income as taxable capital gains.

"Corporate" Tax at a Glance for the USA and Canada:

USA	
Corporate Income Tax Rate	35% (a)
Capital Gains Tax Rate	35%
Branch Tax Rate	35 % (a)
Withholding Tax	
Dividends	30% (b)
Interest	30% (b) (c)
Royalties from Patents, Know-how, etc.	30% (b)
Branch Remittance Tax	30% (b) (d)
Net Operating Losses (Years)	
Carryback	3
Carryforward	15

a) In addition, many states levy income or capital-based taxes. An alternative minimum tax is imposed.

b) Applicable to nonresidents (rates may be reduced by treaty).

c) Interest on certain "portfolio debt" obligations issued after July 18, 1984 and noneffectively connected bank deposit interest are exempt from withholding.

d) This is the branch profits tax.

CANADA	
Corporate Income Tax Rate	29.12% (a)
Capital Gains Tax Rate	21.84% (a) (b)
Branch Tax Rate	25% (c)
Withholding Tax	
Dividends	25% (d)
Interest	25% (d)
Royalties from Patents, Know-how, etc.	25% (d)
Branch Remittance Tax	25% (d)
Net Operating Losses (Years)	
Carryback	3
Carryforward	7

a) The rate is applied to income that is not eligible for the manufacturing and processing deduction or the small business deduction. It comprises a basic rate of 28% plus a 4% surtax. Additional tax is levied by the provinces and territories of Canada, and the combined federal and provincial or territorial rates vary from 38.02% to 46.12%. The basic rate on Canadian manufacturing and Processing income (excluding surtax) is 21%.

b) 75% of capital gains are subject to tax.

c) This tax is imposed in addition to the regular corporate income tax.

d) Applicable to nonresidents (rates may be reduced by treaty).

Describe any special strategies you have to reduce your taxes:

Estimate your tax liability for your first and second year of operation:

FIRST YEAR		Tax Liability as a % of Total Sales	%	Tax Liability in Dollars	$
SECOND YEAR		Tax Liability as a % of Total Sales	%	Tax Liability in Dollars	$

DAY 29

Risk Assessment

Investors want to know how much money they can make if they invest in your business. But they also want to have spelled out to them, what their risks are – *worst* and *best* case scenarios – as well as what evidence you can show them to prove that you have made attempts to anticipate potential problems.

Summarize the main risks your business will face and the risks for any prospective investor:

An Analysis of Competitor's Reactions

Will competitors try to squeeze you out? Will they drop their prices below cost?

Describe how the competition will react to the entrance of your (Product/Service) business into the marketplace.

Contingency Plans

What happens to your business if everything fails? Do you have a "Plan B" or some kind of safety net?

Describe strategies you will implement to reduce risk in the event your original assumptions do not materialize:

Insurance Plan

How much does your insurance costs? What time periods does it cover? Are there any special terms? Who is the carrier? (see GB📖 #31 for "Getting Insurance").

Describe your insurance protection (bankers are keenly interested in seeing that you have adequate insurance coverage):

```
┌─────────────────────────────────────────────────────────────┐
│                                                             │
│                                                             │
│                                                             │
│                                                             │
│                                                             │
│                                                             │
│                                                             │
└─────────────────────────────────────────────────────────────┘
```

Risk-Management Plan

When applying for a loan, banks will require certain types of insurance, depending on the nature of the business and the type of loan.

Show how you plan to deal with specific events that may cause losses to your company. Describe any risk reducing measures you have taken or plans developed if there is a strike, recession, new technology, bad weather, new competition, supplier problems, or shifts in consumer demand. Likewise, describe any risk reducing measures or plans you have if sales projections are off by 30%, sales double, workers quit, or if a key manager quits or becomes sick.

NOTE Some businesses fail because they become too successful, too soon. If your company becomes inundated with orders, what contingency plans do you have for hiring additional staff and contacting additional suppliers?

Sample Risks & Other Variables Statements

Seasonal trends have been considered in our projections. (I/We) believe (my/our) forecasts are conservative.

Identify specific potential risks and how you plan to deal with them:

```
┌─────────────────────────────────────────────────────────────┐
│                                                             │
│                                                             │
│                                                             │
│                                                             │
│                                                             │
│                                                             │
│                                                             │
│                                                             │
└─────────────────────────────────────────────────────────────┘
```

Security Plan

Describe what kinds of security measures you have taken to discourage theft and vandalism, protect inventory, and safeguard important documents.

Describe your security plan. Do you have an alarm system? Do you have a fireproof safe?

Closing Statement

A *Closing Statement* can be used in a business plan to reinforce the purpose of the plan. It can also be used to help direct people to the conclusion you want them to make as well as validate the data contained in your business plan. The "closing statement" shown below can be modified to reflect more than one owner.

Sample Closing Statement

I, the undersigned, declare that the statements made herein are for the purpose of obtaining business financing and are to the best of my knowledge true and correct. I consent to the bank making any inquiries it deems necessary to reach a decision on this information about me to any credit-reporting agency or to anyone with whom I have financial relations.

Date   Signature

Summarize any key points you wish to make in your closing statement:

Write a closing statement:

To Do List

Supporting Documents
Documents Required

✓ Contracts & Lease Agreements
✓ Credit Reports
✓ Income Tax returns
✓ Legal Documents
✓ Letters of Reference
✓ Personal Financial Statements
✓ Résumés
✓ Other Documents

DAY 30
SUPPORTING DOCUMENTS

EXCESSIVE documentation, exhibits and appendixes should not be part of the main business plan. As a separate appendix, they make your proposal look less formidable. In your *Supporting Documents* section, include all records that backup the statements and decisions made in previous sections of your business plan. This section can also include items such as brochures, magazine articles, technical papers, and summaries of market research studies.

NOTE Include only documents and materials that will be of immediate interest to your readers. Keep others where they can be made available on short notice. Also make sure that the information contained in this section adds to and doesn't contradict anything you said earlier.

Contracts & Lease Agreements

Include all business contracts and agreements, both completed and currently in force, such as insurance policies, property and vehicle titles, purchase agreements, service contracts, mortgages, and debentures. Include all ease agreements currently in force between your company and leasing agencies.

Credit Reports

Business credit reports can be obtained from suppliers or wholesalers. *Personal* credit reports and rating can be obtained from credit bureaus, banks and companies who you have dealt with on a credit basis.

Income Tax Returns

Depending on the purpose of your business plan you may want to include copies of federal, state, and local income tax returns for the prior year.

Legal Documents

Include all legal papers pertaining to your legal structure such as articles of incorporation, partnership agreements, and franchise agreements, and proprietary rights such as copyrights, trademark registrations, and patents.

Letters of Reference

Include business or personal letters recommending you as a reputable and reliable businessperson. List the names, addresses, and phone numbers of: banks or other institutions with whom you have had financial dealings (state branch, type of account, type of loan, terms, etc.); accountants, lawyers or other professionals with whom you have had business relationships; and other creditors including long-term relationships with suppliers.

> *Be careful not to go into too much detail in this section.*

> *Compile your list of supporting documents as you work through this guide. While writing about your "business location," for example, you might decide to include a copy of your "lease agreement." Write "lease agreement" in the chart on page 204.*
> **BUINSESS PLAN WRITING TIP**

There is no difference between a plan and a dream, unless there is "action." If a plan is not acted upon it is as useful as a plane without wings.

Personal Financial Statements

Prepare a current *Personal Net Worth Statement*, outlining personal assets and liabilities, for yourself, each partner, or each stockholder owning 20% or more of the stock of your corporation. Banks often require personal financial statements from all owners. They are an important part of your financial package because they: (1) verify your company financial statements; (2) identify hidden liability or equity; and (3) reveal other activities vying for your attention. You should also prepare a *Personal Income Statement*. Both statements should be limited to one page (see page 207 & 208). For new ventures, put these statements in your "Business Financial History" section, especially if they warrant detailed explanation.

Résumés of Management & Key Individuals

Limit to one or two pages at most. Include work history, educational background, professional affiliations, special achievements, and previous businesses owned.

Other Documents

Check other documents and materials required. List other documents or materials required:

❑ A/Ps Summaries (include schedule of payments)	❑ Letters of Intent (potential orders, customer commitments, letters of support)	❑ Mock-ups of Marketing Brochures Describing your Product or Service
❑ A/Rs Summaries (including aging schedules)	❑ List and Description of Major Liabilities (including mortgages)	❑ Names of Suppliers or Possible Suppliers
❑ Appraisals (property, equipment)	❑ List of Fixed Assets (description, age, serial #s)	❑ Personal Property Values (to substantiate the value of your personal guarantee if required)
❑ Backup Info on Competitors	❑ List of Inventory (type, age, value)	
❑ Cash in Bank Statements	❑ List of Leasehold Improvements (description, date made)	❑ Price Lists (to support cost estimates)
❑ Charge Account Statements	❑ List of Prospective Customers	❑ Product Specifications & Photos
❑ Company Investment Portfolio	❑ Location Plans	❑ Publicity Articles and Promotional Pieces
❑ Consulting Reports and Surveys	❑ Marketing & Demographics Studies	❑ Relevant Magazine, Trade Journal, Newspaper Articles
❑ Financial Statements for Associated Companies (where appropriate)		
❑ Job Descriptions for the Management Team		

*List key contracts, agreement, documents, reports, research studies, and other materials that **must be included** in this section:*

Write a summary list of other documents and materials that you may or may not include:

> *I hear and I forget. I see and I remember. I do and I understand.*
> **CHINESE PROVERB**

Conclusion

CONGRATULATIONS! You've completed your business plan! Now, type it out and seek professional consul! Set up a meeting with a Service Corps of Retired Executives volunteer (http://www.score.org) and get some FREE advice via email. There are also SCORE chapters in every state. Next, have your business plan reviewed by people who regularly work with business owners and have come to recognize characteristics of ventures that succeed or fail. Show your plan to a small business banker or an accountant. If you already know people who are running their own successful business, have them look at it. Whatever you do, don't let your plan sit on your desk and collect dust. You've put in long hours and hard work to get it finished. Don't let that work go to waste.

Business Plan Writing Strategies

Before typing your business plan, ask yourself the following four questions:

● What should my business plan look like?

● How long should it be?

● Who will read my business plan?

● What's the best way to get started?

APPEARANCE – Make sure your business plan looks good. Although you may have limited time, limited resources, and should put your efforts where there is the most reward; there is no excuse for a sloppy looking business plan. Put your best foot forward: this commands respect. Copies of your business plan should be printed on quality paper and placed in a blue, black or brown duo-tang, a leather binder, or bound at a local print shop. There should be no typing, spelling, punctuation, or grammar errors.

<u>NOTE</u> A skillful graphic designer can polish a business plan to the point that its physical appearance shines more than its content. Every entrepreneur should be cautioned to avoid losing sight of the real purpose of a business plan. Keep it straightforward and clear. Save the glitz for your marketing campaigns.

LENGTH – Don't make your business plan too long or too short. A 200-page business plan makes a dandy fire, while a three-page business plan makes three dandy paper airplanes. As a general rule, if you are going to a bank or an individual investor, no more than 30 to 40 pages is adequate, including the supporting documents section. Rarely should your plan exceed 50 typewritten pages.

AUDIENCE – Have a good idea WHO will be reading your business plan. There are two main types of business plans: (a) those intended as *roadmaps* for starting, operating and growing a business; and (b) those intended as *sales documents* for raising capital, attracting investors, securing bank loans or securing an operating line of credit from suppliers. In each of the above cases, the intended reader has different expectations and needs. Although the information contained in either type of plan might essentially be the same, the emphasis is different. A plan intended as a roadmap (with the targeted audience being management and/or

> *Prepare a number of copies of your plan and number each one individually. Make sure each copy is appropriately bound with a good-quality cover on which the name of your business has been printed or embossed.*
> **BUSINESS PLAN WRITING TIP**

owners) *wouldn't* need to include extensive biographies of key management figures. However, a plan intended to be used as a sales document for raising capital or obtaining a loan (with the intended audience being bankers or investors) *would*. In fact, the background and experience of management may be what investors consider the most important part of your offering. They want to be convinced that your company is in control of its future before they lay their money on the line.

When typing your business plan, also consider the specific needs of each audience group. Investors, for example, want to know how much capital you are asking for, how much risk is involved, how much potential for profit there is, and whether you are credible, trust worthy, and committed. On the other hand, a banker is more interested in knowing how much money you have at stake, how you will make loan payments, and if you go bankrupt, what personal guarantees you are able to offer.

OUTLINE – Start by rethinking your table of contents. You could complete your business plan by simply typing out the entries made into this guide using the same section titles and headings as shown on page 13. This guide has been carefully organized into a clear yet comprehensive outline. Depending on the purpose of your business plan, you may also decide to rearrange your content to more closely examine other "**Key Areas**" unique to your business, and as a result more effectively meet your needs and the needs of your target audience. If you are seeking a loan from a particular bank or organization, find out the *exact* order they like content to be presented. Loan officers read hundreds of business plans and like to keep things the same so they can kind find important data quickly!

To structure a new outline:

- *Create a heading structure two levels deep.* Write down on a piece of paper all the sections you want to discuss making sure to leave enough room under each second level heading for a list of third level headings. Use the table of contents checklist on page 13 to assist in this task.

- *As you research and outline new sections in your first and second level headings, make a list of additional "Key Areas" or third level headings that need to be researched further.* Express each "Key Area" as one word or a phrase. Organize related "Key Areas" into a logical sequence under each of your second level headings. Go down as many levels into each "Key Area" as needed, however one additional level should be enough. Soon, you will have a new table of contents best suited for your type of business.

- *To start building paragraphs, write concise informative sentences about each "Key Area" by describing the "who," "what," "where," "when," "why," "how" and "how much."* For example, if you're writing about a unique business location, describe *what* kind of building is on the site, *where* it's located, *why* you chose it, and *how much* it costs to rent, lease or purchase. Use the ideas and information entered into this guide, as well as the sample paragraphs provided, as starting points. Always be concise and clear. Eliminate words you don't really need. If your writing lacks vigor and clarity, consult our online Guidebook #57 "Writing and Editing Like a Pro," for additional writing strategies.

PERSONAL INCOME STATEMENT

Name:	Date:	Period:

INCOME

Gross Salaries	
Bonuses & Commissions	
Spouse's Gross Salaries	
Rental Income	
Annuities and Pensions	
Dividends and Interest	
Sale of Personal Capital Items	
1. _____	
2. _____	
TOTAL Gross Income	

Less Taxes

Personal Income Tax	
Other Taxes	
A) TOTAL NET INCOME	

Household

Rent/Mortgage Payments	
Household/Apt. Insurance	
Property Taxes	
Utilities (telephone, power, etc.)	
Maintenance & Repairs	
Furniture & Appliances	
Stereos, TVs, & Computers	
Day Care Services	
Other Household Expenses	

EXPENSES

Transportation

Auto Loan/Lease Payments	
Auto Insurance	
Gas & Oil	
Repairs & Maintenance	
Licenses, Fees & Parking	
Other Transportation Expenses	

Personal

Food	
Clothing	
Laundry & Cleaning	
Music, Movies & Theatre	
Drinking, Dining & Dancing	
Sporting Activities	
Vacation & Travel	
Gifts, Donations & Dues	
Education, Books & Magazines	
Medical/Dental/Life Insurance	
Doctor & Dentist Fees	
Prescription Medicines	
Loans, Debts & Credit Payments	
Investment & Savings Plans	
Other Personal Expenses	
1. _____	
2. _____	
B) TOTAL LIVING EXPENSES	

TOTAL DISPOSABLE INCOME (A - B) $

PERSONAL NET WORTH STATEMENT

Name: **Date:**

ASSETS		LIABILITIES	
Cash		Unpaid Bills	
Cash On Hand		**Credit Cards**	
Checking Accounts		**Income Taxes**	
Saving Accounts		**Insurance Premiums**	
Money Owed to You		**Other Unpaid Bills**	
Investments		Installment Loans	
Mutual Funds		**Automobile**	
Stocks & Bonds		**Other**	
Savings Bonds		Long Term Loans	
Other		**Bank**	
Cash Surrender Value		**Education**	
Annuities		**Home Equity**	
Life Insurance		**Other**	
Pension Fund		Real Estate Loans	
Retirement Plans		**Home**	
Personal Property		**Other**	
Real Estate		Other Liabilities	
Furniture/Antiques		**Alimony Payments**	
Art/Jewlery		**Accounts Payable**	
Vehicles		**Notes Payable**	
Other Assets		**Contracts Payable**	
Accounts & Notes Rec.		**A.** _____	
A. _____		**B.** _____	
B. _____		**C.** _____	
C. _____			

TOTAL ASSETS	$	**TOTAL LIABILITIES**	$
		NET WORTH	$

DAILY PLANNER

SUNDAY   Date:

ABC	TASKS & APPOINTMENTS	🕐

MONDAY   Date:

ABC	TASKS & APPOINTMENTS	🕐

TUESDAY   Date:

ABC	TASKS & APPOINTMENTS	🕐

WEDNESDAY   Date:

ABC	TASKS & APPOINTMENTS	🕐

THURSDAY   Date:

ABC	TASKS & APPOINTMENTS	🕐

FRIDAY   Date:

ABC	TASKS & APPOINTMENTS	🕐

SATURDAY   Date:

ABC	TASKS & APPOINTMENTS	🕐

WEEK #   Date:

ABC	WEEKLY PLANNER

IMPORTANT CONTACTS

COMPANY NAME	ADDRESS	CONTACT PERSON	PHONE/FAX/EMAIL/URL

INDEX